THE BOOK OF THE
MALTESE

THE BOOK OF THE
MALTESE

by Joan McDonald Brearley

Front Cover Photo: Ch. Hazels White Lightening (owned by Hazel Pierson of Stony Point, New York), photographed by Alton Anderson.

Back Cover Photo: Three 12-week-old Maltese puppies (owned by Vera Rebbin, Aurora, Ohio), photographed by Vera Rebbin.

Title Page Photo: Ch. Joanne-Chen's Teddy Bear Dancer (owned by Marcia Hostetler of Des Moines, Iowa), photographed by Adolph Feiler.

ISBN 0-87666-563-6

Distributed in the UNITED STATES by T.F.H. Publications, Inc., 211 West Sylvania Avenue, Neptune City, NJ 07753; in CANADA by H & L Pet Supplies Inc., 27 Kingston Crescent, Kitchener, Ontario N2B 2T6; Rolf C. Hagen Ltd., 3225 Sartelon Street, Montreal 382 Quebec; in ENGLAND by T.F.H. Publications Limited, 4 Kier Park, Ascot, Berkshire SL5 7DS; in AUSTRALIA AND THE SOUTH PACIFIC by T.F.H. (Australia) Pty. Ltd., Box 149, Brookvale 2100 N.S.W., Australia; in NEW ZEALAND by Ross Haines & Son, Ltd., 18 Monmouth Street, Grey Lynn, Auckland 2 New Zealand; in SINGAPORE AND MALAYSIA by MPH Distributors Pte., 71-77 Stamford Road, Singapore 0617; in the PHILIPPINES by Bio-Research, 5 Lippay Street, San Lorenzo Village, Makati, Rizal; in SOUTH AFRICA by Multipet Pty. Ltd., 30 Turners Avenue, Durban 4001. Published by T.F.H. Publications Inc., Ltd., the British Crown Colony of Hong Kong.

Contents

About the Author

Joan Brearley is the first to admit that animals in general—and dogs in particular—are a most important part of her life. Since childhood there has been a steady stream of dogs, cats, birds, fish, rabbits, snakes, alligators, etc., for her own personal menagerie. Over the years she has owned over thirty breeds of pure-bred dogs as well as countless mixtures, since the door was never closed to a needy or homeless animal.

A graduate of the American Academy of Dramatic Arts, where she studied acting and directing, Joan started her career as an actress, dancer, and writer for movie magazines. She studied ballet at the Agnes DeMille Studios in Carnegie Hall and was with an Oriental dance company which performed at the Carnegie Recital Hall. She studied journalism at Columbia University and has written for radio, television, and magazines, and she was a copywriter for some of the major New York City advertising agencies working on the accounts of Metro-Goldwyn-Mayer Studios, Burlington Mills, Cosmopolitan magazine, White Owl Cigars, and World Telegram & Sun newspapers.

While a television producer-director for a major network Joan worked on "Nick Carter, Master Detective"; "Did Justice Triumph"; and news and special feature programs. Joan has written, cast, directed, produced and, on occasion, starred in television commercials. She has written special material for such personalities as Dick Van Dyke, Amy Vanderbilt, William B. Williams, Gene Rayburn, Bill Stern, Herman Hickman, and many other prominent people in the entertainment world. She has appeared as a guest on several of the nation's most popular talk shows, including Mike Douglas, Joe Franklin, Cleveland Amory, David Susskind, and the To-day Show, to name just a few. Joan was selected for inclusion in the *Directory of the Foremost Women in Communications* in 1969, and the book *Two Thousand Women of Achievement* in 1971.

Her accomplishments in the dog fancy include breeding and exhibiting top show dogs, being a writer and columnist of various magazines, and author of over thirty books on dogs and cats. For five years she was Executive Vice-President of the Popular Dogs Publishing Company and editor of *Popular Dogs* magazine, the national prestige publication for the fancy at the time. Her editorials on the status and welfare of animals have been reproduced as educational pamphlets by dog clubs and organizations in many countries of the world.

Joan is just as active in the cat fancy, and in almost as many capacities. The same year her Afghan Hound Champion Sahadi Shikari won the Ken-L-Ration Award as Top Hound of the Year, one of her Siamese cats won the comparable honor in the cat fancy. She has owned and/or bred almost all breeds of cats. Many of her cats and dogs are Best in Show winners and have appeared in magazines and on television. For several years she was editor of the Cat Fanciers Association Annual Yearbook, and her book *All About Himalayan Cats* was published in 1976.

In addition to breeding and showing dogs since 1955, Joan has been active as a member and on the Board of Directors of the Kennel Club of Northern New Jersey, the Afghan Hound Club of America, the Stewards Club of America, and The Dog Fanciers Club. She has been an American Kennel Club judge of several breeds since 1961. She has appeared as a guest speaker at many dog clubs and humane organizations crusading for humane legislation, and has won several awards and citations for her work in this field. She is one of the best-known and most knowledgeable people in the animal world. Joan is proud of the fact that her Champion Sahadi Shikari was top-winning Afghan Hound in the history of the breed for several years, and remains in the number two position today. No other breeder can claim to have bred a Westminster Group winner in the first homebred litter.

Joan has recently been made a Trustee of the Morris Animal Foundation, does free-lance publicity and public relations work, is a Daughter of the American Revolution and the New York Genealogical Society. In her spare time she exhibits her needlework (for which she has also won prizes), haunts the art and auction galleries, and is a graduate auctioneer with the full title of Colonel.

This impressive list of activities doesn't include all of her accomplishments, since she has never been content to have just one interest at a time, but manages to dovetail several occupations and avocations to make for a fascinating career.

Joan lives with her dogs and cats in a townhouse on the oceanfront in Sea Bright, New Jersey.

DEDICATION

to
Aennchen Antonelli
and all her
Maltese Dancers

Aennchen Antonelli awards the ribbons to Ch. To The Victor of Eng, owned and handled by Barbara J. Bergquist.

Preface

Ever since I was a child I have had a great love for dogs—all kinds of dogs—and the friendly, fluffy Maltese were no exception. These snow-white, button-eyed, button-nosed little darlings were always attention-getters, and never before attained such heights of fame as when a lady named Aennchen Antonelli set her mind to the breeding of them.

I got to know Aennchen very well when I was editor of *Popular Dogs* magazine back in 1967. She was my Maltese columnist and we formed a solid friendship based on our mutual love for dogs and Oriental dance.

My fondest memory of Aennchen will always be of one night at the 1966 Westminster Kennel Club as we sat in the first balcony of the Garden and watched her Ch. Aennchen's Poona Dancer and my Afghan Hound Ch. Sahadi Shikari in the ring competing for Best in Show. With tears running down our cheeks we wished each other luck, hoping that if it wasn't our own dog that won it would be the other's, and pondering the irony of our both having sold such beautiful dogs! As it turned out, a wire Fox Terrier won Best in Show that year. But from that night forward, Aennchen and I always recalled this proud moment when we got together.

We can only fantasize what her full impact on the breed would have been had she not died so prematurely. As it is, we can all rejoice in the heritage she left the breed in her short time with us.

Acknowledgments

The author acknowledges with deep appreciation the contributions made to this book. Special thanks go to Kathy DiGiacomo for her enthusiasm and encouragement and inspiration; to Barbara Bergquist, Mary Lou Porlick, and Pamela Brown for their obedience stories and statistics; to Susan Sandlin for special material; to Gail Hennessey for her coverage of the Crufts shows and additional information; to Robert R. Shomer, D.V.M., for his usual counsel; and to all the owners, breeders, and exhibitors of the little white delights that share our lives and who sent photographs and material for this lasting tribute to our breed.

Joan McDonald Brearley

Above: Ch. Aennchen's Poona Dancer, bred by Aennchen and Joseph Antonelli.
Below: Ch. Aennchen's Sitar Dancer, another in a long line of famous "Dancers" from the kennels of Aennchen Antonelli of Waldwick, New Jersey.

Aennchen Antonelli with one of her famous Maltese, the Best in Show winning Ch. Aennchen's Taja Dancer, photographed in 1965.

CHAPTER ONE

Early History of the Dog

Two champions, Tarzan and Sitar, from the kennel of Aennchen Antonelli, whose "Dancer" Maltese were among the most famous winning dogs during their years in the show ring.

Many millions of years ago dinosaurs and other strange-looking creatures roamed the earth. As "recently" as sixty million years ago a mammal existed which resembled a civet cat and is believed to be the common ancestor of dogs, cats, wolves, and coyotes. This animal was the long-extinct Miacis (pronounced *My-a-Kiss*).

The Miacis were long-bodied, long-tailed, short-legged beasts that stalked and chased their prey, grasped it in their long, powerful, fanged jaws and gnashed their food with their teeth. Just 15,000,000 years ago the Tomcartus evolved from the earlier Miacis and provided an even truer genetic basis for the more highly intelligent prototype of the domesticated dog.

It is only fifteen to twenty thousand years since the first attempts were made to domesticate these ferocious, tree-climbing animals. Archeologists have uncovered the skeletal remains of dogs that date back to the age of the cave men, and co-existed with them as members of their families in several ancient civilizations.

There are several schools of thought among the scholars and scientists on the exact location of the very first creatures to cohabit with man. Some contend that the continent of Africa was the original locale. Ancient remains unearthed near Lake Baikal date back to 9,000 years B.C. In the 1950s in an excavation in Pelegawra, Iraq, a canine fossil was discovered and is said to date back 14,500 years, and was appropriately labeled the Pelegawra dog. Siberian remains are said to go back 20,000 years. The Jaguar Cave Dogs of North America have been dated circa 8,400 B.C. Others claim the Chinese wolf to be the ancestor of the dog.

Advocates of the Chinese wolf theory point out that the language barrier was responsible for the Chinese wolf not being known or acknowledged in earlier comparisons. When scientists could not translate Chinese writing, they could not study or authenticate the early Oriental findings. Their theory is also based on the presence of the overhanging bone found in the jawbone of both the Chinese wolf and the dog. This is believed to be significant in the change from their being strictly carnivorous creatures to creatures that eventually became omnivorous carnivores.

The general consensus of opinion among scientists dealing in prehistoric and archeological studies seems to settle on the likelihood that dogs were being domesticated in

11

many parts of the world at approximately the same period in time. Since dogs were to become so essential to man's very existence they were naturally absorbed into family life.

PRIMITIVE TYPES

The three most primitive types originated in three parts of the globe. While all bore certain very exact characteristics, the wolf-type seemed to evolve in southern Asia and Australia, the Pariahs in Asia Minor and Japan, and the Basenjis in Africa.

The Dingo found its way north to Russia and Alaska, across what is now the Bering Straits, into North America. The Pariahs moved far north and learned to pull sleds, and developed into the various northern breeds in the arctic regions. The Basenjis and Greyhounds coursed the desert sands and hunted in the jungles of Africa when they weren't guarding royal palaces in Egypt. As dogs found their way across Europe they served as guard dogs in the castles, rescue dogs in the Alps, barge dogs on the canals, and hunting dogs in the forests. The smaller dogs were bred down smaller and smaller still and became companions and pets for the aristocracy. Kings and queens of the world have always maintained their own personal kennels for their favorite breeds and to suit their own purposes.

BREED DEVELOPMENT

While the cave man used dogs primarily as hunters to help provide meat, and to provide meat themselves, he also made use of their fur as clothing, and for warmth from the dogs' bodies when sleeping, dogs were to become even more functional as time went by and according to the dictates of the climates and geographical regions. Definite physical changes were taking place which eventually would distinguish one dog from another even within the same area. Ears ranged in size from little flaps that we see on terriers to the large upright ears on the Ibizan Hounds. Noses either flattened greatly as they did with Pekingese, or they grew to amazing lengths which we see in the Borzoi. Tails grew to be long and plumey such as those we see on the Siberian Husky, or doubled up into a curl such as those on the Pug. Legs grew long and thin for coursing breeds such as the Greyhound, or were bent and short for the digging breeds like the Dachshund and the Bassett. Sizes went from one extreme to the other, ranging from the tiniest Chihuahua all the way up to the biggest of all breeds, the Irish Wolfhound. Coat lengths became longer or shorter. There were thick woolly coats for the northern breeds and smooth, short coats for the dogs that worked in the warm climates.

SENSORY PERCEPTION

As the dogs changed in physical appearance, their instincts and sensory perception also developed. In some breeds—the German Shepherd for instance—the sense of smell is said to be twenty million times keener than in his human counterpart, allowing it to pick up and follow the scents of other animals miles in the distance. Their eyes developed to such a sharpness they could spot moving prey on the horizon far across desert sands. Their hearing became so acute they were able to pick up the sound of the smallest creatures rustling in the leaves across an open field or in a dense forest.

All things considered, it becomes easy to comprehend why man and dog became such successful partners in their fight for survival and why their attraction and affection for each other is such a wondrous thing.

THE INDIAN FLEECE DOGS

Over 300 years ago when the Indians and the white men were warring over territories in the wilderness, the first auctions came into being. The Indian braves and the colonists every once in a while would declare a one-day truce to trade furs and dogs.

The Indians had three specific types of dogs. The larger ones were used to pull the travois and to hunt along with the braves. The medium sized "common" variety, and small sized dogs were referred to as "fleece" dogs, or Indian dogs.

The fleece dogs were small and white and were sheared and the hair was used for weaving. While the resemblance to the Maltese is slight, the fact that the coat of both the fleece dog and the Maltese is suitable for weaving is significant. The likeness can be seen in a painting by Paul Kane entitled "Clallam women weaving a blanket" that is in the Royal Ontario Museum, Toronto, Canada. The painting is dated 1847.

As recently as 1792 in the Pacific Northwest coast region of this country, Indians were said to have large numbers of these fleece dogs which were shorn once a year, and the Indians themselves wore garments made of this dog hair.

Entitled "Elegance," this pen-and-ink drawing by Kathy Blackard is # 21 of a 200-printed limited edition, rendered in 1982.

A male Maltese, said to be 14 years of age, mounted under glass at the American Museum of Natural History in New York City where it has been since 1914 when it was donated by La Condesa Beatrice di Tavara. Photo courtesy American Museum of Natural History.

CHAPTER TWO

Early History of The Maltese

A fifteenth-century Leipzig painting depicting a witch preparing a philter. While many people associate witches with cats, many other creatures—including dogs—were also found in their company.

While many people believe the Maltese dog originated on the isle of Malta, such is not the case. They could be found on Malta down through the centuries, but the name Maltese is believed to be a corruption of the word Melita, the name of an island in the Adriatic Sea.

In A.D. 25, a scholar named Strabo reported on Maltese dogs as follows: "There is a town in Sicily called Melita whence are exported many beautiful dogs named Canis Melitei." Other dog writers such as Buffon and Linne recognized Melita as their place of origin also. Buffon called them Canis Melitarus and Linne referred to them as Canis Parvus Melitans. Callimachus the Elder, who lived circa 384 B.C. to 322 B.C., Strabo, whom we quoted earlier, lived from approximately 63 B.C. to A.D. 24, Pliny the Elder from 23 B.C. to A.D. 79, and Martialis from around A.D. 38 to A.D. 104, all sang the praises of the fluffy little toy dogs and established their presence during their lives and times.

In truth these little dogs were found on all of the islands of the north side of the Mediterranean Sea, but somehow the Maltese became best known as "the dog of Malta," a name that stuck with it all through the Middle Ages, and for some 3,000 years now. The majority of Maltese dogs on Malta were much larger in size, both then and now, but there is no denying that the smaller, white Maltese were among the most popular and best remembered.

It is safe to say that the Maltese dates back to the pre-Christian era and actually flourished in highly civilized areas where they were referred to as "companions to ladies." Not many breeds have had their history recorded from before the birth of Christ to such an extent, and have enjoyed a reputation as court favorites long before the fall of the Greek and Roman empires and had the distinction of being mentioned in the writings of Aristotle.

THE GREEK AND ROMAN EMPIRES

There is no denying the popularity of these shaggy little dogs during the life and times of Pithias and during the reigns of the Greek and Roman emperors. It was an era in history when most people were devoted to extravagances and self-indulgences and many hours were spent by the ladies playing with and fussing over their cherished lap dogs. While the Melita dogs depicted on Greek and Roman pottery more closely resemble the Pomeranian, with their sharp noses and prick ears, they are still believed to be the progenitors of our modern Maltese.

Evidence of this devotion to their dogs is recorded, though there are those who will dispute it, in the works of the Roman poet Marcus Valerius Martialis which bears out the great affection held for the Maltese by Publius, a Governor of the isle of Malta during the early part of the first century. Publius called his dog Issa, which meant "the beautiful one," and he had a painting commissioned of her. The poet wrote about it in part:

"Issa is more frolicsome than Catull's sparrow. . .
"Issa is purer than a dove's kiss . . .
"Issa is gentler than a maiden child . . .
"Issa is more precious than India gems . . .
"Lest the last days that she sees light should snatch her from him forever, Publius had her picture painted."

True, dogs referred to as "the dogs of Malta" did reach that island during the Middle Ages when Malta was a main trading center between the East and the Western world. They were obviously brought back and forth by the merchant men on the trading ships and eventually acquired the name of "Maltese" because of their tremendous popularity there.

Some claim they were brought to the Mediterranean shores by the Phoenicians. The Phoenicians were originally dog-worshippers and believed in the immortality of dogs. Perhaps they brought Maltese to the isle of Malta as a religious gesture, or gift, much as the Dalai Lama gave his little dogs as gifts to visiting royalty and foreign dignitaries.

Dr. Johannes Caius, physician to Queen Elizabeth I and one of the founders of Caius College in Cambridge, England, wrote in 1576 in his book, *Englishe Dogges,* about them: "They are called Meliti, on the Island of Malta. They are very small indeed and chiefly sought after for the pleasure and amusements of women who carried them in their arms, their bosoms and their beds."

In these very early times it is believed they were also seen in both long and short coats and in all colors as well as pure white. They were small enough to be carried or transported easily in clothing and all sorts of wearing apparel since they were referred to as being about the size of a weasel.

The Maltese is said to have "bred true" to the small size for many centuries. Horrifying stories

have been recorded on the methods through which this was accomplished. If we are to believe ancient reports on procedures, we learn that in some instances wire cages were fitted and built around the bodies of puppies to restrict growth, and only removed when they reached the age—not the size—of maturity.

Others are said to have been enclosed in small boxes designed to prevent exercise so as not to stimulate appetite. It is said that in Egypt they were fed large amounts of salt to encourage thirst, and the vast amounts of water which they craved spoiled their appetites and was thought to retard growth in that manner. When they were fed, they were given only the choicest foods, but in the smallest possible amounts.

Detail from the painting "The Healing of the Demoniac," circa 1495, in which a Maltese dog is evident.

In 1650 a German physician wrote that some of the boxes and cages were lined with fleece so that the dogs would "think coat" at all times, and this would encourage the growth of their hair.

Cages and boxes and bad diets were not the least of the cruelties foisted on the breed to satisfy the whims of the breeders in those early times. In order to keep the noses short, the cartilage was broken shortly after birth. The ends of the noses were massaged vigorously thereafter in the belief that this constant irritation would help keep the nose short.

Linnaeus claimed growth could be controlled by rubbing their spinal columns with spirits of wine mixed with oil.

It is a wonder the breed survived at all . . . As a matter of fact, we know the Maltese was almost extinct on the isle of Malta before the beginning of the 16th century. A traveller to that island reported seeing them there in 1804, but refers to them as being *formerly* kept on the island but had become "almost extinct."

THE STORY OF THE SPANISH ARMADA

While it is believed that the first Maltese reached Britain early in the fourteenth century, it is more than likely they were brought there by the wives of the Roman rulers when they occupied England several centuries before William the Conqueror. There is yet another theory. That is, by the 1600s, during the wreck of the Spanish Armada off the Western coast of Scotland, a Maltese dog made it to shore and when bred to the Scottish Terriers along the coast, was influential in creating the Skye Terrier breed which Lady Macdonald of Armdale Castle pursued and popularized on the isle of Skye. The cross-breeding of the Maltese with the Black and Tan Manchester Terriers is said to be behind the creation of the Yorkshire Terrier also.

Dr. Caius did not share Lady Macdonald's enthusiasm for the little dogs breeding along the craggy coast of Scotland. In this book he referred to them as "beggarly beasts brought out of the barbarous borders from the uttermost countryes northward." However, the drop-eared Skyes at the time did bear a strong resemblance to the Maltese. Mary, Queen of Scots, is said to have had Maltese.

By the thirteenth century, trade had opened up with the Orient and indeed the entire Western world as well. With it came the eventual further exchange of canine specimens and a natural interbreeding of all these dogs.

THE ORIENTAL INFLUENCE

Following the opening and subsequent expansion of the trade routes to China and Japan there was an influx of Oriental dogs. These included the Pekingese, Lhasa Apso and Tibetan Spaniels which were brought back to England by the seamen on the merchant ships, or were presented as gifts to royalty. These little Toy dogs were highly prized and became known as little Lion dogs. The term "lion" was given to them because of the way the Chinese dogs were clipped . . . shaved hindquarters, full mane and tuft of hair on the end of the tail.

It can be imagined that with the scarcity of their numbers in foreign lands some were bred, out of necessity if for no other reason, to other than their own breed, either accidentally or with an eye toward change or improvement.

When the little Lion dogs with their shaggy coats were bred to the solid color Maltese, it naturally contributed to their stamina and coat quality. In fact, coat quality improved to such an extent that they were sometimes referred to as Shock Dogs because of their "shocks" of long hair and thick coats. Profuse coat was a highly desirable feature in small dogs in those times since these small "lap" dogs were used primarily to keep their masters and mistresses warm in the big drafty castles and stone houses on the farms. Central heating was unknown then and the only heat came from fireplaces in the rooms or kitchens. The warmth from the dogs' bodies gave off the necessary heat to merit their special place in such close proximity to their owners.

For this "service" they earned the titles of "gentle Spanyels," or "comforter dogs." The Maltese picked up the "spanyel" reference since so many of the lap dogs were spaniels and surely served as well. Whatever their title, these little dogs enjoyed much success sitting on the laps of the idle rich, always available for the warming of their hands and seeking no greater reward for it than the closeness they shared, and whatever attention, praise or tidbits they might have bestowed upon them.

It was also said the little dogs possessed great healing powers. Dr. Caius wrote that "their moderate vital heat, intermingling as it were with that of the humans, is believed by some people to be beneficial to the patient."

The confusion of the naming of the dog of Malta and classifying the purposes it was to serve continued. We have just mentioned it being referred to as a Spaniel, and a little Lion dog once these Oriental varieties arrived in Great Britain. That was not the last of the confusion. Even today the Tenerife dogs, Bichons and Lowchens are often referred to also as Lion dogs. In earlier times the Maltese were sometimes referred to as belonging to the Poodle family.

In one of H. D. Richardson's books on dogs, published in 1847 he explained the Maltese as being: "... a small Poodle, with silky hair instead of wool, and the short, turned-up nose of the pug ... this is by some naturalists classed with the spaniels; but in the form of its skull, in its erect ears (the type of ear at the time), rough muzzle and determination in the pursuit of vermin, it presents characteristics sufficient to induce me to place it in the present group (terrier) ... it is usually black, but sometimes white, in any case it should be of one colour."

In spite of the reference to both Poodle and Spaniel, the Kennel Club in England described the dog as having "a sharp, terrier-like appearance." Our American Kennel Club states they are Spaniels, not Terriers, and resolved the situation by placing them in the Toy Group. It was a long time before they were generally called Maltese *dogs* rather than Maltese *Terriers*. And we must admit, they certainly carry most of the terrier traits. If it weren't for their silky coat and tiny size they could certainly follow all of the remarkable sporting dog instincts also, and perhaps do quite well in the field. Their enthusiasm, if only for hunting mice, remains with them even today.

At any rate, we can be grateful that our little Maltese did not suffer any "identity crisis" and continued to be known and loved for its remarkable disposition.

THE NINETEENTH CENTURY

While it was believed that the Maltese was enjoying a certain degree of popularity in Britain, a painting rendered by Sir Edwin Landseer in 1830 entitled "Lion Dog from Malta—The Last of his Tribe" seems to cast his personal doubt on it. The painting shows a decidedly healthy-looking little Maltese on a table with the head of an enormous Mastiff-type dog by the table next to it.

It is unlikely, but perhaps the artist meant no more than to indicate that the large dog was about

to devour the little Maltese reclining so conveniently on the table by his head. But at least we can be grateful that the breed did manage to survive and to continue in its recognizable form and in the increasingly desirable all-white color everyone eventually preferred, as is seen in the Landseer painting, and is now required to meet our present day Standard.

Whatever Landseer's intention had been, he realized his "mistake" by 1851 when he painted the Duchess of Kent's Maltese named Lambkin. It was plain to see that the breed was enjoying royal patronage. Indeed, royal recognition from on high came in the form of a letter of condolence from the Queen of England herself when she learned of the death of little Lambkin.

OTHER EARLY IMPORTS

There is no written record, of course, of the earliest imports that arrived in England either about those that were supposed to have come with the invading Romans or on the merchant ships from the Orient. But we do know that in 1841 two Maltese arrived in England with a Captain Lukey who was in the service of the East India Trading Company.

He brought with him from Manila in the Philippines two little Maltese named Cupid and Psyche. Originally intended as gifts for Queen Victoria, after nine months aboard ship their coats had become so neglected that they looked too disreputable to be presented to the Queen. Fortunately for the two little dogs, they found refuge with Captain Lukey's brother, a Mastiff breeder. It was from their matings that the foundation stock of the breed was established and was responsible for the subsequent rise in popularity in the British Isles.

Cupid and Psyche were the first of several Maltese imported from Manila, but while they obviously originated in China (said to be around the first century), they became known as "the dogs of Manila." A dog named Archer, owned by a Mrs. Pidgley, was referred to as "a dog from Manila" at the time she acquired it.

In 1859 a Miss Gibbs of Morden obtained a bitch, also named Psyche, from Mr. Lukey. This descendant of the "original" Psyche weighed just 3¼ pounds, was pure white, with a coat measuring 15 inches long at the shoulders. She was described as being "a ball of animated floss." Miss Gibbs entered her at the June 1859 Newcastle-on-Tyne dog show, England's first dog show. Psyche's true value was partly due to her diminutive size, for others being shown at the time weighed closer to 6 pounds. A Mr. Robert Mandeville, perhaps the most prominent breeder at the time, had a dog named Fido which stood 11 inches tall and weighed 6½ pounds, and was considered to be one of the best around at that time.

As was the custom then, breeders gave the same name to several succeeding dogs in their kennels; it is therefore impossible to judge how prepotent a sire the original Fido was, since there is no way of telling which Fido was doing the siring!

FIRST MALTESE SHOW DOGS IN ENGLAND

As just mentioned, the first dog show in England was Newcastle-on-Tyne in 1859. This was approximately 14 years before The Kennel Club was formed in that country. A scant two decades after the arrival of Cupid and Psyche from Manila the breed had managed to expand and produce fanciers enthusiastic enough to see an entry of forty Maltese at the same dog show. In Scotland by the 1860s the Maltese were also being shown.

The "for sale" prices on Maltese listed in the dog show catalogues ran all the way up to a thousand pounds. This gives evidence of the esteem in which the breed was held, as well as the monetary value placed on them.

Earlier still, some of the better *little* dogs were going for ten gold coins each in Paris, and elsewhere they were sold for as much as forty gold coins!

These early show specimens were reported to be even smaller than our present-day dogs and still had high ear set, though no actual mention is made as to whether they carried prick ears.

"PATRON SAINT" OF THE BREED

Lady Gifford, who showed teams of little Maltese, had been referred to as the "patron saint" of the breed, so it was particularly unfortunate that after her demise the breed began to be demeaned by the general public. There were rumors that breedings were producing pink eyes and copper-colored noses. Some of this stemmed from the fact that in the desperate attempt to keep the size down—though no longer by confining them in boxes—the stamina and constitutions of the little dogs began to deteriorate.

Fortunately, during the next four decades new blood was obtained from European kennels, mostly from Holland and Germany. While the size was large, it did bring back the stamina that had been lost in the breed. Eventually they even managed to reduce the size once again to between four and nine pounds which was thought to be desirable and correct at that time.

NINETEENTH CENTURY BREEDERS

During the early days before the beginning of the twentieth century, there were several breeders who were working diligently to establish the Maltese breed and entered them at the dog shows.

People like J. Woodruff, W. Smallwood, Charles Mitchell, and Alfred Smith were all exhibiting in the area around London.

Another prominent breeder during the mid-1800s was William MacDonald, whose dog Prince won a cash prize of one pound at the 1863 Birmingham show. It is interesting to note the description of the class in which the dog had to be shown. ". . . the extra class for any known breeds of foreign dogs of small size, not used in the fields of sports."

William MacDonald's dog Prince was not to be confused with Mr. Robert Mandeville's dog Prince. Nor was Mr. Mandeville's dog Fido to be confused with Mrs. L. Mandeville's dog Fido. As we explained previously, there were loose regulations regarding names of dogs in those early times. Not only were several dogs in the same kennel given the same names but other kennels also had dogs of the same names, without ever bothering to add Roman numerals, Jr. or Sr., etc., after their names or on registrations.

To continue the pattern, we note a winning Maltese belonging to Mr. Tupper who also owned a "Fido," and Mr. Baker owned a dog Prince. Mrs. Bligh Monck was known for her famous Mopsey, whelped in 1865, and immortalized in a painting by famous dog artist George Earl. There were several Mopseys as well.

Other nineteenth century breeders were Mr. Dewar, Mr. Beattie, Mr. Blackman, Mrs. Sarah Blackman, R. P. Whitlock, Mr. Coleman, Mr. A. Dewey and Miss A. J. Harvey.

Mrs. A. Langton was another well-known breeder-exhibitor in the last two decades of the century as were Mr. C. Pettit, Mrs. Ethel Palmer, Mr. T. W. Leese, L. Weller, Mrs. Fish, Mr. E. Raymont and the extraordinary Lady Gifford.

New Zealand Ch. Garegwen Shining Star was whelped in Australia in January 1977. His sire was Australian Ch. Vicbrita Avalanche (imported from England) out of Manalee Lady Carina. Lady Carina's grandsire was the multi Best in Show Australian Ch. Boreas Bonitas, a Maltese imported from the United States. Owner is Mrs. N. C. Simpson, Carabelle Kennels, New Zealand.

20

CHAPTER THREE

The Maltese in Great Britain

A famous Maltese Terrier from the early days in England. J. Jacobs was the owner of Ch. Pixie, sketched by R. M. Moore.

At the turn of the century an eminent breeder, exhibitor and judge of dogs named Charles Henry Lane wrote a book entitled "All About Dogs." In it he thanks a friend of his named J. Jacobs for acquainting him with the joys of the Maltese breed, and credits him as being the best-known breeder of Maltese at that time. Once again you will note that the Maltese is referred to as a Maltese Terrier in this volume, and Mr. Lane begins his little treatise on the breed by declaring it a breed whose praises he had been singing for years.

To quote in part from his writing in the book, he goes on record as being quite impressed with Maltese, but primarily as a *pet dog*.

". . . and I am delighted to see they are slowly coming back into favour. Those of my readers who remember the Team shown, many years since, by the late Lady Gifford, will, I think, confirm my opinion, that a more beautiful lot of ladies' pet dogs could not be seen. To those not acquainted with the breed, I may say, they resemble very small drop-eared Skye Terriers, with pure white long coats, often sweeping the ground, and almost like floss silk in texture, with short backs and tails curled over them, dark, piercing eyes and black noses.

"They are very smart, cocky little fellows. I admire them greatly, and have done my best for some years past to revive interest in them, and am glad to see better entries at shows which provide classes and judges to suit them. This is

thought to be one of the oldest of the Toy breeds, having been highly prized by the ladies of ancient Greece, and other nations of that historic period."

Mr. Lane goes on to write more of the description of the breed at the turn of the century, and once again mention is made of the Skye.

"Head should be much like that of a drop-eared in miniature. Coat long, straight and silky, often sweeping the ground, quite free from curl, or wooliness. Nose and roof of mouth black, ears moderately long, well feathered, with hair mingling on neck. Tail short, well feathered, and curled tightly over back. Colour, pure white, without markings, or even tints of any other colour. Weight five to six pounds, the smaller the better, other points being equal."

In the credit to his friend Mr. Jacobs he stated, "I have been able to give a portrait of his beautiful little champion." The beautiful little champion he was referring to was Ch. Pixie, featured in the book in a drawing by R. M. Moore and reproduced in this book.

At the turn of the century enough colored Maltese were seen to warrant the starting of special classes for them at the shows, beginning in 1902. For some unknown reason the weight requirements for the colored Maltese and the white Maltese differed. The colored, or "other than white" as they were classified, were not to exceed 8½ pounds and the white were not to exceed 12 pounds.

The colored Maltese were rather common-place in Europe and in England; Mrs. Pryce Hamilton had a corner on the market, but none were seen in the show rings after 1910.

Mrs. A. Langton Money owned both colored and white Maltese. Some of her contemporaries who favored pure white were Miss Smythe, Mrs. M. Moss, Miss M. Fraser-Newalls, Mrs. Dixon, Mrs. R. H. Horlock, Florence Knott, Mrs. Acland Hood, Mrs. Gilbert, Miss K. D. Forest, Mrs. J. L. Stallibrass, Mr. J. Milner, Mrs. L. Milner and Mrs. C. McCarthy.

It was many of these same names that were seen on the pedigrees of the Maltese that began to be exported to the United States. And another of the finest little Maltese ever shown before World War I was Mrs. Horowitz's Ch. Snowcloud of Esperance. This smart little showman had a coat that measured twenty-one inches across from tip to tip.

Mr. J. W. Watts had been active in the breed since before the turn of the century and had dogs named Flossie, Prince Lily White, Pixie, and Little Count. It is to his Ch. Prince Lilywhite (not to be confused with his Prince Lily White—two words in this case) and to Ch. Major Mite that most of the best dogs descended during the early years of the twentieth century.

MALTESE AND THE FIRST WORLD WAR

There is no doubt that the ravages of World War I in the British Isles caused immense hardships on the dog fancy. What quality breeding had been accomplished came to an abrupt halt with the onset of hostilities and the canine world was bound to suffer. It was perhaps to become the very lowest ebb for the Maltese breed in the country.

Fortunately, shortly after the war the Maltese once again returned to favor and new kennels began cropping up that were to bring new impetus to the breed. Many good ones were saved because the breed was small and food could be shared with them, unlike the larger breeds which had to be destroyed because of the vast amounts of food to keep them, and in many cases, they served as food themselves.

Dorothy King was another fancier who represented a third generation of Maltese breeds that managed to span the turn of the century and beyond. Miss King gave up breeding in 1902, but resumed her interest once again in the 1930s after purchasing Invicta White Rose from Miss

M. Neame. Miss King never used a kennel prefix, but her dogs all carried interesting names such as Pilgrim's Progress, Sea Nymph, and so on. Sea Nymph was Best Puppy Bitch at the 1930 Crufts show and won the Fawkham Cup, which was quite an accomplishment at the time.

In 1953, when Virginia Leitch wrote her book on the Maltese, Miss King was still showing but had greatly reduced her activities and had but two Maltese.

Harlingen

After World War I, several quality Maltese came along. None better, though, than Ch. Harlingen Snowman who held a long unbeaten record as winner of fifteen Championship Certificates and over fifty First Prizes. Bred by Miss M. van Oppen in 1926, he won the Southern Counties Canine Association Championship Show in 1927, including four Championship Certificates and his championship title that same year. Snowman died in 1936. Later, as Mrs. C. Roberts, she also bred Newfoundlands.

Harlingen Dolly was a small bitch with Dutch and German background. Another of her famous dogs was Ch. Harlingen Emblem. Emblem was actually bred in 1930 by Mrs. Roberts and was a son of Snowman out of Harlingen Miracle. Emblem won his first Championship Certificate at the 1931 Kennel Club show.

Invicta

Another of the very famous early kennels, started in 1927, was that of Invicta, the prefix given to Miss M. Neame's Maltese. Her Ch. Invicta Bo-Peep was a well-known bitch in her time, as were Invicta Meadowsweet, Urama, Fido and Quip. She also owned Tim of Achmondie and Pendora of Achmondie. Her Invicta dogs were shown at the Ladies Kennel Association Championship show at Olympia in 1932.

It was Miss Neame's contention that at about two years of age the Maltese coat is well developed and continues to blossom until about six years of age. After this time further improvement is unlikely to occur. Further, she contends that while the puppies are born smooth-coated they begin to give indication of how good their coats will actually be at around four or five weeks of age.

At this period in time it was also believed that combing the Maltese coat was better for it than brushing, when as much as eighty percent of the coats were wavy rather than straight, even though it was no more desirable then than a wavy coat is desired today.

In view of the success of Miss Neame's dogs, we can only imagine the added glory they would have brought to breed history had she not maintained a policy of retiring a dog once it had attained its championship.

By the end of the 1960s, Miss Neame had ceased operations of her kennel after more than a half century of devotion to the breed.

Rhosneigr

Perhaps one of the most important kennels of all in the early days was that of Mrs. Marion Crook who used the kennel name of Rhosneigr. Best known of all her dogs might be said to be Rhosneigr Invicta Croesus, winner of Best Toy and Groups and a Best in Show. He had amassed over two hundred fifty cups and awards before his retirement from the show ring.

After becoming Mrs. G. Tighe, her dogs were dispersed and she moved to Spain where she turned to judging Maltese instead of breeding them. In the years that followed, she judged at just about all of the major shows in England, including the 1965 Crufts event and a Dublin, Ireland Championship show.

Her Rhosneigr White Satin was the first of her line to leave for the United States when imported by Commander Shaw of Miami, Florida.

Maltessa Maltese

Dorothy Shepperd, one-time kennel assistant to Miss M. Neame, bred and owned the Maltessa Maltese after leaving Miss Neame's employ. One of her best-known homebreds was Maltessa Ruffles. Her Maltessa Pipkin, whelped in April 1932, was said to be the smallest adult Maltese being shown in his time, weighing in at a scant five and a half pounds. His sire was the popular stud Invicta Joker and he was out of Invicta Pixie.

Ruffles was sired by Joker out of Miss Shepperd's Maltessa Fifinella, and was whelped in August 1932. Bred and shown by Miss Shepperd herself, Ruffles was the winner of many prizes and much acclaim as a true representative of his breed. Her Maltessa Miranda won a Championship Certificate at just one year of age. She, also, was out of an Invicta sire and a Maltessa dam.

Snowman, The Potent Sire

In 1934 a Snowman daughter was bred and exhibited by Mrs. L. H. Card. Her name was Ch. White Chick and she was shown at the 1934 Crufts show and was the winner of many prizes and several Championship Certificates.

Fawkham

Ch. Nicholas of Fawkham was another famous pre-war Maltese owned by Miss Betty Worthington. Her Fawkham Kennels were based on Harlingen lines. Miss Worthington was also a former president of the English Maltese Club. She exported some of her stock to Italy and Africa.

Her outstanding dogs were all big winners during the 1930s and on up to just before World War II.

In addition to Nicholas, some of her most famous dogs were Silverstar of Fawkham, Eulalie of Fawkham and Jeremy, Regency, Angel, and Toinette of Fawkham.

OTHER MALTESE BREEDERS

In 1929 Miss B. MacDonald added Maltese to her Achmondie Yorkshire Terrier Kennels. During the 1930s Mrs. D. Pierre was showing under the Verington kennel name, Mrs. Madeline Beeching and her daughter had the Oldtime Kennels and Mrs. I.C. Brierley had her Leckhampton Maltese since 1937. Her Leckhampton Larkspur was a winner at the 1951 Crufts show which vouches for the success of her kennel over the span of two decades.

Gissing

Mrs. C. M. Hunter began her famous Gissing Kennel in 1945, adding Maltese to several other breeds in which she had become interested. Her first stud dog was Ch. Invicta Phaon. By the 1960s she had produced a long line of Maltese carrying her Gissing name.

In 1968 Mrs. Hunter moved her home and kennel to Portugal via airplane. The news media had a field day reporting on the embarkation of almost 100 Maltese dogs and some cats from Gloucester airport en route to their new home. The entire plane was renovated to accommodate Mrs. Hunter and her entourage at great expense.

Edward Ash on the Maltese

In Edward C. Ash's book entitled *The Practical Dog Book* published by Simpkin Marshall in London, he referred to the Maltese breed as follows:

"The Maltese may be a small dog, but it is very important. A favourite of many Kings and Queens, Lords and Ladies from the times when men went to war in chariots to the present day."

A strong expression of the life and times of the Maltese in that country before and most certainly after World War II.

AFTER THE SECOND WORLD WAR

In 1946 when Mrs. Blanche Mace returned to England with her husband, she became interested in dogs once again. In addition to her first loves—Chows and Pekingese—she eventually got deeply involved with Maltese. Her Yelwa strain was developed and became famous in Great Britain.

Illness prevented her from showing after 1963 but her interest in breeding continued with an accent on preserving the small size in the breed without jeopardy to their health.

Her list of champions is impressive, and she is well-known as the breeder of International Champion Avyola of Yelwa.

THE NINETEEN-FIFTIES

While interest was once again stirring in the breed in the years immediately following the end of World War II, it was well into the 1950s before great progress was made in Maltese. Several years were needed to fully recuperate from the effects of the devastation England suffered. A few of the prominent breeders that were so active during the 1930s survived and continued, on a somewhat smaller scale. We also saw the new breeders coming up in the ranks who were going to "carry on" as the British are wont to say, with what they could recapture from the great lines established before World War II.

Most of the flourishing kennels after the war managed to continue their breeding programs so successfully that there are a good number of them still active today. We can safely say that because of their interest and sincerity, the breed has enjoyed no less popularity than it did at peak periods in the past.

Floriana

Miss Warman's Floriana Maltese began in 1954. Some of her Floriana dogs found their way to Canada and the United States as well. Little wonder she enjoyed much success when her kennel lines were based on Invicta, Rhosneigr, and Yelwa stock. There were other lines brought into her kennel operation, but these three were largely responsible for her excellent specimens.

Maybush

The Maybush Maltese were bred and owned by Mrs. Dorothy Peck who exported some Maltese to the island of Malta, thereby establishing Invicta, Rhosneigr and Harlingen lines there.

Vicbrita

The Vicbrita Kennels were established in 1953 when Doctor and Mrs. Ronald White imported a Maltese from Africa. This one was followed by Golden Dollar of Gissing and Harlingen Coppelia.

By 1970 Mrs. White's Homebred Ch. Vicbrita Sebastian was the top-winning Maltese in Great Britain. Sired by Vicbrita Gambore out of Ch. Vicbrita Samantha, he closed out the first year of this new decade by winning Reserve Best in Show at the Hove Championship Show.

The Vicbrita Kennels are known for many famous dogs including Ch. Vicbrita Tobias that won his first Championship Certificate in 1967 while still a puppy, and eight C.C.'s by 1968. He was also Best Toy at the 1971 Birmingham City show.

Ch. Vicbrita Fidelity was Best in Show in 1963 at the Three Counties show and one of his daughters, Ch. Vicbrita Petit Point won the Best in Show there in 1966. Fidelity was a Group winner at the shows in 1963, 1964, and 1965.

In 1962 Vicbrita Spectacular was launched on a spectacular show ring career. Among her numerous wins was a Best Bitch in Show, and a third place in the final line-up at Crufts. This beautiful bitch represented the third generation of champion bitches for Mrs. White.

Ch. Vicbrita Girlfriend was exported to Frank Oberstar and Larry Ward in the United States for their famous kennel and Mrs. White's International Ch. Vicbrita Pimpernel was exported to Signorina Bianca Tamagnone in Italy where she earned her International title and had a remarkable career on the continent.

Dr. and Mrs. White, and daughter Gilean who became a partner with her mother in 1958, are proud of the fact that Vicbrita is the only British Maltese kennel to have won Supreme Best in Show all-breeds at a championship show *twice*. Their list of champion Maltese that are known all over the world is very impressive.

THE SIXTIES AND SEVENTIES

By the 1960s Elizabeth Morgan came upon the scene with her Glamore dogs, Mrs. G. C. Parkinsen was showing under the Pegaron name, there were the Ellwin Maltese of Mrs. M. Lewin, Mrs. P. J. Pardoe, Mrs. J. Walker, Mrs. M. White, Mrs. P. B. Fraser, the Cotsvale dogs of Miss M. Wild and the Jayleen lines in Ireland.

There were Maltese with kennel prefixes (listed alphabetically) such as Ablench, Abou, Beggarshill, Berrylou, Bleathwood, Brantcliff, Burwardsley, Chryslines, Edmar, Ellwin, Floriana, Francoombe, Garet, Gissing, Gosmore, Harlingen, Hylands, Immacula, Labellas, Lamsgrove, Lilactime, Mannsown, Margretwoods, May-Orko, Maytheas, Movalian, Phieos, Quantos, Rhosneigr, Romvic, Saumarez, Shenala, Snowgoose, Snowsilk, Syrosa, Tolcarne, Triogen, Valday, Vicbrita and Survic.

It is reassuring to notice in this list which takes us into the decade of the 1980s that so many of the famous old kennels are still breeding and winning and maintaining breed Standards.

CRUFTS DOG SHOW

Sometimes referred to as "the greatest show on earth," with all apologies to P. T. Barnum, the Crufts Dog Show was first held in 1891 at the Agricultural Hall in Islington, England. Apart from the war years when most all dog shows on both sides of the Atlantic were affected, and one civil disaster, Crufts has continued to the present date with only one change of ownership. It was originally called the Crufts Great International Show. It is held every February, either just before or just after the February date of the Westminster Kennel Club in New York City.

Ch. Snow Goose Valient Lad, winner at the 1983 Crufts Dog show at Earls Court in London. Bred and owner-handled by Vicki Herrieff, "Benjamin" not only won the C.C. in the breed at this show, but went on to win the Toy Group. Judge Mrs. Peggy Sturgiss gave the C.C. in Bitches to Ellwins Sweet Charity, owned by Mrs. Muriel Lewin, president of the Maltese Club of Great Britain.

While our selection of a February Westminster date depends largely on the availability of the Madison Square Garden facilities, the February date for Crufts was determined by the February closing of the game season, since the show originally featured gun dogs and sporting dogs. It was attended by dogs from many nations until the quarantine for foreign dogs prevented entries from other countries. However, it remains the largest dog show in the world, with entries nearing the ten thousand mark, as we enter the decade of the eighties.

A MALTESE WINS THE CRUFTS TOY GROUP

On Sunday, February 13, 1983 at the Annual Crufts Dog Show in London, a Maltese reached the top of the Toy Group. Ch. Snowgoose Valient Lad and his owner-handler Mrs. Vicki Herrieff, were presented with the Toy Group Trophy by Dame Eva Turner, a well-known British opera star.

Gail Hennessey, who was at the show to cover the Maltese classes for *Maltese Tales* magazine, was on hand to enjoy the victory and to write about it after visiting with the Herrieffs and interviewing Mrs. Peggy Sturgiss, the breed judge. Mrs. Bassett was the judge that awarded "Benjamin" as he is known at home, the coveted Toy Group win that was popular with the ringside crowd. The headlines in the newspapers said it all . . .

"Benjamin Supreme in the World of Toy Dogs."

The C.C. at this show went to Ellwins Sweet Charity, bred, owned and handled by Mrs. Muriel Lewin, President of the Maltese Club of Great Britain. We are grateful to Gail Hennessey for reporting on this major Maltese win.

THE FIRST CLUB CHAMPIONSHIP

The first Maltese Club Championship Show was held on April 16, 1966 in London, and was judged by Mrs. Brierley (not to be confused with the author!) whose prefix, Leckhampton, was well known in the breed even then. Miss M. Wild, who used the Cotsvale name as her kennel prefix, judged the bitches at this show. Mrs. B. Worthington was the referee at this initial event and will return as judge on the golden anniversary jubilee.

At the first show there were twenty-two classes and forty-six dogs entered for a total entry of one hundred nine. The dog Challenge Certificate was won by Mrs. T. Kirk's Immacula Top-O-Pole, winning from the Junior Class. It was his second C.C. Reserve Challenge Certificate was won by Ellwins Pipello, owned by Mrs. Lewin and a future champion.

The bitch Challenge Certificate at this first show was won by Mrs. Darcey's Triogen Toppet and her championship went with it. Better still, she went all the way to Best in Show. Reserve C.C. for bitches went to Mrs. White's Vicbrita Rhapsody. She was a future champion also. Another Vicbrita bitch won Best Puppy. Her name was Vicbrita Genevive.

FIRST BRITISH STUD BOOK

As with every kennel club, one of the first purposes is to establish a stud book record. The first volume published by The Kennel Club covered the period from 1859 to 1874. A total of twenty-four Maltese were included in this first volume. By the beginning of the 1980s, just over one hundred years later, they numbered in the thousands. It would seem safe to say that the future of this breed is assured in the country where it found its early, eventual recognition and continuing success.

REQUIREMENTS FOR THE MALTESE

Originally, Maltese came in various colors and color combinations. However, it was inevitable that the pure white would become the favorite color. Today it is the only color that is acceptable according to the requirements in every country where the Maltese is shown.

The Standard does allow for the lemon or perhaps light tan markings on the ears, but otherwise, the Maltese is required to be pure white.

By the time the Maltese got to be a show ring contender the Maltese Club of Britain did allow for "any self color" and actually offered classes at the shows for "other than white" Maltese between 1908 and 1913.

Size and weight have also been in contention during the years of their increasing popularity. While the British state that the Maltese is not to be more than ten inches at the shoulder, the U.S. Standard strives to determine the breed size by height and weight qualifications, calling for no more than between four and six pounds.

BRITISH STANDARD
FOR THE MALTESE

Characteristics: Sweet tempered and very intelligent.

General Appearance: Should be smart, lively and alert. The action must be free, without extended weaving.

Head and Skull: From stop to centre of skull (centre between forepart of ears) and stop to tip of nose should be equally balanced. Stop should be defined. Nose should be pure black.

Eyes: Should be dark brown, with black eyerims, set in centre of cheeks and not bulging.

Ears: Should be long and well feathered and hanging close to the side of the head, the hair to be mingled with the coat at the shoulders.

Mouth: Level or scissor bite with teeth even.

Neck: Of medium length—set on well sloped shoulders.

Forequarters: Legs should be short and straight. Shoulders well sloped.

Body: Should be in every way well balanced and essentially short and cobby, with good rib spring and the back should be straight from the tip of the shoulders to the tail.

Hindquarters: Legs should be short and nicely angulated.

Feet: Should be round and the pads of the feet should be black.

Tail: Should be well arched over the back and feathered.

Coat: Should be good length, but not impeding action, of silky texture, not in any way woolly and should be straight. It should not be crimped and there should be no woolly undercoat.

Colour: Pure white, but slight lemon markings should not penalise.

Size: Not over 10 inches from ground to top of shoulder.

Faults: Bad mouth, over or undershot; gay tail; curly or woolly coat; brown nose; pink eye rims; unsound in any way.

AMERICAN STANDARD
FOR THE MALTESE

General Appearance: The Maltese is a toy dog covered from head to foot with a mantle of long, silky, white hair. He is gentle-mannered and affectionate, eager and sprightly in action, and, despite his size, possessed of the vigor needed for the satisfactory companion.

Head: Of medium length and in proportion to the size of the dog. The skull is slightly rounded on top, the stop moderate. **The drop ears** are rather low set and heavily feathered with long hair that hangs close to the head. **Eyes** are set not too far apart; they are very dark and round, their black rims enhancing the gentle yet alert expression. **The muzzle** is of medium length, fine and tapered but not snipy. **The nose** is black. **The teeth** meet in an even, edge-to-edge bite, or in a scissors bite.

Neck: Sufficient length of neck is desirable as promoting a high carriage of the head.

Body: Compact, the height from the withers to the ground equaling the length from the withers to the root of the tail. Shoulder blades are sloping, the elbows well knit and held close to the body. The back is level in topline, the ribs well sprung. The chest is fairly deep, the loins taut, strong, and just slightly tucked up underneath.

Tail: A long-haired plume carried gracefully over the back, its tip lying to the side over the quarter.

Legs and Feet: Legs are fine-boned and nicely feathered. Forelegs are straight, their pastern joints well knit and devoid of appreciable bend. Hind legs are strong and moderately angulated at stifles and hocks. The feet are small and round, with toe pads black. Scraggly hairs on the feet may be trimmed to give a neater appearance.

Coat and Color: The coat is single, that is, without undercoat. It hangs long, flat, and silky over the sides of the body almost, if not quite, to the ground. The long head-hair may be tied up in a topknot or it may be left hanging. Any suggestion of kinkiness, curliness, or woolly texture is objectionable. Color, pure white. Light tan or lemon on the ears is permissible, but not desirable.

Size: Weight under 7 pounds, with from 4 to 6 pounds preferred. Over-all quality is to be favored over size.

Gait: The Maltese moves with a jaunty, smooth, flowing gait. Viewed from the side, he gives an impression of rapid movement, size considered. In the stride, the forelegs reach straight and free from the shoulders, with elbows close. Hind legs to move in a straight line. Cowhocks or any suggestion of hind leg toeing in or out are faults.

Temperament: For all his diminutive size, the Maltese seems to be without fear. His trust and affectionate responsiveness are very appealing. He is among the gentlest mannered of all little dogs, yet he is lively and playful as well as vigorous.

Ch. Jo Ann's Merrylane Matchmaker, winner of 75 Bests of Breed, 8 Group Firsts, 12 Seconds, 9 Thirds, and 12 Fourths. Bred, owned, and handled by Jo Ann Dinsmore of Arlington Heights, Illinois, Matchmaker was sired by Ch. Tumblemere's Beau Jester ex Ch. Debbie's Majestic Crysta Lyn. Matchmaker also represented the "Ideal Maltese" in the 1982 issue of *Dog World* magazine. Martin Booth photograph.

CHAPTER FOUR

The Maltese Comes To the United States

Ch. Villa Malta Musi is pictured winning a Group.

The exact date of arrival of the first Maltese in this country is not known or documented. As in other countries, there were no permanent written records kept on dog breedings or detailed pedigrees. Even when the first stud books were beginning to be kept, the entries were usually skimpy and not always accurate. They were based on memory or hearsay. Such was the case with the early Maltese records.

Many breeds of dogs—including the Maltese—were imported by fanciers before there were such things as dog shows, and surely before anyone had the idea of starting a kennel or bloodline of their own in any of the so-called "pure" breeds. We can only assume our little Maltese reached American shores from England as early as 1850, if what we see in old paintings and other art forms can be believed.

We must also realize that most Maltese that found their way to the United States were registered in England (if they *were* registered) and listed in the U.S. as "particulars unknown," since pedigrees and registration papers did not always come with the dogs at that time. We do know, however, that the first registrations with the American Kennel Club were based on early show entries, and the details concerning these early show dogs were gleaned from the pages of those early dog show catalogs or advertisements in the kennel club newspapers.

Most of these early dog show catalogs are on file at the library or show records department at the American Kennel Club and are readily accessible to those who wish to check out all the details and information contained in them on these first imports to this country. A friendly, cooperative staff is available for help in locating all available information on our breed.

THE FIRST MALTESE AT WESTMINSTER

While the very first dog show in America was for sporting dogs only and therefore no Maltese were entered, we do know that there were specimens entered at other shows in the 1870s. We also know that there was an imported "Maltese Lion Dog" entered at the first Westminster Kennel Club show held in Gilmore's Garden on May 8-10, 1877. The exact entry for the Miscellaneous Class, for either dogs or bitches, read as follows:

867. W.F. Morgan, 26 W 10th St., N.Y. Leo, white, 2 years. Imported Maltese Lion Dog. $100.

The price does not speak too well for the value placed on our little Maltese when you consider that an exhibitor named J.M. Crapo of Albany, New York advertised his buff 3-year-old dog Punch for sale for $10,000, and for the price of $100 you could buy Andrew Wagner's brown 2-year-old bitch, Nellie, who had only two legs! It was mentioned in the catalog, however, that both of Nellie's parents had four legs *each*.

Nellie was a small terrier-type dog missing her two front legs and considered such a "draw" for the show gate that a picture of her appeared side by side with several of the other canine attractions in the show newspaper advertisements. Nellie was right in there with Reverend Macdonna's "Rover" valued at $50,000 and Queen Victoria's Deerhounds, Dagmar and Oscar, valued at $100,000. Good company for Nellie and the Maltese Lion Dog, but quite a price spread!

While the Westminster Kennel Foundation reprinted the original catalog for this first show in 1977, the Miscellaneous Class is not marked to indicate the judge's placements. Captain J. M. Taylor officiated, but we will never know if our Maltese Lion Dog won over Nellie.

At the 1879 Westminster Show, our Maltese had yet another description. The entry was listed in the catalog as "colored Maltese Skye Terrier." It further stated it to be six years old, named Carlo, and owned by Dan Miller of New York City. A color distinction was also made at the 1881 show for a dog called London Charlie. It was listed as a Maltese Dog and owned by Steven Mulvey, also of New York City. The color description is confusing to say the least, since it is described as black and white. Was the black for the ears with an all white body or was there a color pattern?

Also at the 1881 show, a Miss Eva P. Russell of New York City entered her imported Maltese Terrier named Mozart. He was entered again the following year and listed as being "priceless."

In subsequent years at the Westminster shows, the Maltese left the Miscellaneous Class and were entered in the Non-sporting Group, eventually finding their rightful place in the Toy Group.

At the 1889 Westminster Show, a bitch listed as an imported Maltese Terrier and named Topsy, whelped in 1883 and owned by Miss Ida Orme (a name we would hear a great deal more of in the future of the Maltese in this country) was entered and priced at $1,000. Topsy was entered again in 1891 and 1892 but after her halcyon years, her value had slipped to $100. Her "ring-mate" at the 1892 show was a Maltese named Tont-tu and that price was $150.

Regulations at shows in those early days were a great deal more relaxed than they are today. Tont-tu was listed as "pedigree and breeder unknown" and Topsy originally was listed in this country as "pedigree unknown" but later "legitimatized" as being by Duke out of Beauty.

At the 1893 Westminster show, two other Maltese were entered with breeding particulars all listed as unknown. Mr. A. Lloyd entered his dog "Doc" and declared him for sale at $150. Another Maltese named Nellie was entered, making a total of two for the show.

At the 1894 Westminster event, Flossie, owned by Mrs. J. P. Wade of Long Island, was offered for sale at $200. A dog named Duke was also entered, owned by Mrs. E. C. Seamans. We can only speculate if this Duke might be the sire of Topsy who was listed as by Duke out of Beauty. However, it should be noted that Duke's background breeding is also listed as unknown.

In 1895, the Bushnell's Maltese, Cuba, was offered for sale for $250 in the Westminster catalog. The breeder was listed as Don Fernando. Cuba was in the 1899 show with new owner, Mrs. G. Keasbury.

In 1896, the Westminster Kennel Club boasted three entries for Maltese. There were Mrs. J. P. Wade's Flossie once again, Mrs. Estelle K. Provost's Madoc, and Mrs. H. Moore's Blanco. By the 1898 show, L. H. Snider entered his "Beauty" and priced it for sale at $500. We can say that during the 1890s the price seemed to rise continually from an original $100 to $150, and to a more substantial $500.

MALTESE MOUNTINGS

While it cannot be said that it was a "custom" at the time, during the 1890s and past the turn of the century, many dog lovers would have their beloved canines stuffed, or mounted, and presented to the American Museum of Natural History in New York City. Several pictures of Maltese mountings are presented in this book.

The author has made inquiries at the Museum, Department of Mammals, since it had been reported that these Maltese specimens could be viewed upon request. Such is not the case. They are deemed fragile and are carefully stored away.

The dog named Duke, mentioned earlier as an entrant at Westminster, was eventually mounted and presented to the Museum, in 1896. The same year a Maltese named Bijou was given to the Museum by Mrs. Mary Good. In 1914, La Condesa Beatrice di Tavara (known also as Beatrice Brown) of Portugal presented for posterity a mounted specimen named Beauty. We can only speculate if this Beauty and Duke were the parents of Ida Orme's Topsy.

THE TURN OF THE CENTURY

Entries at the turn of the century continued to be spotty. While we know the first registrations in 1887 were for two Maltese, one being Mrs. A. Livingston's "Snips," whelped in 1886, it wasn't until 1901 that two more Maltese were registered. These were Mrs. W. L. Draper's Bebe, whelped at her Atlanta, Georgia, residence in 1900,and Mrs. John McCullough's Little Miss Moffett, also whelped in 1900, in Indianapolis.

In 1902, six more were registered from the Chicago area by W. P. Farmer, Union Park Kennels. So we see evidence that the breed had at least reached the midwest by this time. This location also saw Miss Josie Travilla breeding Maltese at her kennels in Kansas City, Missouri.

FIRST BEST IN SHOW WINNER

In 1919 at the New Westminster Show in Canada, Mrs. Anna Judd's Maltese, Ch. Melita Snow Dream won Best in Show, thereby becoming the first Best in Show winner in the breed in that country. But by this time World War I had begun and the swell of popularity in the breed began to subside due to lack of imports and hard times, and the breed just never made a comeback after peace was declared. By 1939 the breed was practically non-existent in this country. From 1888 to 1951, 1,240 Maltese had been registered and 108 championship titles were recorded.

After World War II and the influence of the Villa Malta Kennels, the breed once again began to find a place in the fancy.

"Bijou," a stuffed and mounted Maltese dog, donated in 1896 to the American Museum of Natural History in New York City by Mrs. Mary Good. Photo courtesy of the American Museum of Natural History.

THE FAMOUS VILLA MALTA KENNELS

If there is any single kennel that can be said to have brought the attention of the dog fancy to our breed in the best possible way, it would have to be the Villa Malta Kennels of Dr. and Mrs. Vincenzo Calvaresi. His breed brace and team wins at all the major shows, but especially at Westminster, brought the Maltese a popularity few other breeds have ever enjoyed.

Dr. Calvaresi's first Maltese came from the kennel of his friend, Eleanor Bancroft, who had much success with her Hale Farm dogs. By 1947 the Villa Malta name was synonymous with Maltese and Dr. Calvaresi was winning wherever he chose to exhibit. In 1948, after a trip to Italy, he imported three Electa dogs which he incorporated into his breeding program and his show-winning teams.

It was also Dr. Calvaresi who initiated the finer points of grooming the breed to perfection as well. In 1958 the Gaines Research Center bestowed the Fido Award on him for his many years of contributions to the Maltese breed. The Villa Malta suffix in a pedigree was highly respected and was considered a leading line for several decades. It is still referred to today as one of the all-time famous kennels in our breed.

Some of the leading dogs from Villa Malta were Musi, Fido, Tana, Ricco, Eva Tana, Sir Keno, Faida, Talia II, Merlin, Montego, Sattina, Aramis, Wusi, and Evina—to name just a few who carried the Villa Malta name to the heights of success.

MARGARET M. ROZIK

It was the great good fortune of Margaret M. Rozik of Belle Vernon, Pennsylvania, to fall heir to the Villa Malta Kennels of Dr. and Mrs. Calvaresi when the time came to pass on the torch of victory.

International Ch. Electa Brio is one of the foundation dogs that helped Dr. and Mrs. Calvaresi establish their world-famous Villa Malta line.

Ch. Villa Malta's Talia winning Best in Show in 1960 under the late Percy Roberts. Owned by Margaret Rozik, Villa Malta Kennels, Belle Vernon, Pennsylvania.

The first Maltese Margaret Rozik saw was Ch. Villa Malta's Vivia, in 1940. Vivia was sired by Ch. Cupid of Hale Farms out of Hale Farms Hermanita. Interested chiefly in large breeds, she thought no more about the little white dogs until 1945 when she saw Ch. Issa of Villa Malta, but it wasn't until 1951 that she actually brought one home—and her husband told her it looked like a mop.

It was at this time that she started handling for Dr. Calvaresi, although on a small scale. He showed mainly in the east, while the Roziks were active on the west coast. She also bred dogs for the Calvaresis as well.

Margaret Rozik's Ch. Evina of Villa Malta began the succession of Maltese and she went on to win many Groups and Bests in Show, and finished many champions, including Ch. Musi, Ch. Talia, Ch. Lacy, Ch. Evina, and many more.

On July 23, 1966, Dr. Calvaresi handed Margaret M. Rozik the keys to the Villa Malta Kennels and the breed entered a new era under

her leadership. Forty-five of the best Maltese from Dr. Calvaresi joined the thirty-five dogs at Margaret Rozik's kennel in Belle Vernon when the Calvaresis moved to Florida. They remained in Florida until 1978 when they moved to a small villa in Portugal. Unfortunately, they no longer have dogs.

Margaret Rozik continues to breed and show on a small scale, and has bred many champions bearing the Villa Malta name. Her granddaughter, De Anna Rozik, a lovely girl in her late teens, owns some of her own Villa Malta dogs, and hopes to continue in the fancy after finishing school.

Margaret Rozik is grateful to the Calvaresis for giving her over thirty years of love and affection from owning Maltese, and in 1980 was Breeder of the Year. We are sure that Dr. and Mrs. Calvaresi are proud of the continued love, care, and success she has heaped upon the kennel that helped establish, maintain, and continue the famous name of Villa Malta.

Mexican and American Ch. Villa Malta Lacy, owned by Alma and Cye Statum of Virginia, and shown for them by Marge Rozik. Photo by Larry Kalstone.

THE END OF THE "OLD TIMERS"

Will Judy, head of the dog publishing empire, founded in 1942 a rather unique club he called "The Oldtimers of the Kennel World." Headquarters was in Chicago, where he published books, edited his *Dog World* magazine, and served as the national chairman of the club. Members each had a lifetime membership and proudly displayed or wore the gold-and-white button issued to them if they qualified for membership.

Eligibility was based on ten years of activity in some phase of the dog field; later it was raised to fifteen years of active service to the fancy, then twenty years, and finally to a quarter of a century. The strict enforcement of requiring active participation in the dog fancy kept the roster of members to a minimum, and by the mid-sixties, membership still remained under five hundred.

The purpose of this nonprofit organization was to represent and provide a wealth of information and experience for newcomers who were graciously urged to take advantage of their counsel and advice so they could maintain the highest possible sportsmanship for the fancy.

The great versatility of the membership was clearly seen when the published directory for the club indicated that many of the members owned more than one breed or could recount their many years of service. Maltese breeder Mrs. O. C. Roland of Minneapolis, Minnesota, was one of this illustrious group.

Ch. Parquin's Destiny Prince, bred by Mrs. W. R. Cotton and handled by Win Cotton. "Desi" was whelped in 1974, sired by Margaretwoods Designer ex Parquins Wild Rose.

It is regrettable that the mid-sixties saw the end of this club, which included so many of dogdom's elite who were willing and generous in giving their time to help others. The value of such a group would be appreciated and highly regarded in the fancy today.

OTHER EARLY BREEDERS

With the Villa Malta Kennels leading the way in showmanship, grooming, and show records, others were soon to follow. Some of the names from these early kennels can still be found in the pedigrees of the top winning dogs that made history in the breed. Winifred Cotton was one of these who managed to bring her early interest in the breed in England dating back to the mid-fifties and continuing in this country once she made her home in the United States.

Parquin

Winifred Cotton has been in Maltese since 1956 and began showing the breed in 1960 in England. She has been a member of the American Maltese Association since 1980 and now resides in Joshua, Texas.

During the 1950s, Mrs. Cotton also had Poodles and later Shih Tzu at her kennels, and is a retired American Kennel Club approved judge.

Perhaps her best remembered dog was Ch. Parquin's Destiny Prince, whelped in 1974, which had Gissing, Zurvic, and Rhosneigr bloodlines behind him, as well as Vicbrita.

Aennchen's Maltese

In the mid-1950s we saw the beginning of a new era in the breed. Aennchen and Anthony Antonelli began making a name for themselves in the Maltese world. Their original operation started in a trailer in Lodi, New Jersey. Aennchen taught Oriental dancing and Tony taught art in the local schools. It was not long before their dedication and planned breeding program began to pay off. Together with Aennchen's grooming ability and showmanship, she and her snow-white little "dancers" were setting records not only in the breed rings, but in the Toy Groups and the Best in Show rings.

By 1961 their American and Bermudian Ch. Aennchen's Raja Yoga was named Top Sire of the Year. He was the sire of nineteen champions and grandsire of many others. The same year, 1961, his daughter, Ch. Aennchen's Puja Dancer was named Top Dam of the Year with

Ch. Aennchen's Taja Dancer, bred by Mr. and Mrs. J. P. Antonelli and campaigned by Aennchen Antonelli of Waldwick, New Jersey.

seven champion offspring to her credit. This was the same period that Ch. Aennchen's Shikar Dancer was co-owned and being shown by both Aennchen and Joanne Hesse.

In the early 1970s when the ravages of cancer began to take its toll of Aennchen's strength and she suffered several serious setbacks, it was gratifying to her to see so many friends gather to help

Ch. Aennchen's Laksmi Dancer is pictured winning at a show under judge Anna Katherine Nicholas. The sire was American and Bermudian Ch. Aennchen's Raja Yoga ex Ch. Aennchen's Puja Dancer.

her maintain all her little dogs in full coat. Aennchen and Tony did not believe in keeping the dogs down in oil or their coats wrapped in papers, and once or twice a week their doggy friends would come to groom the dogs so they could be enjoyed more fully.

Aennchen's Savar Dancer was the last dog Aennchen showed before finding it impossible to exhibit in the ring. Puppies sired by him helped to establish the kennels of Dr. Roger and Nancy Brown, Gene and Anne Kannee, and their good friend Nicholas Cutillo. This third puppy was Soomi Dancer. Nick also acquired several other dogs from the Antonellis. After Aennchen's death in the late 1970s, Mr. Cutillo added to her original founding stock by obtaining bloodlines from the Jon Vir and Villa Malta lines.

Ch. Aennchen's Savar Dancer is just seven months old in this photograph.

The list of champions produced from the original foundation stock is long, and through Mr. Cutillo and Joanne Hesse, who has also carried on the line, top quality Maltese have continued to come along to keep Aennchen's name in the forefront of the breed.

Credit must also be given to Anthony Antonelli, who was a major contributor to the breeding of Aennchen's Maltese and certainly a light in her life with their shared joy in the success their dogs had over the years.

Aennchen was well known, well loved, and revered for her integrity and unending willingness to help and guide newcomers in the breed. Those of us who knew her will always remember Aennchen's endearing personality and good sportsmanship in the ring, as well as her consummate breeding program which produced so many beautiful Maltese. Along with Dr. Calvaresi, Aennchen did so much to preserve and popularize the breed.

It's time to stretch for Ch. Marcris Marshmallow, owned by Joyce Watkins of Miami, Florida.

Marcris Maltese

1959 was the year that Joyce Watkins established her Marcris Maltese in Miami, Florida. She states that she has lost track of the number of champions she has finished during the intervening years, but it's a lot. Her membership in the American Maltese Association keeps her in touch with all the happenings in the Maltese world, and she also has had Yorkshire Terriers since 1978. The Marcris name can be found in many of the pedigrees of today's Maltese winners and all those bearing the name are noted for their beauty and temperament.

A champion at eight months of age is Joyce Watkins' Ch. Marcris Marshmallow.

Al-Dor Maltese

American, Bermudian, and Mexican Ch. Fairy Fay's Figaro, owned and shown by Dorothy Tinker of Las Vegas, Nevada. Figaro is also a sire of champions.

Dorothy E. Tinker began breeding Maltese at her Al-Dor Kennels in Las Vegas, Nevada in 1959 and in the ensuing years has finished over twenty champions.

Her first Maltese was Fairy Fay's Figaro, an American champion at just one year of age. He also won the Toy Group in four out of four shows to finish for his Bermudian championship. This was followed by a Mexican championship. His daughter, Ch. Al-Dor Nena made her championship in Bermuda, Canada, and the United States.

Figaro's son, Ch. Al-Dor Pzazz, was among the Top Ten in the breed, and Ch. Al-Dor Randy was one of the top obedience Maltese. Her daughter, Nancy, has won five Bests in Show with their Maltese brace, Figaro and Ch. Fairy Fay's Kapu.

This brace, International Ch. Fairy Fay's Figaro and Ch. Fairy Fay's Kapu, won five Bests in Show in the Brace Classes. Handled by Nancy Tinker for owner Dorothy Tinker.

Dorothy has also imported several of the Vicbrita dogs from Margaret White in England and finished them to their championships. Ch. Vicbrita Tobias was one of the top stud dogs in England and was the sire of several champions in this country. Dorothy has had only Maltese for over a quarter of a century, and owned one of the first Maltese in Las Vegas. Before that, in 1926, she started showing French Bulldogs. She is active in several Maltese Clubs, including the California Maltese Fanciers, and is a charter member of the American Maltese Association. She has served on the Board and in 1983 was vice president for the west. She has been president of the Las Vegas Maltese Fanciers since 1971, and served on the show committee for the first individual Maltese Specialty held in New York in 1971. She and daughter Nancy were cochairpersons for the National Maltese Specialty held in Las Vegas in 1976 and again in 1982, two of the most successful specialty shows the American Maltese Association has held. Dorothy Tinker is also a charter member of the Southeast Missouri Kennel Club, which she helped organize, as well as the Imperial Valley and Silver State Kennel clubs.

Ch. Tutee's Merra Lee wears her queenly crown while admiring a recent trophy. Bred by Trudie Dillon of Graham, Washington, she is owned by Marge Stuber of Lima, Ohio.

Primrose Maltese

Marge Stuber, owner of Primrose Maltese, got into the breed in 1960, after four years in Shetland Sheepdogs.

Since that time, she has finished about forty-five champions and has been extremely active in club work involving the breed. She was corresponding secretary of the American Maltese Association from its inception in 1962 until 1982. She was assistant editor of the A.M.A. monthly publication, *Maltese R_x* for the same twenty year period, and Maltese breed columnist for *Dog World* since 1968.

Marge Stuber with future champion Jeremiah, almost four months old in this picture taken in 1978.

One of her Maltese, Ch. Trina of Primrose Place, had two legs toward a C.D. title, but Marge admits that she does not excel at obedience training even though she has started many of them on their way. Nor does she have any intention of judging the breed, but prefers to enjoy only the breeding and showing of them.

Mrs. Robert L. Stuber's foundation bitch was Ch. Vicbrita Rozeta, who became the dam of four champions. All the dogs at Primrose are raised in her house, and she has finished many champions under the Primrose name. Her Primrose Ceramics business offers a quality line of Maltese figurines. Her jewelry is all hand-painted with China oil paints and fired on porcelain, and includes necklaces, rings, earrings, pins, pill boxes, and framed miniatures.

Russ Ann Maltese

Anna Mae Hardy started breeding Maltese in 1962, and produced a champion in her first litter. Her name was Ch. Gidget of Marcris. The champion in her second litter was Ch. Bobbelee Tammy-Tu of Marcris. However, the most exciting Maltese to come to her was Ch. Russ Ann Petite Charmer. Bred by Emma Taylor in August 1971, she was purchased at eight weeks of age. She took some of her championship points from puppy classes. At three months of age she won a Group at a Match show and it was plain to see she was born to show.

At six months she won the Sweepstakes at the American Maltese Association Specialty in Chicago under Frank Oberstar. In 1974 she was Best Opposite at the National Specialty, and just after eight months of showing, Charm ended up the Number One Maltese bitch in the 1974 Phillips System.

In 1975 she was retired to the whelping box and produced two champions sired by Ch. C & M's Valentine of Midhill, and more champion get resulted from further breedings. In 1978, she won the Veteran Bitch class at the National Specialty and went Best Opposite of seventeen champion bitches. At age twelve (1983) she has produced five litters—truly a great bitch.

A total of seventeen champions have been made by Anna Mae Hardy.

Anna Mae Hardy and her ten-year-old Ch. Russ Ann Petite Charmer. The Russ Ann Maltese are based in Floral City, Florida.

Best Brace in Show in 1967 went to Ch. Pen Sans Cassandra and Ch. Sun Canyon Prelude, handled by Gary Busselman for owner Gloria Busselman of Richland, Washington.

Pen Sans Maltese

Gloria Busselman of Richland, Washington, is the owner of the Pen Sans Kennels where she has been breeding Maltese since 1966. Since she started showing them in 1965, she has finished fifteen champions and a Best in Show winner as well.

She has also had Shih Tzus since 1968 and is a member of the American Maltese Association and the Richland Kennel Club. More recently she has been associated with Pharoah Hounds and is a member of that parent club as well. She is also an American Kennel Club approved judge of both Maltese and Shih Tzu.

While Mrs. Busselman advocates teaching children respect for these small dogs, she is quick to state that she brought up two sons and two daughters during the years she was raising Maltese dogs.

This lovely head study of Ch. Fantasyland Strut N Stuff was photographed by owner-breeder Carole M. Baldwin.

Fantasyland

Fantasyland is the kennel name chosen by Carole M. Baldwin of Novato, California, to identify her Maltese and Miniature Poodles in the show ring. She has been showing Maltese since 1969 and breeding them since 1970. During this time she has finished thirty-four Maltese champions. She has been a member of the Bay Area Maltese Club since 1969 and the American Maltese Association since 1970.

Ch. Fantasyland Billy Jo M.M.A., shown winning Best of Winners and Best of Breed under judge Mildred Heald for a four-point major at the Willamette Valley Kennel Club show. Owner, breeder, and handler is Carole M. Baldwin of Novato, California.

Sun Canyon

Ch. Sun Canyon Co-Star, purchased sight unseen at just eight weeks of age, got the Sun Canyon Maltese started. Star was purchased from Mrs. Gladys Cecil of Santa Maria, California, and established Sun Canyon in 1961.

Miriam Thompson had high hopes for her little bitch, and she lived up to all expectations. She produced five champions, including her Best in Show daughter, Ch. Sun Canyon Starlet, herself the dam of two champions, and Ch. Sun Canyon Maestro, a Group winner and the sire of five champions.

Sun Canyon was a family affair, with daughter Linda helping with the grooming and breeding while Norman Thompson was responsible for the cleaning and feeding of them after his retirement as a rancher and farmer. Dwayne Young also helped with the showing of the dogs since 1959, when the Sun Canyon kennels were actively showing Toy Poodles.

More than forty Maltese earned their championships within the first seven years of activity. These awards included Best in Show, Specialty, and Group winners. Their Ch. Sun Canyon Carousel was also a Group winner in the early days in Sun Valley, California.

Nicholas Cutillo

Nicholas Cutillo fell in love with Maltese after learning about Ch. Aennchen's Poona Dancer and Ch. Aennchen's Toy Dancer, in 1961. It wasn't until 1968, however, that he acquired his first Maltese. Aennchen's Yuki of Aga-Lynn was the name, and it combined the best of both the Aennchen and Joanne-Chen lines. Later Aennchen and Anthony Antonelli presented him with Ch. Aennchen's Tasia Dancer, a half-sister to the great Poona Dancer.

Tasie finished her championship at the 1972 American Maltese Association National Specialty show held in conjunction with the International Kennel Club show in Chicago. She won a 5-point major and was a consistent winner after that, placing in the Toy Group many times.

It was while showing both Yuki and Tasia that the friendship with the Antonellis really grew and they went to many shows together, where Nick learned much about the breed and grooming from the "master" herself—Aennchen. Ch. Aennchen's Pompi Dancer was the next dog at Nick's kennel and proved herself a worthy dam.

The magnificent Ch. Aennchen's Tasia Dancer, bred by Mr. and Mrs. J. P. Antonelli and co-owned by Aennchen Antonelli and Nicholas Cutillo. Size, coat, expression ... all the ultimate in Maltese perfection.

Each of the single puppies from three of her litters went on to become champions, and produced champion offspring of their own.

As Aennchen's illness became more and more acute, Nick was given as a birthday present Ch. Aennchen's Soomi Dancer. This 3¾ pound darling, nicknamed "Sexi" for obvious reasons, went on to become the third champion in an all champion litter which was to be the last litter bred by the Antonellis before Aennchen's demise, in the early 1970s.

Ch. Soomi was awarded a Maltese Merit Award for having sired five champions.

Along with Soomi, Nick Cutillo was to acquire a tiny bitch named Ch. Jetline's Libra Dancer, who was sheer perfection in Maltese and finished with two 5-point majors before being given to Nick's parents as an anniversary present.

Many champions of these excellent lines were to follow, including Ch. Aennchen's Indra Dancer, bred by Mr. Cutillo, finishing in six shows with two 5-point majors. At an American Maltese Association supported entry show, Ch. Indra went Winners Bitch in a class of seventeen and Best of Opposite Sex over a large class of Specials. Inasmuch as Mr. Cutillo obtained his original interest and stock in the late 1960s and early 1970s from the Antonellis, it was Aennchen's wish that he continue his breeding program using the now famous Aennchen prefix.

41

Mr. Cutillo is a fashion designer whose creations have appeared in every major fashion store in the nation, including the windows of Saks Fifth Avenue, Bloomingdale's, and Henri Bendel, and have been seen in *Vogue, Harper's Bazaar,* and other leading publications devoted to couture. He has won honors for his work in oil and acrylic paintings, and he designed the official logo of the Metropolitan Area Maltese Association.

In the early 1980s, Nick Cutillo served as president of the American Maltese Association, the American Kennel Club's recognized parent club, as well as its delegate. He has also served on the Board of the AMA and has been a member of the Maltese Club of Greater Houston, former member of the California Maltese Club, and subscriber to the Bay Area Maltese Club. He has served on the board of governors of the Progressive Dog Club in New York City for over ten years and is a member of the Dog Fanciers Club for more than a decade as well. He has been a member of the Ramapo Kennel Club for longer than a decade and has been a guest speaker on many occasions. He is a contributing writer for the official news magazine of the American Maltese Association and has had articles on the breed published in the *American Kennel Gazette.*

Ch. Aennchen's Cari Krsna Dancer, owned by Nicholas Cutillo of New York City, is pictured winning under the late well-known Toy judge, Ruth Turner.

Brown's Maltese Dancers

Dr. and Mrs. Roger Brown of Omaha, Nebraska, got interested in Maltese in 1963 after an acquaintance with Aennchen Antonelli. In fact, Aennchen gave them authorization to use her "Dancer" suffix after their dogs' names. The Browns were dedicated dog fanciers since 1948 when they had Pomeranians, but they fell in love with the Maltese breed in the early sixties and have been active ever since.

Dr. and Mrs. Roger Brown with Ch. Aennchen's Suni Dancer.

They are founders of the Potomac Maltese Fanciers and members of the Nebraska Kennel Club. Nancy wrote the Maltese column for *Popular Dogs* after Aennchen gave up that assignment. Roger has also served for several years as an officer on the board of directors of the American Maltese Association and has been guest speaker at the American Dog Judges Association Seminar. Dr. Brown is a practicing small animal veterinarian, and is on the Board of Directors for ANCOM, a company which specializes in audiovisual films pertaining to small animals and which has produced 59 films to date.

Ch. Aennchen's Hindi Dancer, pictured winning the Toy Group at a Sioux City, Iowa, show. Bred by Aennchen Antonelli; owned by Dr. and Mrs. Roger Brown, Bel Air Animal Clinic, Omaha, Nebraska.

The Browns still keep in touch with J. P. "Tony" Antonelli whenever they are in the Florida area, just one of the places where Pam and Tracy Brown may be exhibiting their Maltese in the Obedience rings. To date, the Browns have finished nine champions.

Brown's Dandi Dancer, C.D.X., bred by Dr. and Mrs. Roger Brown. Dandi is owned and handled by Mrs. Dennis Brown.

March'en Maltese

Des Moines, Iowa, is the site of the March'en Maltese of Marcia L. Hostetler's kennels.

Earlier Marcia was involved with other breeds. (Boston Terriers in 1945 and Vizslas in 1962) and was active with 4-H groups before becoming involved with Maltese in 1964.

Marcia had purchased some of Joanne Hesse's stock and also uses the "Dancer" suffix on her dogs' names. The artwork on her kennel stationery was done for her by Aennchen's husband, J. P. Antonelli, and she cherishes the gesture.

Marcia Hostetler and Ch. March'en Top Hat Dancer.

Some of her best known dogs are Ch. March'en Kewpie Dancer, and Ch. Joanne-Chen's Mini Maid Dancer, which are behind most of her March'en Maltese. Marcia has been a member of the parent club since 1967 and the Des Moines Kennel Club since 1964. She has served as an officer since 1977 and was president in 1981, 1982, and 1983.

Jo Ann's Merrylane Maltese

Jo Ann Dinsmore of Arlington Heights, Illinois, purchased her first Maltese in 1964 and has been captivated by them ever since. Her first champion was a little dog named Stentaway Sonny Boy, which finished in both the United States and Canada and was bred by Mary Hechinger. She subsequently purchased two bitches, Joanne-Chen's Maja Dancer and Joanne-Chen's Melodee Dancer from Joanne Hesse. They became the foundation stock of her small kennel.

Ch. Maja, who was shown in Specials only four times, won a Best in Show before being retired for breeding. Her Ch. Jo Ann's Majestic Minstrel Man was her first homebred champion.

In the 1980s, Jo Ann Dinsmore is showing her Ch. Jo Ann's Merrylane Matchmaker. As of the end of 1982, he had won 75 Bests of Breed, 9 Group Firsts, 13 Seconds, 9 Thirds, and 12 Fourths. His first litter produced three males

Ch. March'en Kewpie Dancer, bred, owned, and handled by Marcia Hostetler of Des Moines, Iowa. Whelped in 1980, the sire was American and Canadian Ch. March'en Top Hat Dancer ex Ch. March'en Lady Bug Dancer. The judge for this win was Dorothy Nickles.

Ch. Jo Ann's Majestic Minstrel Man with his dam, Joanne-Chen's Melodie Dancer. Both are owned by Jo Ann Dinsmore of Arlington Heights, Illinois.

and all finished their championships. He had four other champions to his credit at the time of this writing.

Jo Ann Dinsmore also is the breeder of the top obedience Maltese for 1980, 1981, and 1982: the notable Ch. Ginger Jake, U.D. and Canadian C.D.X. He is trained and owned by Faith Ann Maciejewski of West Allis, Wisconsin. Jo Ann Dinsmore says "Love is. . .owning a Maltese!"

Ch. Jo Ann's Majestic Minstrel Man, bred, owned, and handled by Jo Ann Dinsmore.

Gulfstream

Mary Lou Porlick of Miami, Florida, established her Gulfstream Kennels in 1968 and began breeding Maltese. She had previously owned and trained in obedience work Cocker Spaniels, a Kerry Blue, and a Doberman. By 1970 she was handling Maltese to their championships and to date has finished seventeen. However, her Maltese have been shown in obedience since 1966 and she has achieved remarkable results with obedience titles on five of them. She has finished three C.D.'s, one C.D.X., and one U.D. In fact, Mary Lou teaches obedience classes and is professionally involved in training and handling.

She is a member of the American Maltese Association, the Greater Miami Dog Club, the Miami Obedience Club, and the Maltese Club of Greater Miami. For many years now she has been compiling obedience records for the breed while continuing with her show ring successes.

The truly remarkable achievements of the little Gulfstream Maltese can be found in the obedience chapter of this book.

Another of the "greats" in Maltese obedience history, Ch. Gulfstream Treasure, U.D. Bred and owned by Mary Lou Porlick of Miami, Florida, Treasure finished her breed championship in 1970, her C.D.X. in 1973, and the U.D. in 1977.

Ch. Gulfstream Chip O'Chalk is pictured winning under Mrs. Fishman at a 1983 show with Mary Lou Porlick, the breeder, handling for owner Dorothy Hatley of Trinity, North Carolina.

Salterr

Sally Thrall Pye is the owner of the Salterr Kennels located in Lutz, Florida, since 1966. A member of the American Maltese Association (since 1968) and the Bay Area Maltese Club in Florida, she has finished five champions.

Her American and Canadian Ch. Salterr Gloryseeker is perhaps her best known champion and a Best in Show winner at a 1975 show. He is the sire of eight puppies, all of which made their championships, and he himself is a son of Salterr Salty of Marcris.

Gloryseeker's total record was 5 all-breed Bests in Show, 32 Group Firsts, 32 Group Placements, and 79 Bests of Breed.

Ch. Salterr Salty of Marcris, bred by Joyce Watkins and owned by Sally Thrall Pye. Salty was fifteen years old in 1983.

This Toy Group winner is by Sally Thrall Pye of Lutz, Florida, photographed in 1975 at the Golden Gate Kennel Club Show.

Today, Frank Oberstar is a judge of many breeds who enjoys this new phase of his life in the dog fancy and looks back on the 1960s with great nostalgia and pride in Poona's show record and her 1967 Quaker Oats Award. Larry Ward also continues his interest in the breed and reflects with joy on the success which Starward has achieved.

Marimack

After being active in Great Danes since 1952, Mary P. McKinnon added Maltese to her Marimack Kennels in 1968. In 1968 she started breeding Maltese and since then has finished six Maltese champions. She has been a member of the American Maltese Association since 1968 and the Pensacola Dog Fanciers Association. The Marimack Kennels are located in Milton, Florida.

Ch. Villa Malta Mister Silks, a treasured gift from Marge Rozik to Eileen Monahan of Levittown, Pennsylvania, photographed in the late 1970s by John Ashbey. The judge for this win on the way to championship was Toy breeder Frank Oberstar; handled by Wendell Sammett.

Ch. Marimack's Sassy Lassy, pictured winning the Breed at a recent show. Her owner is Mary P. McKinnon of Milton, Florida. Rene Roux, handler.

Starward

Frank E. Oberstar and Larry G. Ward of Euclid, Ohio, own the Starward Kennels. The most prominent among the Maltese residents of the famous establishment made history during the 1960s when she was setting the Maltese world on fire. The name of this magnificent little creature was Ch. Aennchen's Poona Dancer. The delightful little Poona also was a Canadian champion and charmed everyone in both countries during her spectacular career.

In 1967, she was not only Top Toy Dog, but also Third in the all-breed finals of the Phillips System.

Bred by Mr. and Mrs. J. P. Antonelli, Aennchen's Maltese in Waldwick, New Jersey, Poona was the undisputed "top dog" among Starward's other little Maltese, including imported dogs from the Vicbrita Kennels in England, and those bred on the premises.

The fabulous American and Canadian Ch. Aennchen's Poona Dancer, owned by Frank Oberstar and Larry Ward of Euclid, Ohio. During 1967 Poona was not only Top Toy and Top Maltese in the nation, but was also Number Three of all breeds and winner of the Quaker Oats Award. She was the top-winning Maltese of all time with a record of 38 Bests in Show, 131 Group Firsts, and 242 Bests of Breed.

Sept 1 1978

Finishing in one weekend is Villa Maltas Chantilly Lace, owned by Jonda and Allen Curry, pictured with Villa Maltas Tonto, owned by Bill Wright. Bred by Margaret Rozik, Villa Malta Kennels, Belle Vernon, Pennsylvania.

This granddaughter of Ch. Parquin's Destiny Prince is Ch. Parquin's Princess Lilibet, owned and bred by Mrs. W.R. Cotton of Clovis, New Mexico.

Opposite page: (Above) Ch. Aennchen's Arjuna Dancer, co-owned by Nicholas Cutillo and Betty M. Charpie. (Below) Ch. Winget of the West, bred by Marge Stuber of Lima, Ohio, and owned and handled by Lorraine West of Salt Lake City.

Ch. Russ Ann A Touch of Class wins the Toy Group at the 1979 Central Florida Kennel Club show. "Johnny" is handled by breeder-owner Anna Mae Hardy, Russ Ann Kennels, Floral City, Florida.

Opposite page: Ch. Pen San Widget of Ethridge is pictured winning at the 1979 Richland Kennel Club show under noted Toy judge Frank Oberstar. Bred and owned by Gloria Busselman of Richland, Washington.

Ch. March'en Kewpie Dancer stands for examination by the judge with owner-breeder-handler Marcia Hostetler of Des Moines, Iowa.

American and Canadian Ch. Titanic's Moppet's Bolero of Normalta is owned by Barbara Searle, Titanic's Lovely Maltese, Salt Lake City, Utah.

Ch. Fantasyland Pete R Wabbit is pictured winning Best of Breed under judge Mrs. Dorothy Carson at a 1981 show. Bred, owned, and handled by Carole M. Baldwin of Novato, California.

A doubleheader for Mary Lou Porlick's Gulfstream Maltese at the Trenton show in 1981. Ch. Gulfstream Smooth Sailing (at left) finished for championship as Best of Winners from Puppy Class, and Ch. Gulfstream Radiant Rhapsody took Best of Breed first time out in Specials Class. The judge was Keke Blumberg. Miss C.L. Rawlings handled Sailor. Co-breeder and owner Mary Lou Porlick is on the right.

Ch. Su-Le's Turkey, winner of the Sweepstakes at the Thirteenth National Specialty show in 1977 under judge Joanne Hesse. The sire was Ch. To The Victor of Eng ex Ch. Su-Le's Jacana. Bred and owned by Barbara Bergquist of the Su-Le Kennels in New Boston, Michigan.

56

Ch. Salterr Glory Found, son of American and Canadian Ch. Salterr Glory Seeker. Bred and owned by Sally Thrall Pye of Lutz, Florida, he was Best of Breed over champions when both seven and nine months of age on the way to his championship.

Ch. Tennessa's Fitzhue of Weewyte winning a Group Placing under the late judge Peter Knoop. Owner-handled by Kathy Blackard, Weewyte Maltese, Brooklyn, Connecticut.

Monika Moser's beautiful Martin's Samuel-Cid, ready to go into the ring at eighteen months of age.

Opposite page: Ch. Martin's Rachel-Cid. Bred, owned and photographed by Marjorie Martin, Martin's Maltese, Columbus, Ohio. Whelped in 1980, Rachel was sired by Ch. Martin's Michael-Cid.

Rita and Arvid Dahl with two of their champion Dil-Dal Maltese winning at a show. The Dil-Dal Kennels are in Keyport, Washington.

Ch. Oak Ridge Melissa is shown winning under judge Marion Mangrum. Barbara Alderman handled for owners Linda and Lee Coleman, Lin-Lee Maltese, Finleyville, Pennsylvania.

Ch. Kathan's Tangerine, relaxing after finishing for her championship at the 1982 Tuxedo Park Kennel Club show. Co-owners are Kathy DiGiacomo, Claudia Grunstra, and Tom Pierro.

Weewyte's Mistletoe, owner-handled by Kathy Blackard, Weewyte Maltese, Brooklyn, Connecticut.

Professional handler Peggy Hogg with Ch. Maree's Tu-Grand Kandi-Kane, owned by Nancy H. Shapland.

Ch. Malone's Snowie Roxann is pictured in action as she competes in the Toy Group finals at the 1979 Westminster Kennel Club show with handler Peggy A. Hogg. Roxann is owned by Nancy Shapland, and is winner of 15 all-breed Bests in Show and 52 Group Firsts. She also is a multi-specialty winner and took Best of Breed at Westminster twice.

Peggy A. Hogg

Peggy Hogg is best known as a professional handler and, as such, has finished many Maltese champions. In the early 1970s she became a member of the American Maltese Association. Since 1974 she has added Shih Tzu to her list of favorite breeds, and she also handles them to perfection.

Best in Show for the magnificent Maltese male, Ch. Maree's Tu-Grand Kandi-Kane, pictured winning one of his eleven Bests in Show with handler Peggy Hogg, under judge Maxine Beam. Owned by Nancy Shapland, "Kandi" also has 47 Groups to his credit and was a Quaker Oats Award winner. Photo by Twomey.

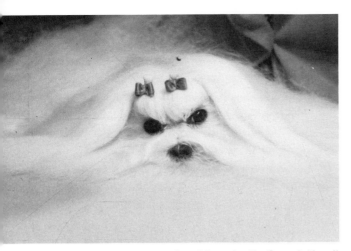

Nancy Shapland's Ch. Maree's Tu-Grand Kandi-Kane, many times a Best in Show winner with his handler, Peggy Hogg.

From her base of operations in Chapin, Illinois, Peggy has had the privilege of handling numerous outstanding Toy dogs for a list of distinguished clients who recognize her proficiency and the impeccable grooming of all her little charges. In the ring and out of the ring, Peggy Hogg is recognized as an authority on Maltese care and showmanship, and can be counted on to give the incomparable performance which has brought much fame and admiration to our breed.

American and Canadian Ch. Villa Malta's Encore Le Ore. Encore was Winners Bitch at Maltese Specialties in Texas with four Bests of Breed out of five shows, handled by Peggy Hogg for owner Mr. B. Bissell of Las Vegas, Nevada.

Dragonwyck

Norman L. Patton, who, along with J. Chip Constantino, owns the Dragonwyck Kennels in St. Louis, Missouri, has been in the dog fancy for many years.

Ch. Melodylane Raggedy Andy Luv is pictured winning under judge Dorothy Nickles at a 1982 show. Shelwyn photograph.

It was 1954 when Norman Patton began in dogs, and was active in the showing of Shih Tzu in 1969. He finished several champions in the ensuing years. Along with J. Chip Constantino, 1969 was the year the Maltese were added; they are currently showing their Ch. Melodylane Raggedy Andy Luv, whose show record includes 9 Bests in Show and 26 Group Firsts within a seven-month period.

Norman Patton is an American Kennel Club approved judge of all Toy Breeds and the Non-Sporting Group.

Barbara Searle and her American and Canadian Ch. Titanic's Lovely Madonna, the first champion finished by her.

Titanic's Lovely Maltese

Barbara G. Searle of Salt Lake City, Utah, started breeding Maltese in 1968. She started showing her dogs in 1970 and has since finished ten champions. She is a member of the Intermountain Kennel Club since 1970, as well as a member of the American Maltese Association.

American and Canadian Ch. Titanic's Moppet Star, owned by Barbara Searle.

Lepetit Maltese

In 1968 Cathy Lepetit fell in love with her sister-in-law's Maltese puppy and determined to have one for herself. Within a few months she had purchased one and has not been without a Maltese since. Pixie of Villa Malta was that first little dog that spent his entire lifetime as a pampered pet, traveling about in Cathy's handbag!

Diamond Jim was the name of Pixie's puppy, and with his remarkable intelligence, was entered in obedience classes—finishing for his C.D. title within a year.

Pixie and Diamond Jim, C.D., with owner Cathy Lepetit of New Orleans, Louisiana.

A bitch named Chanty, from the Hi-Ho Kennels, became the foundation bitch of the Lepetit Kennels in New Orleans, Louisiana, and her first son, Ch. Lepetits McCloud, became Cathy's first homebred champion.

Next Cathy Lepetit added Ch. Sun Canyons Ichi-Ban to her kennel lineup. He introduced many of his fine qualities to her line, and his first daughter, Lepetit's La Blanche, finished her championship at eleven months of age. Champion Lepetit's Paris of Troy is a recent champion tracing back to McCloud and a granddaughter of Ch. Joanne-Chen's Maya Dancer.

There have been five Maltese champions finished to date, as Cathy Lepetit continues her interests in both the breed and obedience rings.

Ch. Lepetits McCloud (above) with handler Peggy Lloyd at a 1978 show, and Ch. Lepetits La Blanche (below) at a 1976 show.

Su-Le

In 1968, Barbara Bergquist found the exact six-month-old puppy she desired in a litter bred by Anna Engstrom, but which was not for sale. Fortunately, Barbara's husband Robert wouldn't take "no" for an answer and persisted until he presented her with "Robin" as a present on Christmas Eve.

Two months later, Barbara and later American and Canadian Ch. Robin were in the show ring and went reserve. At the next show, Robin took the Breed from puppy class over Specials for a 4-point major win, at the Detroit show under William Kendrick.

Robin later raised a litter of three puppies, two of which won their titles and her son, Ch. Su-Le's Roadrunner, won a great many Groups, and was a sire of champions.

The other "love of her life" was her first stud dog, Ch. To The Victor of Eng. He was the top-producing stud in the history of the breed, with 63 champions by 1983. Among his get are many Best in Show, Specialty, and Group winning

Ch. Su-Le's Robin of Eng, owned by Barbara J. Bergquist. This Best of Breed win came under judge William Kendrick at the 1969 Kennel Club of Detroit, Robin's second show.

dogs as well as dogs rating the title of Top Producers. His fifth major for his championship title was awarded by Aennchen Antonelli herself, of which Barbara is very proud.

The Su-Le dogs are named after birds; the kennel name itself is taken from the names of the Bergquists' two children, who grew up with the dogs. Both Susan and Lisa have shown the dogs in junior showmanship and the breed rings, making Su-Le truly a family affair.

Ch. Su-Le's Roadrunner is pictured winning the Toy Group at a 1972 show. This 3½ pound winner is a Maltese Merit Award winner and is a "Robin" and "Victor" son, owned by Barbara Bergquist.

Dogs bearing the Su-Le prefix are responsible for starting many other kennels on their way in the breed, and have won handsomely for their new owners. As of this writing (1983) Barbara Bergquist has finished 104 champions—truly a record to be proud of.

Another Specialty winner for Barbara Bergquist's Su-Le Kennels, Ch. Su-Le's Man-O-War Bird takes Best of Winners award at the 1975 American Maltese Association show under judge Robert Graham.

Ch. To The Victor of Eng, owned and shown by Barbara J. Bergquist of the Su-Le Kennels, New Boston, Michigan.

Barbara's second bitch, American and Bermudian Ch. Su-Le's Wren, was her first Best in Show winner and produced two champions for her.

Barbara also has bred and owns the all-time top producing Maltese dam, Ch. Su-Le's Jacana, who has fifteen champions to her credit. She is the only bitch to win the H.I.S. top producing dam award more than once, at least up to the time of this writing. She earned it three times: in 1975, 1976, and 1978.

Victor won the H.I.S. Publications top sire certificate in 1972, 1976, 1977, 1979, 1981, and 1982. He was awarded the Gold Certificate in 1981. Barbara has been a member of the American Maltese Association since 1970 and a board member of the Breeders Action Board.

70

JuLaine Maltese

Judith Elaine Johnson-Gil obtained her first brood bitch from the Bobbelee Kennels (which was owned by the late Roberta Harrison) in Hialeah, Florida. She started showing Maltese in 1970 and bred on a limited basis for her own kennel line in 1973. To date she has finished fourteen champions.

Bobbelee Constant Comment became an American and Mexican champion before being bred. She finished her American championship within months, just days before being bred to American and Mexican C.D.X. title holder Al-Dor Randy. She is a daughter of the Best in Show winning Ch. Bobbelee Hanky Panky.

The first show dog for JuLaine was Sun Canyon Kiku, purchased from Miriam Thompson many years ago. While too small to be bred, she was a delight to show and was responsible for Judith Johnson-Gil falling in love with the breed. Together with Helen Hood of the Non-Vel Maltese in Lubbock, Texas, she bred her recently retired American, Mexican, and International F.C.I., Canadian Ch. JuLaines Chim Chim Chip, surely one of the most titled little Maltese we have in the breed to date.

American and Mexican Ch. Bobbelee Constant Comment with her owner, Judith Elaine Johnson-Gil.

LaVonne Roach

LaVonne Roach (Bonnie, as she is better known in obedience circles) has trained three Maltese to top awards, and a third is warming up in the waiting ring.

Two of her dogs have both their American U.D. as well as their Canadian C.D. titles. They are R and B's Little Sonny Boy and R and B's Kriss Kringle. Her R and B's More Bounce Per Ounce is a C.D.X. and will soon be back in the ring working on his U.D.

Best in Show Maltese R & B's More Bounce per Ounce, C.D.X. Owned by LaVonne Roach of Omaha, Nebraska, and bred by Marjorie Lewis and Phyllis McCarthy, Bounce earned the titles by 1974. The sire was Ch. Almar's Kriss Kringle ex Mac Joy Mary-Z-Ha of Almar.

The magnificent American, Mexican, International, F.C.I., and Canadian Ch. JuLaines Chim Chim Chip, bred and owned by Judith Elaine Johnson-Gil of San Diego, California.

All three have placed many times in the obedience rating systems and their records can be found in the obedience chapter of this book, but additional mention can be made of the fact that in 1978 Kriss received the Highest Scoring Utility award from the American Maltese Association, and in 1979 Sonny received the same award. Sonny also received the award for Highest Scoring combined score in Open and Utility that same year.

Bonnie Roach might well be the first person to have two Maltese owned and shown by the same person to win highest scoring utility dog year after year. Sonny and Kriss have also been shown many times in brace class, which could also be a "first."

She takes her little dogs out in public to give obedience demonstrations at nursing homes, children's homes, and the like.

R & B's Kriss Kringle, U.D. and Canadian C.D., and his pal R & B's Little Sonny Boy, U.D. and Canadian C.D. These titlists were trained by owner LaVonne Roach. Sonny Boy was bred by Marjorie Lewis; Kriss by Marcia Hostetler.

Ch. Tennessa Grand Trunk, R.S., is pictured winning as a puppy before being specialed starting in the summer of 1983. Owned by Annette S. Feldblum.

American and Canadian Ch. Nyssameads Jonah of Tennessa was listed as a Top Producer in the 1978-1979 *Kennel Review* magazine for having sired twenty-four champions. Owned by Annette S. Feldblum of Charlton, Massachusetts.

Tennessa Maltese

Annette S. Feldblum has finished nineteen Maltese champions for her Tennessa Maltese kennels in Charlton, Massachusetts, since it began in 1970.

She has been a member of the American Maltese Association since 1970, and in 1975 added Whippets to her list of breeds. While Annette Feldblum has no plans to judge at this time, or to finish her Maltese to obedience titles, she is completely sold on the Maltese temperament and their magnificent over-all appearance in the show ring.

Mykiss Kennels

Sharon Roberts of Byron, New York, is the owner of the Mykiss Maltese Kennels where she has finished twelve Maltese champions since 1972. She is also active in obedience and has finished one Maltese to a title.

Sharon is a 4-H leader in dogs and also has had German Shepherds since 1960. In 1973 she became a member of the American Maltese Association, and in 1975 joined the all-breed Tonawanda Valley Kennel Club.

Reward for a good performance in the ring. Sharon Roberts, owner of the Mykiss Kennels, congratulates one of the champions bred at her kennel.

Ch. Martin's Christel-Cid, whelped in 1981 and pictured winning on the way to championship with breeder-owner-handler Marjorie Martin of Columbus, Ohio. Sire was Ch. Martin's Michael-Cid. Judge Thomas Baldwin.

Marcris Fame of Mykiss winning a three point major under judge Crouse at just eight months of age. Owned by Sharon Roberts of Byron, New York.

Martin's Maltese

Marjorie Martin is the owner of Martin's Maltese located in Columbus, Ohio, where she has been breeding since 1974. She has finished eight champions during this time and is a member of the American Maltese Association.

In 1978 Marjorie Martin whelped her Ch. Martin's Michael-Cid, who was to become a leading sire at her Martin's Maltese kennel and is featured on her stationery. After his show ring career, he became the sire of many of the Martin Maltese, all with names to which she added a hyphen and the name "Cid." Some of these include Ch. Martin's Rachel-Cid, Ch. Martin's Chanel-Cid, Martin's Samuel-Cid, Ch. Martin's Jewel-Cid, and so on.

Ch. Martin's Christel-Cid, bred and owned by Marjorie Martin. This beautiful portrait was taken by Ms. Martin.

Marjorie Martin also writes about dogs, including articles on grooming and boarding, and she is involved in photography, drawing cartoons, and creating crossword puzzles.

Weewyte Maltese

Kathy Blackard of Brooklyn, Connecticut, started showing Maltese in 1972. Breeding began in 1974, and she has shown her dogs on a rather infrequent basis ever since.

Kathy Blackard is an accomplished artist who concentrates on capturing the beauty of the Maltese in her work. She has also been a member of the American Maltese Association since 1972, was secretary of the Central New England Maltese Association from 1979 until 1981, when she took over the duties of president. She is also a member of the American Dog Owners Association.

Kathy Blackard considers her Maltese an integral part of the family and her three-and-a-half year old daughter, Keri Beth Blackard, helps care for and train their little dogs.

Noble Faith Maltese

Almost within a decade of first getting involved with Maltese, Faith Knobel achieved the ultimate—she owned a show dog that was to reach the top. Her White Tornado, better known as Torre, boasted a show record of 9 Bests in Show, 26 Group Firsts, 29 Group Seconds, 24 Group Thirds, and 16 Group Fourths. Torre was a champion at eight months of age, and was never defeated in the classes from the 6-9 month puppy class.

Torre's sire was multiple Best in Show Ch. Oak Ridge Country Charmer, and she was out of Multiple Group winning Noble Faith's Phoebe's Finale.

Noble Faith's Maltese have attained twenty championships and C.D. titles as well. Faith is active in the Ft. Lauderdale, Florida, Dog Club and since 1971 has been a member of the American Maltese Association and the Maltese Club of Greater Miami. Before becoming active in Maltese in 1971, Faith Knobel was involved with exhibiting Basset Hounds (since 1959) and finished fifteen of them to their championships.

Paintings by Kathy Blackard, acrylic on glass and wood from her personal collection.

Dil Dal Maltese

In 1972 Rita and Arvid Dahl and their teenage daughter Angela began the Dil Dal Kennels in Keyport, Washington.

It was Angela, active in 4-H Club work for over ten years, who has by now finished twelve Maltese champions and stays active in obedience and junior showmanship work with the dogs since its beginning.

At state fairs, Angela has been Junior, Intermediate, and Senior State Champion. She has been featured in many newspaper articles in her home state relating her experiences and accomplishments in the dog show rings as she and her family and troupe of little Maltese travel around the country in their motor home to compete in the show rings.

Tutee Primrose Picca Dilly winning a three-point major as Best of Winners at the 1979 Gallatin Kennel Club show in Montana. The handler is Angela Dahl of the Dil Dal Kennels.

Angela Dahl with her American and Canadian Champion Dil Dal's Lit'n of Anitas. The Dil Dal Kennels are in Keyport, Washington, where breeding and showing Maltese is a "family affair."

The Dahls are members of the American Maltese Association, the Evergreen Maltese Club, the Peninsula Dog Fanciers Club, and have served in many executive capacities. The Dahls are a truly active family devoted to their dogs.

Lin-Lee

Linda and Lee Coleman of Finleyville, Pennsylvania, started showing their first Maltese puppy, Oak Ridge Melissa, in August of 1973. She became their first champion in a little over a year's time, handled by owner Lee Coleman, who was strictly a novice at the time.

Their next Maltese, Su-Le's Teal, came along in the classes while Melissa was doing her thing in Specials Class. Teal finished in 1975, also owner-handled by Lee Coleman. Melissa went on to win eleven Toy Groups and two all-breed Bests in Show plus numerous Group Placements.

76

By this time a small breeding program was planned and they acquired Villa Malta's Maestro of Lin-Lee, who finished his championship with all majors in just five shows. Ch. Maestro is owned by Mrs. Chieko Toda of Japan, but was bred to Melissa before leaving the country. This mating resulted in two stud dogs named Lin-Lee's Marquis and Lin-Lee's Magnum. These

Ch. Su-Le's Teal, owned by Lin-Lee Maltese and handled by Lee Coleman of Finleyville, Pennsylvania.

Ch. Villa Malta Maestro of Lin Lee, owned by Lin-Lee Maltese, at a show in 1977.

two males went to Canada in 1978, where Marquis won the Puppy Toy Group in his first three Canadian shows, and in 1979 both finished for their Canadian titles along with the Coleman's Canadian Ch. Lin-Lee's Melodie.

Marquis went on to win four Bests of Breed and three Group wins from Open Dog Class while finishing for his American championship in 1979, owner-handled by Lee Coleman. Magnum followed in Marquis' pawprints in eight following shows, also handled by Lee. Marquis became the first Maltese in 1980 to win an all-breed Best in Show.

While Linda and Lee Coleman intend to keep their breeding program on a small scale, they have already produced several champions and will continue to breed and show on a limited basis.

American and Canadian Ch. Lin-Lee's Marquis is pictured winning the Toy Group at the Macon, Georgia, Kennel Club show in 1979.

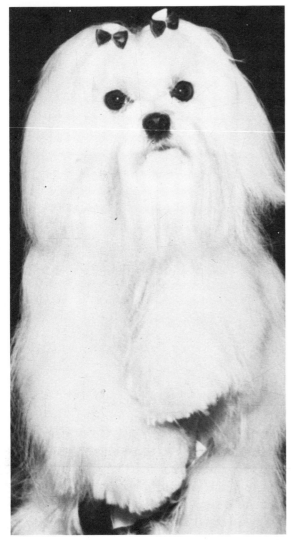

Ch. Viceroy Kathan Honeycomb, owned by Laura Ford, was bred by Kathy DiGiacomo and Claudia Grunstra. The sire was Ch. Su-Le's Atlantic Brent ex Ch. Kathan's Honey of Viceroy.

Kathan

One of the most popular exhibitors in the Maltese breed is Mrs. Kathy DiGiacomo, Kathan Maltese, located in Fair Lawn, New Jersey. Since 1974, Kathy DiGiacomo has owned or bred more than fifty Maltese champions. Kathy's little dogs are easily recognizable in the ring by their quality and beautiful grooming.

Over the years, Kathy DiGiacomo has served the fancy in other ways too—as the director for the eastern division of the American Maltese Association as well as a past vice president and director, and past director of the Progressive Toy Dog Club and the Ramapo Kennel Club. She is also a member of the Kennel Club of Northern New Jersey and the Union County Kennel Club.

Kathan's Little GTO is pictured after winning a three-point major at just seven months of age.

Kathy has been known to show Maltese for friends and always makes a winning combination in the ring with her little charges. In the early 1980s, Kathy teamed up with the late Peg Vicedomini of Ithaca, New York, to co-breed an additional five champions during the 1981-1982 season, including Ch. Kathan's Honey of Viceroy, Ch. Kathan's Layla of Viceroy, Ch. Kathan's Torquay of Toyland (Peg Vicedomini's original kennel prefix for her fifteen years in dogs), Ch. Viceroy Kathan Nite Owl, and Ch. Kathan Viceroy Mr. Blue. These champions in turn are also producing champions that will carry on the Viceroy name, even after Peg Vicedomini's death in 1982.

Ch. Kathan's Torquay of Toyland, is co-owned by Peg Vicedomini and Kathy DiGiacomo, who also bred and handled to this win under judge Keke Blumberg.

Ch. Su-Le's Bluebird, pictured at thirteen months of age while still owned by his breeder, Barbara Bergquist. Several months later, Bluebird went to Kathy DiGiacomo's Kathan Kennels, where he sired more than twenty champions during the next seven years.

Ch. Kathan's Blu Danube of Amour, owned by Ruthann Ferguson and handled for her by breeder Kathy DiGiacomo. Blu Danube is one of five champions from the litter sired by Ch. Su-Le's Bluebird ex Angie Baby.

These three typey puppies were bred by Kathy DiGiacomo, Kathan Maltese, Fair Lawn, New Jersey.

A lovely headstudy of Ch. Inge of Winddrift, owned by Diane Davis of Haines City, Florida.

Windsong

Diane Davis of Haines City, Florida, uses the Windsong name for her little Maltese since starting in the breed in 1974. After owning Shih Tzu for a year, she added Maltese to her group and since that time has finished or owned over twenty-four champions including two Specialty and Best in Show winners.

Diane Davis is active in several aspects of the dog fancy and is interested in neo-natal intensive care, grooming, etc. She has been a member of the American Maltese Association since 1975 and is also a member of the Lakeland Winter Haven Kennel Club in the Florida area.

Ch. Inge of Winddrift, handled by Glynnette Cass for owner Diane Davis to a three-point major win in 1976 under Mrs. Heywood Hartley.

Country Villa Maltese

1975 was the year that Stan and Dee Halley of Blue Grass, Iowa, became involved with Maltese. They have finished two champions, Ch. Galas' Misty Mountain Top and Ch. Country Villa's Tinker Toy, and have belonged to the parent club and also the Quad-Cities Obedience Club since 1978. They also have Greyhounds, Afghan Hounds, and Whippets. In the future, Stan Halley would like to do some judging and has judged at match shows so far.

Ch. Gayla's Misty Mountain Top is going Winners Bitch at the 1977 Westminster Kennel Club show. Bred and handled by Darlene Wilkinson, she is owned by Delores Halley of Blue Grass, Iowa. Judging was Mrs. S. Rowe.

Vera A. Graham

In 1976, after thirteen years in Yorkshire Terriers, Vera A. Graham of Alexandria, Virginia, joined the American Maltese Association because she had became so enamored of the Maltese beauty, temperament, and intelligence.

Veronica M. Clark

The same year also saw Veronica M. Clark of Chattanooga, Tennessee, get into Maltese after breeding Miniature Schnauzers and training them for obedience. Veronica Clark is also a professional dog groomer with her own shop.

Ch. Stentaway Zeus, whelped in 1973, became the top stud dog at Carol Yaw's Kennel.

Eileen Monahan

Eileen Monahan of Levittown, Pennsylvania, is owner of the Mac Monte Kennels where she started breeding Maltese in 1976 and showing in the following year. She has also been a member of the American Maltese Association since 1977 and would love to judge at some time in the future.

Ch. Mac Monte's Benny Button, owned by Eileen Monahan, on the way to championship with handler Wendell Sammett.

Carol Yaw

Carol Yaw of Newport, Nebraska, had been in dogs since 1964, owning and breeding Cockers and Yorkies after Saint Bernards and Samoyeds. She has purchased three champions, two males and one female, to enhance her breeding program, and has been active with her children in 4-H programs. She is a member of the parent breed club as well.

The fabulous Ch. Ginger Jake, U.D., shown going through his paces, also has his Canadian C.D.X. and is one of the obedience "greats" in the history of the breed. Owned by Faith Ann Maciejewski of West Allis, Wisconsin.

Faith Ann Maciejewski

One of the most active and successful of all contenders in the fancy during the mid-1970s was Faith Ann Maciejewski, whose Ch. Ginger Jake, U.D., Canadian C.D.X, and Bahaman C.D., is one of the most successful of all obedience titlists. Faith Ann Maciejewski was also active in 4-H projects as a trainer and started with German Shorthaired Pointers in 1956 before becoming active with Maltese.

Caro's Maltese

Carole Bashford of Las Vegas, Nevada, began showing her Maltese at Sanctioned Maltese matches in 1977. Her first litter was bred in 1979 and all her dogs and puppies are raised in an unrestricted environment as active members of the family along with the children. She is a member of the parent club, the American Maltese Association.

Sno-Doll

Danny M. and Edith N. Dollar of Pine Bluff, Arkansas, are owners of the Sno-Doll Kennels. They started showing in 1977 (at which time they joined the American Maltese Association) and began a breeding program in 1981. Their best known dog is Sno-Doll Dandalion of Almar.

Sanibel

Manya Dujardin of Oxford, Connecticut, can boast of a champion in her first litter back in 1977. While she had dogs since 1960, her first Maltese came along in 1976 and since then she has finished twelve champions. She also has Yorkies, Suffolk Sheepdogs, and Rottweilers at her Sanibel Kennels. She is a member of the A.M.A. and the Central New England Maltese Association.

Quiet mood reflected by Butdon, owned and trained by Vera Rebbin of Aurora, Ohio.

The Aurora Companion Dog Training School is Vera's special interest and she is a marvelous photographer, as evidenced by numerous pictures in this book. She has taken many photographs of her dogs and has won prizes in photos contests with several of them.

Vera Rebbin takes Best Toy Group Brace at the 1981 Mad River Valley Kennel Club show, with one of the dogs only six months old. The judge was Joe Gregory.

Ch. Sanibel Jessica Tate is pictured winning under judge Dr. Ed McGough.

Sixpence Kennels

Vera and John Rebbin own the Sixpence Kennel in Aurora, Ohio. Vera, who is active in obedience training, has had other breeds of dogs for over 40 years and in 1978 became involved with Maltese.

Vera Rebbin also boards and breeds, shows, and teaches obedience. She has finished several C.D. and C.D.X. titles on her dogs. Vera and John Rebbin belong to many dog clubs in their area and have held office in many of them.

Twelve-week-old brother and sister, Jingles and Happy Holly, owned and photographed by Vera Rebbin.

Jingles snuggles up to Vera Rebbin at their home in Aurora, Ohio.

Three of Vera Rebbin's six-week-old puppies dress up in their canine tee shirts for this photo, taken in 1983.

Ch. Richelieu's Sassy Lizette, the first champion finished by Elsie Burke for her Louan's kennel in Farmington, Michigan.

American and Canadian Ch. Louan's Cherokee Sunshine finished for championship in fourteen shows and with Group First, Second, and Third in Canada. Sunshine is now training for an obedience degree with the Showmen's Dog Club. This 1982 win with owner-breeder-handler Elsie Burke was for a five-point major under judge Richard Hensel.

Louan

Elsie L. Burke of Farmington, Michigan, owns the Louan Kennels. She started showing Maltese in 1978 and was breeding by September 1979. While she is more active in obedience than in conformation classes, she has finished five champions and usually takes her dogs from the championship classes to their obedience training.

She has belonged to the American Maltese Association since 1977 and has two pet-quality Poodles at Louan as well as her Maltese. In her opinion, however, the Maltese breed has no faults and she appreciates their personality and the fact that they are a clean, non-shedding breed.

Maltese in motion . . . in ceramic, from the collection of Pamela Rightmyer.

Sundaze

1978 was the year Pamela G. Rightmyer started her Sundaze Kennels in Xenia, Ohio. Breeding on a very small scale, Pamela Rightmyer is about to start one of her puppies in obedience training and perhaps breed again. She has been a member of the American Maltese Association for several years and was in Borzoi since 1978. Among other breeds she has had are Miniature Schnauzers (since 1972), Yorkshire Terriers (1980), and Whippets (1982).

Lindy's Surprise From Weejun, bred and owned by Lindy Fuller of Colorado City, Texas.

Lindy's Maltese

Maltese have shared the kennel with Yorkshire Terriers at Lindy Fuller's kennel in Colorado City, Texas, since 1982. The Maltese arrived first, however, in 1978. Since then Lindy Fuller has finished two champions and has been a member of the American Maltese Association.

Fable's Little Match Girl is pictured with her breeder-owner Elyse R. Fischer of Port Washington, New York.

Our Enterprizes

Susan S. Grubb and Karol Geiger are partners in the Our Enterprizes Kennels in Norwalk, Ohio. Started in 1978, they have finished three champions to date. They are BeBe, Su-Le Bird, and Su-Le Goldcrest, all bearing the Our Enterprizing prefix. Susan and Karol are members of the American Maltese Association.

Ch. Our Enterprizing BeBe wins Best in Show. Owned by Susan S. Grubb and Karol R. Geiger, Our Enterprizes Kennel, Norwalk, Ohio, this adorable 4½ pound Maltese bitch has won several Bests in Show.

Fable Maltese

Elyse R. Fischer of Port Washington, New York, started her Fable Maltese line in 1978 when she became interested in obedience training. She has finished one dog with an obedience title and three champions since that beginning. She is a member of the American Maltese Association and the Progressive Dog Club, which is for Toys only. Her obedience affiliation is with the Nassau Dog Training Club.

She is co-owner with Kathy DiGiacomo of Ch. Su-Le's Mynah II, and is currently showing Fable's Little Match Girl which she co-bred with Manya Dujardin.

Her very first Maltese was Little Miss Ragamuffin III, C.D., who earned her title at seven years of age.

Ch. Su-Le's Mynah II, owner-handled by Elyse R. Fischer, takes Best of Breed in 1982 under judge Merrill Cohen.

86

The Original Petit Point

Susan M. Sandlin, owner of the Original Petit Point Maltese got her first Maltese in 1979. Ch. Kathan's Petit Point Alfie finished at fourteen months of age handled by Susan. Two weeks later her second Maltese, Ch. Kathan's Petit Point Sugaree, finished with back-to-back majors at just eleven months of age. She returned to Kathy DiGiacomo for her third, Kathan's Petit Point Blu Velvet. This Maltese won a three-point major at six months of age and later was sold to South America where she represented the breed in that country.

A woollen macrame Maltese, designed and executed by Susan M. Sandlin.

Susan M. Sandlin and her first Maltese champion, fourteen-month-old Ch. Kathan's Petit Point Alfie. Susan is owner of The Original Petit Point Maltese in Arlington, Virginia.

Other breedings show remarkable quality and promise in the show ring and keep Susan's interest in the breed going strong. She is also known for her remarkable miniatures which always include her beloved Maltese figurines and have been sold all over the world where Maltese and her artwork are well known.

Petit Point Pique is pictured winning Best of Breed at just fourteen months of age. Her breeder-owner-handler is Susan M. Sandlin of Arlington, Virginia.

From Barbara Bergquist, Susan then purchased Peersun's My Valentine, which was bred to Alfie and which produced a litter of four puppies so good that she kept two for herself. One of these was Petit Point Pique, which at the time of this writing was nearly finished and also pointed in Bermuda and Canada, as was littermate Petit Point Poker Chip.

Chelsea

Gail Hennessey is the owner of the Chelsea Maltese in Wappingers Falls, New York.

It was in 1979 that her Kathan's Bluflower of Chelsea was campaigned and picked up her first 3-point major at the Bronx County Kennel club show (with Kathy DiGiacomo showing her under judge Bessie Pickens). Bluflower finished at the Delaware Water Gap show in May of the same year. Bred by Linda and Nicky Kenney of Hopelawn, New Jersey, "Lily" began her obedience training right after championship.

Danny's Jude of Chelsea, bred and owned at that time by Gail Hennessey and shown for her by Lani Howell, is pictured winning on the way to championship under judge Ed Jenner.

Gail Hennessey's "Lily" with handler Kathy DiGiacomo.

Ch. Danny's Jude of Chelsea piloted by handler Tim Lehman, takes Best of Breed under judge Dr. William Field. Danny is currently owned by Mrs. Shirley Sherwood of Sands Springs, Oklahoma.

By 1981 Bluflower's son Ch. Chelsea Dee-Jaay began his show ring career handled for Gail Hennessey by Lani Howell, and finished for his championship at just twelve months of age, with two 4-point majors. He also went on to Best of Breed with one of the 4-point majors. Another of Gail Hennessey's winners is Danny's Jude of Chelsea, handled by Lani Howell or Tim Lehman.

Gail is known in the breed for her enthusiasm in all aspects of the show world, and was lauded for her encouragement at the time *Maltese Tales* was initiated by Muriel Hunt. She also attended the 1983 Crufts Show and her report on that show of the Maltese that won the Toy Group at that prestigious show is reported in this book in an earlier chapter.

Tical

Maurice Melvin of Dallas, Texas, owned the Tical Maltese dogs and his Ch. Joanne-Chen Aennchen Tiny Tim was used to represent the breed in the 1980 issue of *Dog World* magazine. Bred by Joanne Hesse and whelped in May 1978, Timmy finished for his championship at sixteen months of age with several Bests of Breed from the classes.

OTHER MALTESE FANCIERS

Others who perpetuated the breed over the years are Alice Pond of Ohio with her Alpond Kennels; Patricia Howell with Boreas, who is also author of the book, *The Modern Maltese;* Mrs. Boyd Clark; Arlene Grady and her D'Arlene; Fran Duncan in Norfolk, Virginia; and Russell Jackson and his Faience Kennels in Collegeville, Pennsylvania.

Mrs. Eckes called her kennels Eve-Ron; Elvera Cox in Missouri had Fairy Fay; Harriet Taylor called her Maltese Folklore at her California Kennels; Rita Brickley gave her Maltese the Gaybrick prefix in Kansas; and Good Time Kennels were owned by Robert and Eloise Craig in Illinois. The Craigs were a driving force in the American Maltese Association and also columnists for the American Kennel Gazette wherein they spread the "good word" about our breed.

There were the LaModa Maltese from Salem, Oregon; and Lonesome Lane; and Virginia Evans' Maltacello Kennels in Bethel Park, Pennsylvania. Malta Gables was located in Tiffin, Ohio, owned by Florence Hopple and Michael Wolf, so famous in many breeds, but especially Pekingese exhibited successfully under his Mike-Mar Kennel name.

Vivian Horney operated out of Miami with Windrift as her kennel prefix, and Mrs. H. W. Wilson was known for her Whispering Pines. Sunglow was the name chosen by Mrs. Bernie Crowe of Louisville, Kentucky, and the name Ronell was chosen by Mrs. Rose Anhell in Quincy, Illinois. Others were Jean Rand, Mrs. Ruth Roath, Dorothy Palmerston, and Mrs. Claudette LaMay, whose Sugar Town Kennels produced American, Canadian, and Bermudian Ch. Nyssamead Dhugal. Nyssamead was owned by Susan M. Weber.

There are undoubtedly many more. Any omissions, however, are purely unintentional and still others are represented elsewhere in this book.

THE HUNDREDTH ANNIVERSARY BOOK

In 1976 the Westminster Kennel Club published a 100th Anniversary Book which contained a history of the kennel club and show records, as far back as possible.

Three of our Maltese were included among the prestigious Toy Group winners, starting in 1964 with Ch. Co-Ca-He's Aennchen Toy Dancer, owned by Anne Maria Stimmler.

The second Maltese to win the Toy Group at Westminster was Ch. Aennchen's Poona Dancer in 1966. Poona was a great show winner and all during her career was co-owned by Frank E. Oberstar, her handler, and Larry G. Ward. Mr. Oberstar had an entry of twenty-nine Maltese when he judged the 1983 Westminster Kennel Club show.

In 1972 Ch. Joanne-Chen's Maya Dancer won the Toy Group for owner Mamie R. Gregory.

It is worthy of note that all three of these little Maltese were of Aennchen Antonelli's breeding with her "Dancer" names—a great credit to her superb breeding program.

Mamie Gregory's beautiful Maltese dog Ch. Joanne-Chen's Maya Dancer, is groomed and ready to go into the ring with handler Peggy Hogg.

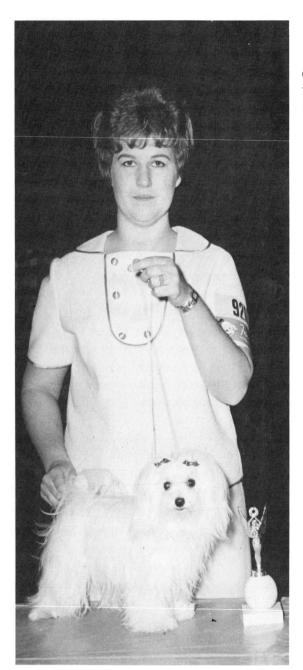

Ch. Pen Sans Cassandra was a winner in 1966 at the Seattle Kennel Club show. Owned by Gloria Busselman of Richland, Washington.

Brown's Keri Mia, bred by Dr. and Mrs. Roger Brown and owned by Mrs. Helen Nelsen, is pictured winning at the 1971 Maryland Kennel Club show.

Ch. Lin-Lee's Magnum at a 1979 show. Owned by Lin-Lee Maltese, Finleyville, Pennsylvania.

Ch. Su-Le's Bittern winning under the late judge Ruth Turner. Kathy DiGiacomo handled for owner Gail Hennessey, Chelsea Kennels, Wappingers Falls, New York.

Ch. Russ Ann Repeat Performance on her way to championship in 1979 with owner-breeder-handler Anna Mae Hardy.

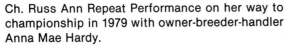

Ch. Jay Dora's Scarlet Touch, owned by Anna Mae Hardy of Floral City, Florida.

American and Canadian Ch. Lin-Lee's Marquis winning under judge Mrs. Yan Paul. Barbara Alderman handled for owners Linda and Lee Coleman, Lin-Lee Maltese.

Ch. Kathan's Petit Point Sugaree winning at eleven months of age with her owner Susan Sandlin of Alexandria, Virginia.

Ch. Villa Malta's Olivia is owned by Jennie Malone, who handled her to this 1980 Best of Breed win under judge Edna Voyles.

Salterr Glory Times is pictured winning another major on the way to her championship. Owned and bred by Sally Thrall Pye of Lutz, Florida.

WINNERS
CLEARWATER
KENNEL CLUB
JULY 1981
Graham PHOTO BY BONNIE

Ch. Gordon's Legend of Russ Ann, pictured winning in 1981 with owner Anna Mae Hardy of Floral City, Florida.

Ch. Fantasyland Legacy takes Best of Winners under judge Ann Stevenson at a 1981 show. Owner-handler is Mr. M. Basiszta.

Dil-Dal's Moonshine on the way to her championship. Moonshine is owned by Rita Dahl and Trudie Dillon. This win was at the 1981 Peninsula Dog Fanciers Club in the state of Washington.

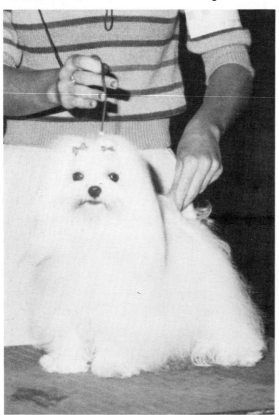

Ch. Martin's Annabel-Cid winning with handler Barbara Alderman under judge Kenneth E. Miller. Whelped in 1980, Annabel is bred and owned by Marjorie Martin, Martin's Maltese, Columbus, Ohio.

Ch. Aennchen's Ashur Dancer, owned by Nicholas Cutillo of New York City.

Ch. Kathan's Elusive Butterfly, bred, and handled by Kathy DiGiacomo, is co-owned with Kathy by Cheryl Sledge and represents her first champion Maltese. The judge is Cyril Bernfeld.

Ch. Joanne-Chen's Maya Dancer with handler Peggy A. Hogg of Chapin, Illinois. Maya Dancer was owned by Mamie Gregory; bred by Joanne Hesse.

CHAPTER FIVE

The Maltese
Parent Club

Marge Stuber of the famous Primrose Maltese Kennels in Lima, Ohio, with Primrose Flower. Photo by Mills.

The American Maltese Association is a national organization and recognized by the American Kennel Club as the parent club for the breed. All Maltese fanciers are invited to become members.

The purpose of the association is to protect the interests of the Maltese, to help newcomers with problems they may encounter with their first dog, to educate the general public on the merits of the breed, and to insure ethical standards.

The American Maltese Association holds an annual National Specialty show, each year in a different area of the country, and also publishes a little monthly publication entitled *Maltese R*$_x$ which includes all pertinent information on the breed.

Corresponding secretaries and club activities change frequently, so those wishing to join this parent club are advised to write for the name and address of the current secretary to the American Kennel Club (51 Madison Avenue, New York, New York 10010) for the latest information.

PARENT CLUB MATERIALS

The American Maltese Association makes available a brochure on various phases of Maltese care, as well as back issues of their publication and an illustrated top knot instruc-

tion sheet. For current prices, get in touch with the club secretary. There often are books about the Maltese available through the club and information about other books and materials. Notepaper and Maltese jewelry and ceramic figurines are also available by writing the club secretary.

THE FIRST PARENT CLUB SPECIALTY

The American Maltese Association held its first individual Maltese Specialty Show in New York City on Sunday, February 14, 1971. The beautiful Georgian Room at the Statler Hilton Hotel was the setting. Four previous Maltese Specialties had been given, but only in connection with all-breed shows and in various locations.

This first Specialty was the culmination of a dream for A.M.A. President Gini Evans of Bethel Park, Pennsylvania. Her plans for this major event were announced when she and her husband, Dr. J. S. Evans, were attending a veterinary convention in Las Vegas and were given a dinner in their honor by the Las Vegas Maltese Fanciers. President Dorothy Tinker introduced Gini Evans, who told of her plans to hold a Specialty of their own with a judge of their choosing and a special catalog. Their willingness to underwrite any loss made the event possible.

97

Ch. Annamarie's White Panther, the Number Three Maltese in 1968, owned by Dr. and Mrs. Kenneth Knopf of Forest Hills, New York.

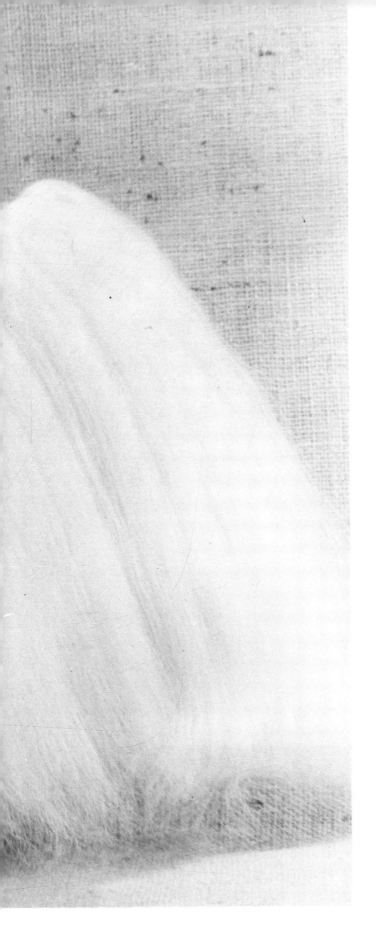

ENTRIES AND WINNERS

Sixty-five Maltese entered for a total of 96 positions with 30 puppies entered in the Sweepstakes. Breakdown was 30 bitches, 18 dogs, 16 Specials, 1 Veteran, and 1 Brace Class entry. Sweepstakes were judged by Mrs. Shirley Kalstone, and Louis Murr judged the regular class.

Best Puppy in the Sweeps was Maltacello's El Cid, owned by Dorothy White. Best Junior Puppy was Joanne-Chen's Kiddles Dancer, owned by Wendy and Jean Corioll. Winners Dog was Mike-Mar's Gwenbrook, owned by Gwen Holbrook. Reserve Dog was Ha-Lo's Mini Mite Dancer, owned by Haskel and Loretta Zuckman. Winners Bitch was Dazzlyn Dinah Mite, owned by Jeanne Underwood. Reserve Bitch was Kol-Lu's Powder Puff, owned by Grace Keller. Best of Breed went to Ch. Pendleton's Jewel, owned by Dorothy and Norman White. Best of Winners was Dazzlyn Dina Mite and Best of Opposite Sex was Ch. Anna Marie's White Panther, owned by Dr. and Mrs. Kenneth Knopf.

OFFICERS AND COMMITTEE MEMBERS

Dr. Knopf was chairman for the banquet later that evening; after a Board meeting of the American Maltese Association it was agreed the event was an enormous success.

The show committee was comprised of Gini Evans, president, and Kathie Mooney, Dorothy Tinker, Helen Schively, Anna Mae Hardy, Florence Hopple, Michael Mooney, Marjorie Lewis, Roberta Harrison, Grace Hendrickson Anderson, Vivian Horney, Harriet Taylor, Gloria Busselman, and Nancy Tinker.

Officers of the American Maltese Association were president, Mrs. Gini Sunner Evans; vice president east, Mrs. Thalia Meacher; vice president midwest, Mrs. Patricia Howell; vice president west, Mrs. Priscilla Kannarr; recording secretary, Mrs. Melda Lee Duxbury; treasurer, Mrs. Mary Sapovchak; corresponding secretary, Mrs. Marge Stuber. The delegate to the American Kennel Club was Mr. Stewart Pendleton, and the board of directors was comprised of Bobbie Floriabo, Roberta Harrison, Joanne Hesse, Florence Hopple, Gloria Busselman, and Sandra Dennan.

This first independent specialty show for the American Maltese Association was also a financial success, and the club owes Gini Evans a vote of gratitude for having the foresight to see the club's future success in the fancy and for making her dream come true.

International, South American, and Argentinian Ch. Peggotty von Igolta, owned by Adolfo and Elena Spector of Buenos Aires, Argentina.

100

Enlargement of a Sharjah postage stamp featuring a Maltese dog. Many countries issue stamps featuring animals indigenous to their areas.

Maltese Around The World

Since the earliest Maltese are believed to have come from the Malta/Melita area, it was only natural that they should spread to Italy during the days of the Roman Empire. It is perhaps the earliest known place for the dog we now know as the Maltese, and this is evidenced by their appearance in early paintings.

Maltese are said to have been seen in Switzerland as early as 1791 on a visit by Lord and Lady Sheffield during that year. First registration in Switzerland, however, was in 1908.

In Belgium the Maltese also got an early start. A dog named Thim, whelped in 1878, was registered that year; two named Marquis and Martha were registered the following year. They were listed as "pedigrees unknown" and were owned by Mme. Bodinius. Marquis and Martha were awarded prizes at the 1882 Spa Show in Belgium.

Apparently the breed was never very popular in that country, and by 1970 there were no known breeders or dogs there, or any registrations in their stud book, the *Livres Des Origines Saint Hubert*.

By 1850 the breed was seen in Germany and there were five entries at an International Show in 1882. The first stud book registration, however, was about 1900. In 1893 a Maltese named Kleine Nelly was whelped in Holland and was entered in the stud book. Nelly was owned by Mr. W. Howens in Rotterdam.

Strange as it may seem, as far away as the Union of South Africa there were Maltese entered in dog shows as far back as 1881, and in Canada there were records of Maltese in 1889.

The first Maltese was registered in Sweden in 1903, and it was at the turn of the century that the first Maltese was entered in the Norwegian stud book. However, that was a German-bred dog named Mignon, owned by K. H. Hornemann of Oslo, and listed as "pedigree unknown." Mr. Hornemann's Bijou, the second dog registered, was believed to have been whelped in 1910. By 1912 a Russian-bred Maltese, named Milka, was the first to appear in the stud book of Finland.

There are records of Maltese in New Zealand around 1900. In Australia, Maltese were exhibited at Melbourne shows in the 1920s.

By 1922, the first Maltese was registered in Ireland, and then not another one until 1935. One of the first breeders of Maltese in Ireland was Mrs. P. B. Gordon Fraser. Mrs. Fraser is still breeding Maltese today, and three of her Suirside Maltese (namely Blossom, Rosabelle, and Show Man) were sent to the American lawyer, Virginia Leitch, author of *The Maltese Dog*. Mrs. Fraser's Suirside Brigid was also the first Irish-bred Maltese to win the championship title in both Canada and the United States. She won the Breed at the Westminster Kennel Club show in 1952 over an entry of seventeen, one of the largest ever at that event. She also won a Best in Show during her ring career.

The first Maltese registered in France was a dog named Fatty, whelped in 1922 and registered in 1927. France is said to have had Maltese as far back as the fifteenth century, and they are seen in artwork dating back to that period.

Australian Ch. Snopampas Lord George, whelped in 1980 and owned by Mrs. G.A. Hodges of Essendon, Victoria, Australia. The sire was Australian Ch. Toolong George out of Snowgold Pampas Angel.

Maltese reached East Africa by 1935. These were English imports owned by L. Abbey, though further details are not known. In 1953 Miss Tora Roede was said to be the only breeder of Maltese in Denmark. Her original stock came from Sweden in the 1940s.

While this much evidence of their presence in other countries has been recorded, there seems to be a general lack of information on the prominent breeders down through the years. Even today, we have difficulty finding out in which countries they were rather popular or rather scarce. The breed clubs seem to be about the best method of keeping track of them.

International and Colombian Ch. Kathan Sugar Baby, winner of 3 Groups, 8 Best Puppy in Group, and 32 Bests of Opposite Sex. Owned by Becky Brauer of Bogota, Colombia, South America. The sire was Ch. Su-Le's Bluebird ex Kathan's Tallahassee Lassie.

THE BREED IN JAPAN

While Maltese were never a popular breed in Japan at any early time, the quality of those that were there was high. During World War II, however, the Japanese were cut off from most other countries and the importation of new bloodlines came to a standstill. By the 1950s interest in the breed began to increase once again, and while it was a considerable time before the quality improved markedly, the present day Japanese Maltese are considered excellent and the breed has become rather popular.

A-S Gloria's Snow Mayan Dancer II, is pictured with owner Akira Shinohara and one of Mayan's newborn babies at their home in Osaka, Japan. Mr. Shinohara is a breeder, judge, and member of the Osaka Maltese Club as well as the American Maltese Association.

The Japanese imported dogs from the United States, Great Britain, and Australia to get them started once again, and during the 1950s and 1960s we saw the names of Mr. Kazumasa Garshi, Mr. Yoshimichi Sakai, Mr. Kinji Sana, and Mr. Saichi Hasegawa as having been the stalwarts in the breed in that country. During this period the author wrote articles for the magazine *Inu-nu-saki,* the Japanese Dog World publication, in which many Maltese imports were mentioned in their advertising.

A-S Gloria Kennels

By the mid-sixties, a gentleman named Akira Shinohara, of Osaka, became interested in the breed and was to become one of Japan's leading devotees of the Maltese. By 1967 his A-S Gloria Kennels were established and he was also importing a great many Maltese from the United States. Mr. Shinohara is still a member of the American Maltese Association and belongs to the Kennel Club of Japan and the Osaka Maltese Club. He is also a judge in Japan.

Mr. Shinohara first became entranced with Aennchen Antonelli's little "dancers" and was determined to import some of them to establish his kennel bloodlines after admiring their photographs in the pages of *Popular Dogs* magazine. American Ch. Aennchen's Susi Dancer and Mar-T's Tiny Snow Dancer were the first to make the trip overseas.

On May 19, 1966, a litter was whelped at the A-S Gloria Kennels, the first in Japan of American parentage, with Susi as dam and Ch. Aennchen's Mastyr as sire. All four from this litter became Best in Show winners in Japan. They were Snow Dancer Junior, Snow Prince, Snow First Lady, and Snow Princess, all bearing the Ch. A-S Gloria prefix.

Mr. Shinohara then purchased Ch. Anna of Aromatic Peak, the record holder of most Bests in Show in Japan, followed by American Ch.

Japanese Best in Show winner, Ch. A-S Gloria's Snow Dancer Junior, sired by Ch. Aennchen's Mastyr Dancer ex Ch. Aennchen's Susi Dancer, and owned by Akira Shinohara.

Mike-Mar's Shikar's Replica. Replica, bred to Anna, produced three more Best in Show winners, named Snow Queen, Snow Jewel, and Snow Hi Lady. All of these also produced many champions for his line.

These are the winners of a 1977 Maltese Specialty Show in Nagoya, Japan. The judge is Akira Shinohara. Photo courtesy of Dorothy Tinker.

After seeing Aennchen's Shikar Dancer's picture in the December 1965 issue of *Popular Dogs* magazine, and after a full year of negotiations, Mr. Shinohara managed to purchase and import this great dog to Japan. Shikar was followed by American Ch. Joanne-Chen's Sweet He Dancer and American Ch. Joanne-Chen's Aga Lynn Dancer. It wasn't long before Shikar produced three Best in Show winners for him; namely, Snow Select Boy, Snow Shikar Dancer, and Snow Samanther. Many more champions were to follow.

In the spring of 1972, Mr. Shinohara imported American Ch. Joanne-Chen's Siva Dancer and Joanne-Chen's Mayan Dancer, daughter of American Ch. Joanne-Chen's Maya Dancer. By 1974 he imported American Ch. Joanne-Chen's Sweet Man Dancer. These important imports and advice from Mrs. Joanne Hesse have given Mr. Shinohara and his kennel a substantial base for quality Maltese in Japan.

American Ch. Joanne-Chen's Shikar Dancer was exported to Japan by his breeder Joanne Hesse, who is pictured with him here. This photo was taken in Japan at the Lineage Show given in his honor by owner, Akira Shinohara.

Japanese Best in Show winner, Ch. A-S Gloria's Snow Select Boy, owned and bred by Akira Shinohara of Osaka. The sire was his American Best in Show import, Ch. Joanne-Chen's Shikar Dancer.

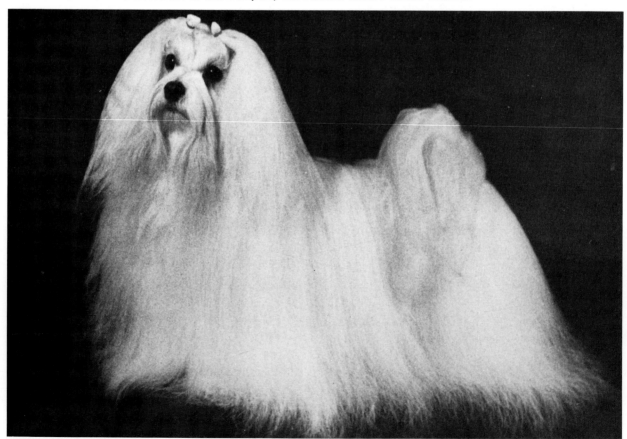

Japanese Best in Show winner Ch. A-S Gloria's Snow Shikar Dancer, owned by Akira Shinohara, was sired by American Ch. Joanne-Chen's Shikar Dancer ex American Ch. Joanne-Chen's Aga-Lynn Dancer.

In 1974 Mr. Shinohara staged a special Lineage Show honoring American Ch. Joanne-Chen's Shikar Dancer. He produced an excellent catalog for the show, honoring all the dogs sired by this great little dog. A Hall of Fame was also included in the catalog and Mrs. Joanne Hesse was one of the honored judges and guest of the club, with a wonderful party afterward.

Japanese Best in Show winner Ch. A-S Gloria's Snow Fair, a beautiful little Maltese bitch owned by Umeko Yamaga of Japan. The sire was Japanese Ch. A-S Gloria's Snow Sweet He Jr. ex A-S Gloria's Snow Suci Dancer. The breeder was Akira Shinohara.

The Osaka lineage party given for American import Ch. Joanne-Chen's Shikar Dancer in Japan, 1974. The two American judges for the show are seated front and center and include Shikar's breeder, Joanne Hesse.

American Ch. Joanne-Chen's Siva Dancer, the beautiful male exported to Japan as a stud dog in the A-S Gloria Kennels.

Ch. A-S Gloria's Snow Marilin, owned by Yoshimichi Tanaka of Japan. The sire was Ch. Joanne-Chen's Shikar Dancer ex Ch. Anna of Aromatic Peak.

Japanese Ch. A-S Gloria's Snow Doris Dancer, owned by Umeko Yamaga of Japan. The sire was Japanese Ch. A-S Gloria's Snow Mars Dancer ex Joanne-Chen's Sweet Tai Dancer.

Other Breeders and Exhibitors

Some of the other breeders and exhibitors in Japan are Masters Maltese, owned by Hajime Masuda; Snow Park Maltese, owned by Umeko Yamaga; M.Y. White Graces Maltese, owned by Yashuko Matuo; Lovely Fairy's Maltese, owned by Yoshimichi Tanaka; Cherry Land, owned by Yashuko Togawa; Villa Bay, owned by Chihara Mashima; White Birch, owned by Seigo Urata; Pearl Palace, owned by Yasuo Takahashi; Fine Piece Maltese, owned by Shumiko Takeuchi; Beautiful Fairy Maltese, owned by Shigemi Komatu; Nagoya Rainbow Maltese, owned by Toshie Takeichi; Ace Aizawa, owned by Kasumi Aizawa; Moriyama Hotta Maltese, owned by Hiroshi Hotta; Her-Mines, owned by Taeko Numano; Lets Go Maltese, owned by Shohzoh Takahashi; Garden Shine Wood Maltese, owned by Nobuko Mori; Kasaoka Takagi Kensha, owned by Mitsuo Takagi; Ebino Echoes Maltese, owned by Tadao Eto; Nagoya Taki Sow, owned by Kimiko Taki; Daiwa Sow Maltese, owned by Kazuko Oya; Rustic Maltese, owned by Minako Miyamoto; and Acacia Kennels, owned by Minako Matsui.

Ceremonial celebration at the 1974 Lineage Show in honor of American import Ch. Joanne-Chen's Shikar Dancer in Japan. Host and owner of Shikar is Akira Shinohara, owner of the A-S Gloria Maltese Kennels of Osaka, Japan.

Japanese Ch. A-S Gloria's Snow Shikar Young is pictured at two months of age. Bred and owned by Akira Shinohara, the sire was American Ch. Joanne-Chen's Shikar Dancer ex Patricia of Beautiful Fairy.

Others are Diamond Arrow, owned by Kimiko Kubo; Little Stars, owned by Ayako Kato; Effelgent Bambi, owned by Teruichi Takahashi; Star Like, owned by Hiroko Jinno; Branch M.O., owned by Kazue Ogura; Rain Wood, owned by Fusae Amemori; M Action, owned by Tamie Haraday; Fukuyama Sazanami Sow, owned by Ryoko Kobayashi; Song Mountain, owned by Eiko Yoneda; and in Japan, not New York—Long Island Kennels, owned by Mashae Tsukuda.

The charming ceramic Maltese figurines awarded at Japanese shows are fashioned after the famous American and Japanese Ch. Joanne-Chen's Shikar Dancer.

DOGS IN THE SOVIET UNION

The Soviet Union acknowledges both local and national champions, and these regional titles can be won many times, though there is usually only one regional show per year. Every few years there is a show called an All National, and the national champion from this show is the top winning dog in the USSR. Dogs are rated excellent, very good, fair, poor, or unacceptable, depending on both performance and conformation.

Russia held its first dog show in 1923, and shows have survived all regimes and political changes, though they are on a smaller scale than in other countries.

As elsewhere in the world, a dedicated core of devoted breeders manages to preserve important bloodlines in the existing breeds, although reports of Maltese in Russia would be hard to authenticate. However, we do know that registrations for Maltese can be found in the stud books of Finland for a Maltese named Milka, born in 1912 in St. Petersburg, Russia.

If you wish to buy a dog in the Soviet Union, you must do so through a local dog club. The cost will depend on the quality and success of its sire and dam. You must register the dog with the club after receiving the dog's papers, and if you wish to breed it, you must consult the breeding section of the same local club. Dogs which are permitted to be bred must have a show mark of X or VG (excellent or very good) for dogs, and G (good) for bitches. They must also have an obedience or utility degree.

Dogs are registered with three independent branch organizations under Toy, Hunting, or Service Dog categories, and then also individually by breed. These service dog clubs can be found in all major cities of Russia, and they are the central body overseeing all the activity under the name of the Federation of Service Dog Breeding.

There is no advertising of "puppies for sale," since there is always a demand for puppies and, therefore, the need to advertise does not exist. Russian show dogs are a healthy lot, since veterinary care is free. There is, however, a tax (of an approximate equivalent to fifteen dollars in United States money) on each dog.

During the researching of this book there was information concerning almost thirty or more clubs for the different breeds of dogs popular there, with memberships totaling almost six thousand. Regrettably we found none for the Maltese breed.

Jose A. Fraguada and Lillian Vializ Velazquez of Puerto Rico, with dogs Dickey of Rodvel and Linda Fuster Rodvel.

MODERN OVERSEAS FANCIERS

Today the leading breeders in foreign countries represent their Maltese through club affiliations. In Italy, the Baroness Tamagnone is a leading Maltese fancier in Genoa; Mrs. W. M. Hill and Mrs. M. Jensen are active in New Zealand, as is Mrs. E. Pogson and Miss P. Nicholson. South Africa is the home territory of Mrs. P.A. Scott in Sandton and Mr. and Mrs. Klassnick in Johannesburg. Sweden has Miss B. Bericson in Tustared and Miss B. Lanserius in Hindas. Kiel, Germany, is the home of Mr. Scharfenburg and his Maltese; and Madrid, Spain, is where Senor and Senora Favier represent the Maltese in their country.

Three six-week-old Carabelle Maltese puppies are pictured with their proud sire, New Zealand Ch. Garegwen Shining Star, an import from Australia. Owned by Mrs. N.C. Simpson.

American and Canadian Best in Show winning Ch. Four Halls Conversation Piece, Canada's Number One Maltese and Number Four Toy Dog for 1978, won five Bests in Show, ten Group Firsts, and thirteen other Group Placements. Bred and owned by Glenna Fierheller of Vancouver, British Columbia, the sire was Canadian Ch. Maltacellos Friendly Ghost ex Joanne-Chen's She Dancer.

International, South American, and Argentinian Ch. Peggotty von Igolta, owned by Adolfo and Elena Spector of Buenos Aires.

New Zealand Ch. Sara-Jayne of Carabelle, whelped in 1981 and pictured here at fifteen months, is owned by Mrs. N. C. Simpson of New Zealand.

Argentinian and South American Ch. Garet David, winning at a 1974 show in Buenos Aires, is owned by Elena Spector. The judge is Arivoldo Amoni of Brazil.

American and Canadian Ch. Revlo's Louis Riel is owned by Mrs. Gerry Taylor of Dugald, Manitoba, Canada. The sire was Canadian and American Ch. Mike-Mar's Sirius of Revlo ex Canadian Ch. Revlo's El-Alamein, II.

Ch. Delysia of Carabelle, born in 1973 and owned by Mrs. N. C. Simpson of New Plymouth, New Zealand, is a multiple all-breed Best in Show winner sired by New Zealand Ch. Ckisjane Dreamboy, an Australian import, ex Ch. Sweetheart of Carabelle.

Canadian Ch. Four Halls Creme de la Creme is shown here at eleven months of age and celebrating her championship title. Bred and owned by Glenna E. Fierheller of Vancouver British Columbia, the sire was American and Canadian Ch. March'En Top Hat Dancer ex American and Canadian Ch. Four Halls Conversation Piece.

Number One Maltese, Number One Toy, and Number Six All-breeds in Canada in 1982, American and Canadian Ch. Revlo's Ringo Star of Midway, owned by Douglas and Mary Olver, Revlo Maltese, Prince Albert, Saskatchewan.

Canadian Ch. Su-Le's White Scoter pictured at the 1979 American Maltese Association Specialty Show under judge Merrill Cohen. The sire was Am. Ch. Tennessa's Bobolink of Su-Le ex Su-Le's White Ibis. Owned and shown by Lesley Kerr, Prince George, British Columbia, Canada.

American and Mexican Ch. Sun Canyon KiKu pictured winning at a 1973 show under judge Edd Bevin. Owner is Judith Elaine Johnson-Gil of San Diego, California.

Ch. Emma-Jane of Carabelle, 5½ pounds of joy and a top show winner in New Zealand. Sired by New Zealand Ch. Garegwen Shining Star, an import from Australia, out of Ch. Delysia of Carabelle. Owned by Mrs. N.C. Simpson of Westown, New Plymouth, New Zealand.

New Zealand Ch. Carabelle Coeur-de-lion photographed at thirteen months of age. Sired by New Zealand Ch. Garegwen Shining Star out of New Zealand Ch. Whiteglory Dreamtime, both Australian imports. Owned by Carabelle Kennels.

American, Canadian, and Mexican Ch. Villa Malta's Encore Leore pictured winning at a Mexican show. Owned by William Bissell of Las Vegas, Nevada.

Little Ghost's Mariana, Best Puppy in Show at an 1982 event in Argentina. Owned by Adolfo and Elena Spector of Buenos Aires.

Ch. A-S Gloria's Snow Daisy, owned by Hajime Masuda of Japan. The sire was Ch. Joanne-Chen's Sweet He Dancer ex A-S Gloria's Snow Young Lady.

A-S Gloria's Snow Mayan Dancer II, owned and bred by Akira Shinohara of Osaka, Japan. The sire was American Ch. Joanne-Chen's Shikar Dancer ex Joanne Chen's Mayan Dancer.

Japanese Best in Show winner Ch. A-S Gloria's Snow Fair with friend, Ch. Little Star's Show Girl.

Ch. Myi's Sun Seeker, Best in Show winner in the United States before being exported to Japan, where he is owned by Akira Shinohara.

American and Canadian Ch. Dil-Dal's White Lit'n of Anitas, co-owned by Rita and Angela Dahl, Keyport, Washington, is pictured winning a Group Third at a recent show.

Canadian and American Ch. Revlo's Louis Riel pictured winning Best in Show under judge Knut Egeberg at the 1981 Parkland Canine Club in Canada. Owned and handled by Mrs. Gerry Taylor, Ridgegreen Kennels, Dugald, Manitoba, Canada. The breeders were Mary and Douglas Olver, Revlo Kennels, Prince Albert, Saskatchewan, Canada.

This Encore Maltese from the Alma Line earned her American and Mexican championships for owner William Bissell of Las Vegas, Nevada.

Best in Show winning American and Canadian Ch. Four Halls Conversation Piece.

Eight-month-old Mandarin, owned by Glenna Fierheller. The sire was Am., Can. Ch. March'en Top Hat Dancer ex Am., Can. Ch. Four Halls Conversation Piece.

High in Trial at the 1983 Bahamas Kennel Club Show in Nassau was Ch. Ginger Jake, U.D., one of the few dogs to earn both a conformation and obedience title. Jake now lists a Bahamian C.D. title in addition to his American U.D. and Canadian C.D.X. credits. Owned and trained by Faith Ann Maciejewski of West Allis, Wisconsin.

Linda and Dickey on the terrace of their home in Puerto Rico. Owners are Jose A. Fraguada, Lillian Vializ Velazquez, and Lymari Rodriquez.

Ch. Gayla's Piccolo Pete M.M.A., owned by Mr. Yoshimitsu Murakami.

122

These four Maltese beauties owned by Norma Belford, of Soddy, Tennessee, are pictured below in a more formal pose.

Norma Belford's Maltese captured in this studio photograph are Floriana Bernice, Ch. Su-Le's Bunting, Precious Penelope Peach, and Jolly Olly Orange.

"Nikki" and "friend Fritz" are owned by Vera Graham of Alexandria, Virginia. Nikki was eight years old in 1983.

Ch. Fantasyland Pete R Wabbit, photographed by breeder-owner Carole M. Baldwin of Novato, California.

Coat cared for to perfection! This crowning glory displayed by American and Canadian Ch. Titanic's Moppet's Bolero of Normalta is just one of the beautiful characteristics of the Maltese at Barbara Searle's Titanic Maltese Kennels in Salt Lake City, Utah.

In another pose is American and Canadian Ch. Titanic's Moppet's Bolero of Normalta, owned and shown by Barbara Searle.

Ch. Martin's Chanel-Cid "in her Poodle disguise." Whelped in 1980, Chanel is pictured after her show ring career, "cut down" for her impending motherhood. Bred and owned by Marjorie Martin. Columbus, Ohio.

Lovely formal portrait of Elyse Fischer's Ch. Su-Le's Mynah II. Elyse Fischer's Fable Kennels are in Port Washington, New York.

Martin's Samuel-Cid, owned by Monika Moser, is pictured wrapped between shows. Bred and photographed by Marjorie Martin.

CHAPTER SEVEN

Grooming
Your Maltese

Kathy DiGiacomo puts the finishing touches on one of her beautiful Kathan Maltese before going into the show ring.

No matter how much acclaim was given to our breed in the past, no one in those olden days could have imagined by the farthest stretch of the imagination the glorious beauty we see in the sparkling, shimmering flowing white coats we see on our dogs today. And all made possible through our modern grooming aids, the benefits of correct nutrition, and the indulgence of caring owners who are well aware that it takes all three, plus a certain inheritance factor, to produce our modern day beautifully-coated Maltese.

All dogs, including the short-coated breeds but especially the long-coated breeds such as our Maltese, require regular, careful grooming. Done on a regular basis, it can be a relatively simple task. With regular basic care, your dog can remain a fully-coated Maltese which proudly wears the silky, luxurious coat the breed Standard requires and is a joy to behold, in and out of the show ring.

Once it is ruined, or let go beyond repair, the coat will take endless time and energy on your part to restore it to its original natural luster and length.

To establish grooming as a common practice in your daily routine, you'll find matters simplified by choosing a particular place for grooming the dog each time. You'll make it easier for yourself by placing the grooming table where the light is good and where the dog will have the fewest distractions. Make the table top a rather small area which will reduce the temptation for the dog to "wander off," and eliminate temptations by keeping toys, bones or biscuits or other family pets out of sight of the grooming area. The dog will become restless if he thinks he's missing something. Make the dog realize there is work to be done and that you mean to do it. Be firm—but gentle—about it.

How you choose to position your dog for the various phases of grooming is a matter of choice for your own convenience. Teaching the dog to be comfortable in various positions will aid and speed the grooming. First consideration should be that the table be steady and doesn't wiggle, and is covered by a rubber mat so that the dog has firm footing and feels secure at that height.

You must establish your own amount of time for grooming. There is no set time for grooming a Maltese. Naturally the more heavily coated the dog, the more time must be allotted for going over the entire dog each time it is put up on the table. What you skip on one grooming session will be twice as hard to remedy by the time the next grooming time rolls around.

129

A portrait study of Ch. Malone's Snowie Roxann shows off her magnificent coat to best advantage. Owned by Nancy Shapland, this darling little Maltese has 11 all-breed Bests in Show to her credit, as well as 52 Group Firsts and Best of Breed at Westminster for two years. She has also won Specialties with Peggy Hogg, her handler throughout an impressive career.

SPECIAL CONSIDERATIONS

Every Maltese owner will have his own ideas of the perfect method for grooming. However, each dog is different and may require special methods. Generally speaking, the natural bristle hair brush should be used and the coat should be brushed out in layers from the skin to the ends of the hair. If the brush is gathering too much hair on one side of the bristles you are not holding it properly. The dead hair you brush out should be evenly distributed all over the surface of the bristles. The coat should be brushed in the direction in which it is to fall. The one exception to this is in the case of puppies. Here the method of grooming or brushing the coat can be said to be "in every which way." At this tender age, it does the hair itself no actual harm and stimulates the skin and hair cells to encourage the growth of the

coat. Hair on the legs and face can be fluffed up and add to that typical, darling puppy expression.

Particular attention should be given to the feet. The feet are usually the first part of the dog to get dirty and may stay that way. Wiping them off with wet paper towels will help, especially in winter if the dog has been walking on sidewalks that have been sprinkled with salt to help melt ice. It is irritating to the feet and not good for the dog if it licks its feet.

Nails should be trimmed periodically with great care given to not cutting them too short. If the quick is cut, excessive bleeding may result which will upset the puppy. Bleeding can be stopped by applying wet cotton to the nail, smearing it with a little vaseline or using a styptic pencil. Ice applied directly to the nail tip sometimes helps also.

GROOMING EQUIPMENT

Following is a list of recommended items that you are likely to need for grooming your Maltese. There are, obviously, additional pieces of equipment that you would want to have on hand.

Natural bristle brush
A wide and a narrow width comb
Spray bottles or atomizers
Wrapping paper—rice, wax, porous paper, net or handiwraps cut to size
Baby powder and/or cornstarch
Tangle remover lotion
Shampoo—a brand best suited to your dog's coat
A dry shampoo for between baths
Balsam creme rinse
Hair control spray
Knitting or crochet needle (for making the part)
Rubber bands for top knot or wrappings
Hair bows
Nail clippers

GROOMING AIDS

The stores are filled with various kinds of grooming aids and coat conditioners that can help you keep your dog well groomed and smelling like a rose. It is up to you to decide which is best suited to your particular dog and gives you the best results. They are on sale at all pet shops and at the concession booths at all the dog shows. Consult the breeder of your dog if you have any questions and learn what they use. For the most part these coat conditioners are sprayed on the coat with atomizers and brushed into the coat. However, it is wise to read—and re-read—the instructions on the bottle.

If your Maltese is outdoors a great deal, or lives in a city where soot and excessive dirt will show on the white coat, you will more than likely want to use one of the dry shampoos or lather dry bath preparations between tub baths. Do not expect miracles from these man-made preparations. They are only "aids" that will help you maintain a clean, healthy coat.

Groomed and ready to go into the ring are two Mykiss Maltese owned by Sharon Roberts of Byron, New York.

GROOMING POSITIONS

The first thing to look for when grooming your Maltese is any tangles that might have gathered since the last grooming session. These will probably be found on the under side of the dog and behind the elbows. One of the easiest ways to eliminate these is to turn the dog over on its back on your lap, or perhaps on the table. Spray the mat with a tangle remover and brush loose hair gently away from the area around the mat. Take a little bit of the mat in your hands and try to separate it gently with your fingers. Next, take a comb and carefully work it out from the ends of the hair first and work up toward the body, until you get to the skin. When the mat has all been separated, start brushing out the tangled hairs until all remaining hairs are free. Then brush them back into the rest of the coat.

While the puppy or dog is on its back, it is a good time also to trim the nails. If the puppy is trained to lie in this position at an early age it will save you much grief in later months when a heavier coat may tangle. Rubbing the puppy's stomach, and talking to it will also help in getting it to tolerate this position. The puppy should also be taught to lie on its side, as well as to stand still so that the body coat can be given full attention in all areas. Standing for grooming is also good practice for the show ring. The noose on the grooming arm can help accustom the dog to the feel of a show lead also. Just be certain that the noose does not "hang" the dog or he will not like grooming or the show ring! Need we mention, NEVER leave the dog alone when he is attached to the grooming arm. If the dog should slip off the table, it could break its neck or hang itself. If the telephone or door bell rings, put the dog on the floor or take it with you.

When the coat is all brushed out, use the knitting needle to make the part from the nose to the tip of the tail and brush the coat downward on each side.

Ch. Gaylord of Primrose Place sports a coat seven inches long and still growing. The breeder was Marge Stuber, Primrose Kennels, Lima, Ohio.

When grooming the head, special care should be taken to protect the eyes. Steel combs and sharp bristles on the brush can damage eyes permanently and the dogs themselves seem to sense this danger. They will be extremely uncomfortable while you are working in this area once they have been "nicked." A little reassuring conversation at this point will help tremendously.

Ch. Aennchen's Suni Dancer, bred by Mr. and Mrs. J. P. Antonelli and owned by Dr. and Mrs. Roger Brown of Omaha, Nebraska.

THE TOP KNOTS

One of the most charming features of the Maltese is the traditional little top knots over the eyes. This is the gathering of hair from the top of the head secured with a rubber band, barrette or ribbon bows. Rubber bands will hold it adequately, but ribbons, being more decorative, are seen in the show ring, as well as for every day use at home.

The small rubber bands can be purchased at most variety stores, pet shops or concession booths at the dog shows, or by direct mail from ads appearing in breed magazines devoted to these toy breeds. There is also available a specially designed elastic band that does not risk pulling out as much hair as the regular rubber bands. These are especially recommended for show dogs where every hair must be preserved.

When learning to make the top knots, you will find you get the best results by observing and learning from others—for instance, the person from whom you bought your dog. But basically the hair is gathered from the outside corner of the eye to the part in the center of the head, doubled over and secured with the rubber band, letting the hair fall to the sides of the face.

Sporting the single top knot is Kandy Hollis, owned by Maxine Hollis of Oklahoma City, Oklahoma.

Many Maltese owners prefer the single top knot that we see on the Yorkshire Terrier which is gathered at the top of the head secured with a rubber band with the hair falling down the back of the neck.

Once the rubber bands are secured, be certain that the knot is not so tight that it pulls the eyes or ears out of their natural position, or that loose hairs not caught in it are pulling the skin. Move the bands back and forth and around in place to be sure there is no pulling or the dog will scratch at them and break off a lot of the hairs in an attempt to ease the tension. If there is any tension or tightness, loosen the hair between the band and the skin until the tautness is relieved. Then attach the little bows and praise the dog for its beauty!

Once you put the dog down on the floor, watch it for a moment to see that it does not scratch at the rubber bands or try to rub them off against the furniture, floor, or with its paws. If it does try to get them off, remove the band gently and immediately and repeat the procedure, until you get it right. Remove the rubber bands with scissors if possible. Trying to slip them off the hair tends to break the hair and can be painful for the dog.

Practice makes perfect, and there is a knack to preparing top knots correctly. Once you learn, it quickly becomes second nature. You might want to practice on a wig, or on a doll, before risking the hair on your dog. At any rate, you will soon become adept at making top knots, or *pien ji* (pronounced *been dye*), as the Chinese call them!

133

Ch. Aennchen's Suni Dancer is pictured at the peak of her show ring career. Bred by Mr. and Mrs. J. P. Antonelli, Suni was owned and shown by Dr. and Mrs. Roger Brown of Omaha, Nebraska.

MALTESE EARS

Naturally, you want your dogs' ears to be clean and clean smelling. There is no set time limit on how often to do this. Once again it will depend on each individual dog. While some dogs may require daily maintenance, others need to be checked only once a week or every several days.

A periodic test with a cotton swab will soon give you an indication of what your dog requires and you can act accordingly. The main thing to remember is that the ear is an extremely sensitive organ and must be handled with care. Do not "dig" down or try to penetrate the inner ear canal. A hint would be to draw an imaginary line from the ear base to the nose along the side of the face and keep the swab in that direction. Gently twirl the cotton-tipped swab rather than rub out any matter you may find there. If it continues to build up or becomes dark in color a visit to the veterinarian is recommended, since this may indicate a more serious condition than normal ear wax.

Use eyebrow tweezers to pull out any matted hair from within the ear canal. The air thus allowed to enter the cleared ear canal will help keep the ears clean. The hair on the outer ear will prevent dust and dirt from entering the canal.

Ch. Villa Malta's Roxie of Lyndale is shown on the day she completed her championship for owner Lillian Harrington of Vestal, New York.

MALTESE EYES

As with all breeds of dogs that are close to the ground, the Maltese do suffer from watering eyes. This constant tearing has a tendency in about 90% of the dogs to cause a brownish stain on the fur around the eyes.

This brown discoloration is not only unattractive and detracts from the adorable expression on their faces, but is a particular problem for show dogs when perfection in grooming is a must. There are many "variations on a theme" for keeping this problem under control and very likely as many methods of preventing it as there are Maltese owners and exhibitors.

Some Maltese have runnier eyes than others, and some stain darker than others. It is also an established fact that when Maltese are teething they have a tendency toward watery eyes—and when the pollen count is high, or when the air is filled with what might be considered irritants, i.e., room deodorizers, sawdust, and so on.

Most Maltese owners prevent this problem by daily rinsing the eyes with Eyebrite. Eyebrite is obtainable at any drug store and comes with complete instructions as to use, and results. There is another commercial product on the market called Diamond Eye which is put on the hair—not in the eye—which will prevent brown stain. Careful attention with these two products, one for use *in* the eyes, and one for use on the hair around the eyes, will minimize the stain, if not eliminate the problem entirely.

With puppies or grown dogs at home, boric acid powder applied on the hair around the eyes after it is wet will also prevent brown stain. However, if other puppies or the mother lick it off the fur, boric acid powder can make them sick.

GROOMING THE FACIAL HAIR

Even if you tie the side and bottom "whiskers" in papers or rubber bands while your Maltese eats, food will undoubtedly stick to the fur and a washing will be necessary to prevent the hair from developing an unpleasant odor. If rubber bands are used you can rinse the whiskers in a small bowl of water, squeeze dry with paper towels, sprinkle them with cornstarch and brush them dry. You must be sure that all food is rinsed away. Make sure that, when applying the rubber bands, the chin hairs are not pulled so tight that they will interfere with the dog's ability to eat. If the lips, for instance, are pulled back too tightly he may not even *want* to eat, or may not be able to chew or swallow naturally. After applying the bands, and/or wraps, check to see if the mouth is held in a normal position.

WRAPPING THE COAT

Many owners, especially owners of show dogs, put up their dog's coat in "papers" between shows to prevent the ends of the hair from breaking off and to insure the longest possible growth. Coats that trail on the floor have a tendency to break or wear off and never attain any greater length.

Ch. Sun Canyon Classy Clancy (1968-1982). This flashy little Maltese was owned by Mary P. McKinnon of Milton, Florida.

The art of putting the coat up in papers, netting, or any of the other things used for this purpose is truly an "art" which requires observation, learning and lots of practice in order not to do more harm than good to the coat. *How* to wrap the hair, *where* to wrap the coat, *how long* to keep it wrapped and *what* is best to use for wrapping the coat are all very much a matter of individual preference and experience if you are to do it at all.

It is possible to have a show dog's coat in good condition without wrapping it. Rather than do it wrong, it is better not to do it at all if you don't learn from a good teacher. There are specific and very definite ways to cut and fold the "wraps" and to apply the rubber bands to hold them in place and still have them be comfortable for the dog.

In humid climates a more porous material should be used as a wrap. It must also be remembered that a dog cannot be wrapped and left that way indefinitely. The wraps must be removed at least every couple of days and the coat given a complete grooming to assure the coat gets sufficient air and the skin proper stimulation. Wrapping should never be considered a substitute for grooming.

Consult the breeder or person from whom you bought your dog for advice on how to do the wraps, or take your dog to a grooming salon and have them show you how. Actually it is a breeder's obligation as a normal courtesy to teach you all necessary procedures required to maintain your dog. So do not hesitate to seek his help. Breeders should be familiar with the wrapping procedure and grooming aids that best suit their bloodlines. A breeder who is proud of his line will willingly offer this advice. It might not be easy for you to learn the technique at first, but it will be well worth your while over a long period of time to take the best possible care of that long beautiful coat.

If you haven't done so already, study the diagrams on the wrapping procedure in this book, and if there are any questions in your mind as to whether or not you are doing it correctly, seek help *before* you ruin your dog's coat.

Pictured between appearances in the show ring, with his coat wrapped in papers, is Japanese Best in Show winner Ch. A-S Gloria's Snow Shikar Dancer, owned by Akira Shinohara of Osaka, Japan.

Maltese Wraps

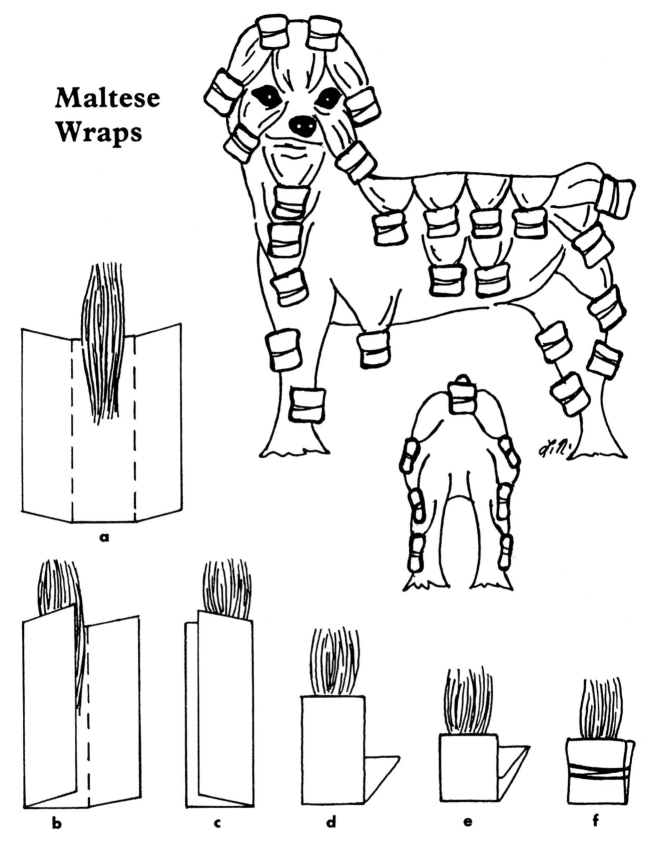

The diagrams above may be helpful in understanding the procedure for wrapping a Maltese. After folding a strip of paper into thirds and then re-opening it, (a) lay hairs about halfway down the center section, (b) fold one of the thirds over the center section, and (c) fold the other third also over the center section. Then (d) fold the paper under once, (e) fold it under a second time, and (f) put rubber bands around the final package to keep it securely together. Since this procedure will be repeated perhaps as many as thirty times each time you wrap your Maltese, be sure you have an adequate supply of papers and rubber bands available before you start.

Ch. Brown's Joni Dancer, as she looks between appearances in the show ring, was bred and is owned by Dr. Roger and Nancy Brown of Omaha, Nebraska.

WRAPPING INSTRUCTIONS

You will be dealing with between 26 and 28 wraps, depending on the length and thickness of your dog's coat and the size of your dog. Cut your papers ahead of time, once you've decided on what you are going to use. Wax paper is most commonly used, although many people are now using "Handi-wipes" or other specially impregnated paper products because they are porous and allow the hair to "breathe." A porous wrap is essential in a damp climate.

These papers should be approximately eight inches long by three inches wide. They should never be put on over a dirty coat, or one that is matted. And only the longer hair need be wrapped. Fold your wrap in three sections length-wise. Open the paper. Place a strand of the hair half way down the middle section. Fold one of the outer sections over the hair; then fold the other outer section over the hair. Fold up and under once and then fold up under once again. Wrap your rubber band twice around the entire folded section.

Test to see if there is any hair being pulled uncomfortably, and on the tail and ears especially be sure you have not included any skin or ear leather. You can do this by making sure you can get a comb through the hair between the paper and the skin. Check to see that the eyes and lips and ears are not pulled out of shape so that the dog is uncomfortable and will scratch at the papers.

See illustrations for all the places the wraps can be placed and remember that practice makes perfect!

SPECIAL MALTESE HAIRCUTS

Many people who love the breed and own Maltese either do not have the time or the ability to keep their little dogs in show coat all the time. Even those of us who specialize in show dogs find that after a Maltese is no longer being shown and we have new little hopefuls coming along who deserve their fame in the show ring, there is less and less time available to keep all the "stay-at-homes" in show coat.

A number of us have come to realize that there are alternatives which make their care quite simple and that will still keep them close to looking like the show dogs they used to be. These alternatives consist of several different kinds of "haircuts" which make grooming much easier without drastically changing the appearance or characteristic expression we have come to love in the Maltese. These special haircuts also allow the owners, and those who cannot find the time to groom their pets as often as they should, the opportunity to care for the breed by making just a few adjustments to the normal coat pattern.

While the true, staunch breed advocates gasp at the shaved dog, with only fluffy ears, top knots and feathery tail left after the visit to the grooming parlor or after they've taken a scissors to the dog themselves, there are far too many Maltese seen trimmed down to the skin. The list of selections for other grooming patterns allows for variations that are far more acceptable and more becoming. For instance, there is no reason at all that a Maltese cannot be put back into a puppy length coat. Then there is the pattern seen on many Cocker Spaniels that can be applied to the Maltese. The major portion of the body hair is cut down and the hair on the legs thinned out and shortened. The ears are trimmed down to just below the ear leather, whiskers shortened, top knots and the tail shortened. There is also the cut to which the Old English Sheepdog owners often resort: cutting the hair down to one inch in length over the entire body but leaving the head intact. With this cut, the top knots remain and the cute little bows can be put on, but the body coat is too short to mat.

Of course, people who are handy with a pair of scissors can also create their own personal haircut that will make grooming easier for them. However, the grooming parlors are also getting to know the various short cuts and might make suggestions for other haircuts that would suit your dog. If you tell them what you want, they will very likely do a good job, no matter which pattern you choose.

GROOMING BEHAVIOR

If your Maltese wiggles and squirms and backs off and fights you every bit of the way when grooming time rolls around, chances are you are being a little too rough. True, there are dogs that never do get to like being groomed, and these dogs require extra patience and, quite possibly, extra work, since they will employ every scheme known to canines to put you off and hamper your progress. But more than likely, if you meet resistance, it's because the dog is genuinely uncomfortable.

The most important thing is to be gentle. Be even more gentle in the sensitive areas such as the groin, the feet, under the tail, around the eyes, the testicles, etc. The calmest of dogs will flinch when he sees the shiny teeth of a steel comb flashing overhead. You can be pretty brisk on the body and chest, but such fervor in the tender regions can resemble the Chinese torture in the wrong places.

Since we are dealing with a long-coated breed, it will pay off later to get the dog to like being groomed from the time he is a very young puppy. Grooming may never seem easy even if you are doing it right, but it can be a gratifying experience for both dog and owner if approached with common sense and patience. Let your dog see that you take a definite pride in taking care of him. He will appreciate the attention and it will result in a closer communication between you and your dog through this time spent together. And he'll certainly look more beautiful.

"Bullet" gets ready for her first ring appearance at a Match Show. Bred and owned by Diane Davis, she won Best in Match at just five months of age.

Try starting the grooming process when the puppy is just a few days old, using a baby's toothbrush for the coat. Play with the puppies' feet, singling out the toes, standing the puppies briefly in future show pose and propping up their tails and holding up their heads, giving a little scratching under the chin at the same time. Repeat the words "stay," and "good dog," as a clue to future ring procedure. It all adds to a bright future and an outgoing personality.

BATHING THE MALTESE PUPPY

Here again there are two schools of thought on the advisability of bathing the very young puppy. If you are an advocate of the bath, the same technique that is advised for the grown dogs can be used for the puppy. Drafts are very dangerous for puppies especially. Also, *never* leave a puppy only partially dry, or put it out in the cold while it is still damp.

If you believe a bath exposes and endangers a puppy unnecessarily, it is wise to know about the dry shampoos mentioned before when a cleaning job is deemed necessary. These dry shampoos, plus regular brushings, will keep a puppy reasonably clean as well as stimulate the hair follicles and encourage the natural hair oils necessary for a good coat.

Bathing a dog can be hard work, and if you don't know a few of the tricks of the trade, it can be a disaster with a long-haired dog, with everyone and every thing ending up equally wet. We would suggest you wear a rubber apron or an old, lightweight raincoat with the sleeves cut off at the elbows as proper attire, because sooner or later your dog is going to start shaking himself.

139

This basket full of charm, owned by Norma Belford of Soddy, Tennessee, includes Precious Penelope Peach, Jolly Olly Orange, Ch. Su-Le's Bunting, and Floriana Bernice. Photo by their owner.

BATHING THE ADULT MALTESE

There are probably as many theories on how, and how often, to bathe a dog as there are dog owners. There is, however, no set rule on frequency or method, although it is certain that show dogs, or dogs that are outdoors a great deal in all kinds of weather will require a bath on occasion.

Once you've made up your mind that the time for the bath has arrived, and all mats have been removed from the coat, a wad of cotton in each ear and perhaps a drop of mineral oil in each eye to prevent soap burning, you are almost ready to begin. Provided, of course, you have already placed a rubber mat in the bottom of the sink for sure footage, gathered the towels and shampoos, rinses, combs, and brushes and a dryer.

For dogs the size of Maltese, a kitchen sink is about the best place for a bath, and the water pressure and drainage is ideal for the several soapings and many rinsings you will want.

Soaping should provide a good thick lather, and this can best be achieved by giving the dog a thorough rinsing with warm water first. You must decide if your dog requires one or two shampoos, (usually two is better) and then follow with a good, long rinsing to make sure every last bit of soap is out of the coat.

Start the rinsings and soapings at the rear of the dog. The noise and feel of the water will be more readily accepted if it is away from the face and first touches the more heavily coated areas of the body. Let a little water gather in the sink so that the feet are soaked well; it will help melt away any heavy dirt that might be stuck to the pads or toes. When you get to the head, be sure to hold the head back and protect the eyes from any direct stream of water or soap. Cup water in your hands to wet the head at first and gradually work up to the spray. Separate the coat as you rinse. Use the cream rinse after the two shampoos and follow the directions on the bottle very carefully. Once you are sure that you have given several good rinsings, do it once more for good measure!

WHITENING THE COAT

Many breeders use a special rinse for white dogs. Here again it would be wise to consult the breeder of your dog about what is best for the particular coat your dog has. Many of the pet shops have personnel who can also advise you on brands that are available and you can perhaps try different ones until you are completely satisfied with the results. Follow the directions carefully.

THE DRYING PROCESS

Let the water from the rinsings run off and make sure the feet have not gathered any of the soap or residue washing down the sink. Let the dog "drip dry" for a few minutes while you gently squeeze out the heavily coated parts of the body. Then throw a turkish towel over the dog and gently squeeze the coat dry with the towel. Always squeeze the coat; never rub it or you will tangle the coat.

Once you have most of the drippings in the towel, lift the puppy, wrapped in the towel, out of the tub and onto the grooming table. While the excess is still soaking into the towel, turn on your dryer and let it warm up before you direct the air current at the dog for the blow-dry. This will also give the dog time to get used to the sound of the dryer as well. We must remember that their hearing is much more acute than ours, and this must be a most unpleasant sound for them.

When the dryer has warmed up, place the dog in the air stream and with the brush, start gently going over the entire body brushing within the current of warm air. Allow approximately one foot of space between the dog and dryer and once again brush in layers or in the direction in which the coat is to fall. Be sure to dry evenly all over the body and not just in one spot.

When brushing the feet and legs, it is helpful to place the dog's feet at the edge of the table so that you can brush from the skin to the ends of the hair without hitting the table.

Never dry just the ends of the hair while the remaining hair next to the skin stays wet. Don't bathe the dog unless you are prepared to finish the job once you have started it. When the dog is completely dry continue with the normal grooming final touches.

Some Maltese love the water, but not a bath. So be sure to talk to your dog and reassure it so the next bath will be even easier. Every once in a while pick it up and hug it and take a whiff of that marvelous sweet freshness! It can make all the effort seem worthwhile.

Some of the Dil-Dal Maltese line up on the couch in the Dahl's motor home for a siesta under the dryer while on the dog show circuit.

How often to bathe is a personal decision—as often as necessary for the pet dog. The general consensus of opinion among exhibitors of show dogs seems to be around every seven to ten days. Others hold with once a month, or when necessary.

PREPARING THE SHOW DOG

If your Maltese is to be a show dog, there are several additional phases which will further enhance its coat and appearance in the ring. Sooner or later every Maltese owner or exhibitor comes up with what they consider the ideal way to prepare a Maltese for the ring, having achieved what they believe to be the best combination of sprays, cream rinses, oils, shampoos, etc. This is not as simple as it may sound. All one has to do is to pass a concessionaire's booth at a dog show and view the myriad of grooming aids and products on display to realize how long it takes to give all of them a fair trial before settling on the "perfect" way to present your dog.

With so many combinations available, the entire process might seem to be one of trial and error. Since all products, with rare exception, are of good quality, the selection can be said to be "to each his own" when selecting products. It is for this reason that it is advisable to spend a great deal of time observing others until you learn the technique and profit from their experience.

Let professionals groom your dog until you have the procedures down pat. Watch the pros groom at the dog shows. You will almost be able to pick out the winners in the grooming area by the outstanding way the dogs look and behave while still up on the grooming tables. Do not expect the handlers to take time out to teach you while they are preparing to go into the ring. You must learn from observation here. And the breeder of your dog should be able to advise you about learning for yourself by attending a grooming school.

USING CLIPPERS

Many exhibitors will use the corner of an electric clipper to trim away excess hair around the anus, and to clean off the hair on the stomach. This is another procedure which requires practice and skill, to avoid cutting or burning those delicate areas of the body. A good teacher should be consulted before attempting this.

All scissors used to shape the feet, cut whiskers, etc., should have blunt ends and be kept away from the dog's eyes.

CONDITIONING

While we have already discussed the fact that diet plays a large part in a good coat, and inheritance another, and wrapping yet another, there are additional aids if a dog is inclined to have a poor, dry coat. Hot oil treatments or "putting a dog down in oil" between shows is yet another contributing factor to a good coat.

Warm olive oil applied to the roots after a bath and gently worked into the coat clear out to the ends will help if heat is also applied by means of hot towels or a warm dryer for several minutes. Mineral oil, baby oil, corn oil, cocoanut oil or perhaps other oils are sometimes used, but caution must be taken to see that the oil does not discolor the white coat. You must also be careful that the dog does not stain the furniture while down in oil and before you have had a chance to wash it out. Once again, it is advisable to check with your breeder or someone experienced with Maltese conditioning for advice on how to do it, or if it is necessary to do it at all.

Never brush if the coat is dirty and when it is dry. Even a spraying with water as you brush will help. After a bath a spray of half water and half cream rinse will put a lovely finishing touch on the coat.

BRAIDING THE COAT

In recent years more and more Maltese have been seen with their hair braided or plaited. While in the past the hair was put up in top knots with a bow and falling in a cascade, we are now noticing little braids, perhaps with bows at the ends.

These tiny little braids serve several purposes. They keep the hair out of the eyes and also train the "part" for the correct fall of the hair. It alleviates the need for barrettes, bows or rubber bands in most cases and the dogs seldom scratch at them if they are done properly. The braids are easy to do, and they should lie close to the body and not stick out from it. The silky quality of the hair gives it a natural tendency to fall down so if the braids stick out, re-do them. Just as you must take down the wrappers every few days, the braids should be redone also. The hair must be quite long to make a decent braid so don't give up on it too soon.

Not that braiding Maltese hair is anything new. It is interesting to notice in photographs of Mrs. M. Neame's dogs taken in 1932 that her Maltese had braids in their hair around their faces.

Canadian and American Ch. Revlo's Louis Riel is pictured as he is seen between appearances in the show ring. A copy of the picture appeared in a Winnipeg, Canada, newspaper in December of 1981 with mention of Louie's appearance at a local dog show. His owner is Mrs. Gerry Taylor, Dugald, Manitoba, Canada.

American and Canadian Ch. Lin-Lee's Melodie is pictured winning under judge Sue Kauffman on the way to championship at a 1978 show. Handled by Lee Coleman, who co-owns with Linda Coleman.

CHAPTER EIGHT

The Dog Show World

Bar None Harold Square, winner of the Bred by Exhibitor Class at the 1984 Westminster Kennel Club show. Now near championship, she won the largest class at the Maltese Specialty in 1983. Owner-handled by Michele Perlmutter of Ghent, New York.

Let us assume that after a few months of tender loving care, you realize your dog is developing beyond your wildest expectations and that the dog you selected is very definitely a show dog! Of course, every owner is prejudiced. But if you are sincerely interested in going to dog shows with your dog and making a champion of him, now is the time to start casting a critical eye on him from a judge's point of view.

MATCH SHOWS

For the beginner there are "mock" shows, called match shows, where you and your dog go through many of the procedures of a regular dog show, but do not gain points toward championship. These shows are usually held by kennel clubs, annually or semiannually, and much ring poise and experience may be gained there. The age limit is usually reduced to two months at match shows to give puppies four months of training before they compete at the regular shows when they reach six months of age. Classes range from two to four months, four to six months, six to nine months, and nine to twelve months. Puppies compete with others of their own age for comparative purposes. Many breeders evaluate their litters in this manner,

choosing which is the most outgoing, which is the most poised, the best showman, and so on.

For those seriously interested in showing their dogs to full championship, these match shows provide important experience for both the dog and the owner. Class categories may vary slightly, according to number of entries, but basically include all the classes that are included at a regular point show. There is a nominal entry fee and, of course, ribbons and usually trophies are given for your efforts as well. Unlike the point shows, entries can be made on the day of the show right on the show grounds. They are unbenched and provide an informal, usually congenial atmosphere for the amateur, which helps to make the ordeal of one's first adventure in the show ring a little less nerve-wracking.

POINT SHOWS

It is not possible to show a puppy at an American Kennel Club sanctioned point show before the age of six months. When your dog reaches this eligible age, your local kennel club can provide you with the names and addresses of the show-giving superintendents in your area who will be staging the club's dog show for them, and where you must write for an entry form.

Danny's Jude of Chelsea took Best of Breed and a Toy Group placement at his first Match Show. Handled at this 1980 event by Sabrina Keenan for owner Gail Hennessey.

The forms are mailed in a pamphlet called a premium list. This also includes the names of the judges for each breed, a list of the prizes and trophies, the name and address of the show-giving club and where the show will be held as well as rules and regulations set up by the American Kennel Club which must be abided by if you are to enter.

A booklet containing the complete set of show rules and regulations may be obtained by writing to the American Kennel Club, Inc., 51 Madison Avenue, New York, N.Y., 10010.

When you write to the dog show superintendent, request not only your premium list for this particular show, but ask that your name be added to their mailing list so that you will automatically receive all premium lists in the future. List your breed or breeds and they will see to it that you receive premium lists for specialty shows as well.

Unlike the match shows where your dog will be judged on ring behavior, at the point shows he will be judged on conformation to the breed standard. In addition to being at least six months of age (on the day of the show), he must be purebred for a point show. This means he and both of his parents are registered with the American Kennel Club. There must be no alterations or falsifications regarding his appearance. Females cannot have been spayed, and males must have both testicles in evidence. No dyes or powders may be used to enhance the appearance, and any lameness or deformity or major deviation from the standard for the breed constitutes a disqualification.

With all these things in mind, groom your dog to the best of your ability in the area specified for this purpose in the show hall, and *exercise your dog before taking him into the ring!* Too many Maltese owners are guilty of making their dogs remain in their crates so they do not get dirty, and the first thing the animals do when they start to show is stop to empty themselves. There is no excuse for this. All it takes is a walk *before* grooming. If your dog is clean, well groomed, *empty*, and leash trained, you should be able to enter the show ring with confidence and pride of ownership, ready for an appraisal of your dog by the judge.

Vera Rebbin waits to enter the ring with one of her little Maltese.

Angela Dahl and Lit'N wait to go into the ring at a 1982 show.

The presiding judge on that day will allow each and every dog a certain amount of time and consideration before making his decisions. It is never permissible to consult the judge regarding either your dog or his decision while you are in the ring. An exhibitor never speaks unless spoken to, and then only to answer such questions as the judge may ask—the age of the dog, the dog's bite, or to ask you to move your dog around the ring once again.

However, before you reach the point where you are actually in the ring awaiting the final decisions of the judge, you will have had to decide in which of the five classes in each sex your dog should compete.

POINT SHOW CLASSES

The regular classes of the American Kennel Club are: PUPPY, NOVICE, BRED-BY-EXHIBITOR, AMERICAN-BRED, OPEN; if your dog is undefeated in any of the regular classes (divided by sex) in which it is entered, he or she is *required* to enter the Winner's Class. If your dog is placed second in the class to the dog which won Winner's Dog or Winner's Bitch, hold the dog or bitch in readiness as the judge must consider it for Reserve Winners.

PUPPY CLASSES shall be for dogs which are six months of age and over but under twelve months, which were whelped in the United States or Canada, and which are not champions. Classes are often divided six and (under) nine, and nine and (under) twelve months. The age of a dog shall be calculated up to and inclusive of the first day of a show.

THE NOVICE CLASS shall be for dogs six months of age or over, whelped in the United States or Canada, which have not, prior to the closing entries, won three first prizes in the Novice Class, a first prize in Bred-by-Exhibitor, American-bred or Open Class, nor one or more points toward a championship title.

THE BRED-BY-EXHIBITOR CLASS shall be for dogs whelped in the United States which are six months of age and over, which are not champions, and which are owned wholly or in part by the person or by the spouse of the person who was the breeder or one of the breeders of record. Dogs entered in the BBE Class must be handled by an owner or by a member of the immediate family of an owner, i.e., the husband, wife, father, mother, son, daughter, brother, and sister.

Canadian Ch. Chatelaine's Kirsten is pictured taking Best of Winners from the Junior Puppy Class for a three-point major under judge William Bergum. Kirsten completed her championship the next day under Mrs. Olmos-Ollivier at just eight months of age. Owned by Lesley Kerr, Prince George, British Columbia, Canada.

THE OPEN CLASS is for any dog six months of age or over, except in a member specialty club show held for only American-bred dogs, in which case the class is for American-bred dogs only.

WINNERS DOG and WINNERS BITCH: After the above male classes have been judged, the first-place winners are then *required* to compete in the ring. The dog judged "Winners Dog" is awarded the points toward his championship title.

RESERVE WINNERS are selected immediately after the Winners Dog. In case of a disqualification of a win by the American Kennel Club, the Reserve Dog moves up to "Winners" and receives the points. After all male classes are judged, the bitch classes are called.

BEST OF BREED OR BEST OF VARIETY COMPETITION is limited to Champions of Record or dogs (with newly acquired points, for a ninety-day period prior to American Kennel Club confirmation) which have completed championship requirements, and Winners Dog and Winners Bitch (or the dog awarded Winners if only one Winners prize has been awarded), together with any undefeated dogs which have been shown only in non-regular classes; all compete for Best of Breed or Best of Variety (if the breed is divided by size, color, texture, or length of coat hair).

BEST OF WINNERS: If the Winners Dog or Winners Bitch earns Best of Breed or Best of Variety, it automatically becomes Best of Winners; otherwise they will be judged together for Best of Winners (following Best of Breed or Best of Variety judging).

BEST OF OPPOSITE SEX is selected from the remaining dogs of the opposite sex to Best of Breed or Best of Variety.

OTHER CLASSES may be approved by the American Kennel Club: STUD DOGS, BROOD BITCHES, BRACE CLASS, TEAM CLASS; classes consisting of local dogs and bitches may also be included in a show if approved by the American Kennel Club.

Ch. Gulfstream Radiant Rhapsody waits for the next command from Mary Lou Porlick, her owner-handler. This is one of the few owner-handled Maltese to win a Group as well as numerous other Group placings.

Fourteen-year-old Angela Dahl with Tutee's Chutzpah winning a four-point major under judge Mrs. Thomas Gately at the 1979 Seattle Kennel Club show. Angela's mother, Rita Dahl, is owner of the Dil-Dal Kennels in Keyport, Washington.

The MISCELLANEOUS CLASS shall be for purebred dogs of such breeds as may be designated by the American Kennel Club. No dog shall be eligible for entry in this class unless the owner has been granted an Indefinite Listing Privilege (ILP) and unless the ILP number is given on the entry form. Application for an ILP shall be made on a form provided by the American Kennel Club and when submitted must be accompanied by a fee set by the Board of Directors.

All Miscellaneous breeds shall be shown together in a single class except that the class may be divided by sex if so specified in the premium list. There shall be *no* further competition for dogs entered in this class. Ribbons for First, Second, Third, and Fourth shall be Rose, Brown, Light Green and Gray, respectively.

OBEDIENCE TRIALS

Some shows also offer Obedience Trials, which are considered as separate events. They give the dogs a chance to compete and score on performing a prescribed set of exercises intended to display their training in doing useful work.

There are three obedience titles for which they may compete: first, the Companion Dog or C.D. title; second, the Companion Dog Excellent or C.D.X.; and third, the Utility Dog or U.D. Detailed information on these degrees is contained in a booklet entitled *Official Obedience Regulations* and may be obtained by writing to the American Kennel Club.

JUNIOR SHOWMANSHIP

Junior Showmanship competition is for boys and girls in different age groups handling their own dogs or ones owned by their immediate family. There are four divisions: Novice A (10 to 12-year-olds) and Novice B (13 to 16-year-olds) for competitors with no previous Junior Showmanship wins, Open A (10 to 12-year-olds) and Open B (13 to 16-year-olds) for competitors with one or more JS awards.

As Junior Showmanship at the dog shows increased in popularity, certain changes and improvements had to be made. As of April 1, 1971, the American Kennel Club issued a new booklet containing the Regulations.

149

LAKEHEAD KENNEL CLUB
BEST IN SHOW - 1960

One of the great Maltese of the 1960s was International Ch. Fidino of Villa Malta, pictured winning Best in Show at the Lakehead Kennel Club under Alva Rosenberg, one of the most famous dog men of all times. Shown by Mrs. Andrena Brunotte of Caistor Centre, Ontario, Canada, for Fidino's owner, Mrs. J. C. Morgan.

DOG SHOW PHOTOGRAPHERS

Every show has at least one official photographer who will be more than happy to take a photograph of your dog with the judge, ribbons, and trophies, along with you or your handler. These make marvelous remembrances of your top show wins and are frequently framed along with the ribbons for display purposes. Photographers can be paged at the show over the public address system, if you wish to obtain this service. Prices vary, but you will probably find it costs little to capture these happy moments, and the photos can always be used in the various dog magazines to advertise your dog's wins.

TWO TYPES OF DOG SHOWS

There are two types of dog shows licensed by the American Kennel Club. One is the All-Breed show which includes classes for all the recognized breeds, and groups of breeds; i.e., all Terriers, all Toys, etc. Then there are the specialty shows for one particular breed which also offer championship points.

BENCHED OR UNBENCHED
DOG SHOWS

The show-giving clubs determine, usually on the basis of what facilities are offered by their chosen show site, whether their show will be benched or unbenched. A benched show is one where the dog show superintendent supplies benches (cages for toy dogs). Each bench is numbered and its corresponding number appears on your entry identification slip which is sent to you prior to the show date. The number also appears in the show catalogue. Upon entering the show you should take your dog to the bench, where he should remain until it is time to groom him before entering the ring to be judged. After judging, he must be returned to the bench until the official time of dismissal from the show. At an unbenched show, the club makes no provision whatsoever for your dog other than an enormous tent (if an outdoor show) or an area in a show hall where all crates and grooming equipment must be kept.

Benched or unbenched, the moment you enter the show grounds you are expected to look after your dog and have it under complete control at all times. This means short leads in crowded aisles or getting out of cars. In the case of a benched show, a "bench chain" is needed. It should allow the dog to move around, but not get down off the bench. It is also not considered "cute" to have small tots leading enormous dogs around a dog show where they might be dragged into the middle of a dog fight.

IF YOUR DOG WINS A CLASS

Study the classes to make certain your dog is entered in a proper class for his or her qualifications. If your dog wins his class, the rule states: *You are required* to enter classes for Winners, Best of Breed and Best of Winners (no additional entry fees). The rule states, "No eligible dogs may be withheld from competition." It is not mandatory that you stay for group judging. *If your dog wins a group,* however, *you must stay for Best In Show competition.*

"There may be trouble ahead . . ." might be the thought foremost in the mind of eight-month-old Chatelaine's Tiara, owned by Lesley Kerr of Prince George, British Columbia, Canada.

THE PRIZE RIBBONS AND WHAT THEY STAND FOR

No matter how many entries there are in each class at a dog show, if you place first through fourth position you will receive a ribbon. These ribbons commemorate your win and can be impressive when collected and displayed.

All ribbons from the American Kennel Club licensed dog shows will bear the American Kennel Club seal, the name of the show, the date and the placement. In the classes, the colors are blue for first, red for second, yellow for third and white for fourth. Winners Dog or Winners Bitch ribbons are purple, while Reserve Dog and Reserve Bitch ribbons are purple-and-white. Best of Winners ribbons are blue-and-white; Best of Breed, purple-and-gold; and Best of Opposite Sex ribbons are red-and-white.

In the groups, first prize is a blue rosette or ribbon, second placement is red, third yellow, and fourth white. The Best In Show rosette is either red, white, and blue or incorporates the colors used in the show-giving club's emblem.

QUALIFYING FOR CHAMPIONSHIP

Championship points are given for Winners Dog and Winners Bitch in accordance with a scale of points established by the American Kennel Club based on the popularity of the breed in entries, and the number of dogs competing in the classes. This scale of points varies in different sections of the country, but the scale is published in the front of each dog show catalogue. These points may differ between the dogs and the bitches at the same show. You may, however, win additional points by winning Best of Winners, if there are fewer dogs than bitches entered, or vice versa. Points never exceed five at any one show, and a total of fifteen points must be won to constitute a championship. These fifteen points must be won under at least three different judges, and you must acquire at least two major wins. Anything from a three to five point win is a major, while one and two point wins are minor wins. Two major wins must be won under two different judges to meet championship requirements.

American Ch. Myi's Sun Seeker is pictured winning the Toy Group in the United States before being exported to Japan for owner Akira Shinohara of Osaka.

Windsong's Solitaire takes her third major for a four-point win under Dr. William Field at a 1980 show. Barbara Alderman handled for breeder-owner Diane Davis of Haines City, Florida.

PROFESSIONAL HANDLERS

If you are new in the fancy and do not know how to handle your dog to his best advantage, or if you are too nervous or physically unable to show your dog, you can hire a reliable professional handler who will do it for you for a specified fee. The more successful or well-known handlers charge slightly higher rates, but generally speaking there is a pretty uniform charge for this service. As the dog progresses with his wins in the show ring, the fee increases proportionately. Included in this service is professional advice on when and where to show your dog, grooming, a statement of your wins at each show, and all trophies and ribbons that the dog accumulates. Any cash award is kept by the handler as a sort of "bonus."

When engaging a handler, it is advisable to select one that does not take more dogs to a show than he can properly and comfortably handle. You want your dog to receive his individual attention and not be rushed into the ring at the last moment because the handler has been busy with too many other dogs in other rings. Some handlers require that you deliver the dog to their establishment a few days ahead of the show.

Other handlers will accept well-behaved and trained dogs that have been groomed from their owners at ringside, if they are familiar with the dog and the owner. This should be determined well in advance of the show date. NEVER expect a handler to accept a dog at ringside that is not groomed to perfection!

There are several sources for locating a professional handler. Dog magazines carry their classified advertising. A note or telephone call to the American Kennel Club will also put you in touch with several in your area.

DO YOU REALLY NEED A HANDLER?

The answer to that question is sometimes yes, sometimes no! However, the answer that must be determined first of all is, "But can I *afford* a professional handler?" or, "I want to show my dog myself. Does that mean my dog will never do any big winning?"

Do you *really* need a handler to win? If you are mishandling a good dog that should be winning and isn't because it is made to look bad in the ring by its owner, the answer is yes. If you don't know how to handle a dog properly, why make your dog look bad when a handler could show it to its best advantage?

Some owners simply cannot handle a dog well, and still wonder why their dogs aren't winning in the ring, no matter how hard they try. Others are nervous and this nervousness travels down the leash to the dog, and the dog behaves accordingly. Some people are extroverts by nature, and these are the people who usually make excellent handlers. Of course, the biggest winning dogs at the shows usually have a lot of "show off" in their nature, too, and this helps a great deal.

Australian Ch. Dainty Gem of Carabelle is a multiple Best in Show winner, whelped in 1973 and owned by the Carabelle Kennels in New Zealand.

American and Canadian Ch. Gina of Villa Malta, owned by Mrs. J. C. Morgan and shown for her in the 1960s by Mrs. Andrena Brunotte of Ontario, Canada.

THE COST OF CAMPAIGNING A DOG WITH A HANDLER

At present many champions are shown an average of twenty-five times before completing a championship. In entry fees at today's prices, that adds up to over $250. This does not include motel bills, traveling expenses, or food. There have been dog champions finished in fewer shows, say five to ten shows, but this is the exception rather than the rule. When and where to show should be thought out carefully so that you can perhaps save money on entries. This is one of the services a professional handler provides that can mean a considerable saving. Hiring a handler can save money in the long run if you just wish to make a champion. If your dog has been winning reserves and not taking the points and a handler can finish him in five to ten shows, you would be ahead financially. If your dog is not really top quality, the length of time it takes even a handler to finish it (depending upon competition in the area) could add up to a large amount of money.

Campaigning a show specimen that not only captures the wins in his breed but wins Group and Best in Show awards gets up into the big

money. To cover the nation's major shows and rack up a record as one of the top dogs in the nation usually costs an owner between ten and fifteen thousand dollars a year. This includes not only the professional handler's fee for taking the dog into the ring, but the cost of conditioning, grooming, board, advertising in the dog magazines, photographs, and so on.

There is great satisfaction in winning with your own dog, especially if you have trained and cared for it yourself. With today's enormous entries at the dog shows and so many worthy dogs competing for top wins, many owners who said "I'd rather do it myself!" and meant it, became discouraged and eventually hired a handler anyway.

However, if you really are in it just for the sport, you can and should handle your dog if you want to. You can learn the tricks by attending training classes, and you can learn a lot by carefully observing the more successful professional handlers as they perform in the ring. Model yourself after the ones that command respect as being the leaders in their profession. But, if you find you'd really rather be at ringside looking on, then do get a handler so that your worthy dog gets his deserved recognition in the ring.

Kathan Blu Flower of Chelsea goes Best of Winners for a three-point major at the 1979 Bronx show under judge Bessie Pickens. Kathy DiGiacomo handled for owner Gail Hennessey of Wappingers Falls, New York.

154

Australian and New Zealand Ch. Sebastion of Carabelle is owned by Mrs. N. C. Simpson, Carabelle Kennels, New Plymouth, New Zealand. Whelped in 1974, his sire was New Zealand Ch. Crisiane Dreamboy, an Australian import, ex Ch. Atawhai Lexie.

TATTOOING

Ninety percent success has been reported on the return of stolen or lost dogs that have been tattooed. More and more this simple, painless, inexpensive method of positive identification for dogs is being reported all over the United States. Long popular in Canada, along with nose prints, the idea gained interest in this country when dognapping started to soar as unscrupulous people began stealing dogs for resale to research laboratories. Pet dogs that wander off and lost hunting dogs have always been a problem. The success of tattooing has been significant.

Tattooing can be done by the veterinarian for a minor fee. There are several dog "registries" that will record your dog's number and help you locate it should it be lost or stolen. The number of the dog's American Kennel Club registration is most often used on thoroughbred dogs, or the owner's Social Security number in the case of mixed breeds. The best place for the tattoo is the groin. Some prefer the inside of an ear, and the American Kennel Club has ruled that the judges officiating at the AKC dog shows not penalize the dog for the tattoo mark.

The tattoo mark serves not only to identify your dog should it be lost or stolen, but offers positive identification in large kennels where several litters of the same approximate age are on the premises. It is a safety measure against unscrupulous breeders "switching" puppies. Any age is a proper age to tattoo, but for safety's sake, the sooner the better.

The buzz of the needle might cause your dog to be apprehensive, but the pricking of the needle is virtually painless. The risk of infection is negligible when done properly, and the return of your beloved pet may be the reward for taking the time to insure positive identification for your dog.

K-9 TRANSPORTATION

Shipping puppies by air, or sending bitches away for stud service is frequently a disturbing decision. The horrible tales of unfortunate mishaps linger in our ears as we tuck our little Maltese into their crates and turn them over to the men who load them aboard those enormous aircraft. We always wonder if they will be suffocated, or crushed under other baggage, or put off at the wrong destination. We have all heard these stories, and Maltese are so tiny!

However, when we compare the large number of dogs that are safely shipped these days to the relatively few bad experiences, perhaps we can take heart and hope that with a few ordinary precautions, a safe journey can be almost assured.

Planning ahead of time is the key to a smooth trip. Making the reservations ahead of time for non-stop flights—even if it means considerable traveling on each end—is good for starters. And not shipping puppies in summer heat is another important consideration. Night flying is always

One of Sharon Roberts' Mykiss Maltese seems to be asking for an opinion on his show stance.

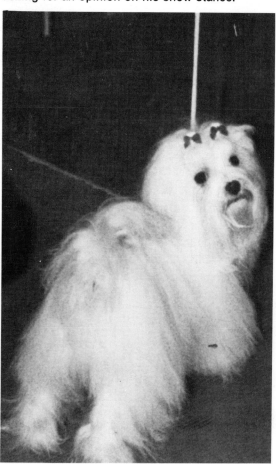

an advantage, and so is shipping your dog midweek when vacationers are not also traveling, in order to avoid crowded conditions. Try, if possible, to ship your dog in your own crate as it will smell of home. Also include a toy or blanket that is comforting and familiar. Just make sure the crate is substantial and large enough to meet plane requirements, and won't get lost "in the shuffle." Crates may be purchased at the airport, and you can work it out with the party on the other end as to who will pay for it.

A visit to the veterinarian is another prerequisite. Each state has different rules and regulations concerning vaccinations, so there is no purpose in stating them here. But it is wise to call the airline to find out the current rules and vaccinations necessary at that time. Most airlines also require the animal to be present at least two hours before the flight departure time. Needless to say, feed a light diet on the day of the flight, and walk the dog before crating it. This practice not only enables the dog to relieve itself, but gives it exercise, and hopefully it will be able to sleep en route. Make sure water is included in the crate. Not so much as to spill over, but enough to give it a drink en route.

The ideal way to ship is to take the dog on board with you in a small carrier to be put under your seat. Most airlines will allow this if reservations are made far enough in advance, and if not too many pets are booked on the same flight. Some airlines will permit only one dog in the cabin at a time. So plan ahead!

If the dog must travel in the baggage section, make sure the crate is marked "LIVE ANIMAL" with full instructions as to where it has come from and where it will be going, complete with telephone numbers. If the trip takes a reasonable time, leave instructions not to remove the dog from the crate. If it is a matter of several days, be sure to leave complete instructions and a leash attached to the crate. Dog biscuits will usually suffice as food. On long trips, put a heavy layer of sawdust or newspaper on the bottom of the crate. Secure the door to prevent an accidental bump from opening the crate and having your dog escape. However, do not lock the crate in case of an emergency.

Once the dog is airborne, head for a telephone and let the people on the other end of the line know all the details: when it ate last, what it eats, arrival time, and so on. Then go home and wait by the phone to learn of its safe arrival!

Best in Sweepstakes at the 1980 National Specialty Show was future Ch. Su-Le's Litonya, bred, owned, and handled to this win under judge Pauline Dick by Barbara Bergquist of New Boston, Michigan.

The Maestro himself! The famous Dr. Vincenzo Calvaresi conducts one of his teams of Maltese to a win at Westminster, bringing further fame to the Villa Malta kennels.

CHAPTER NINE

Showing and Judging the Maltese

March'en Love Bug Dancer and March'en Sassy Dancer are ready to enter the ring in this 1979 photo. Breeder-owner is Marcia Hostetler, Des Moines, Iowa.

Ever since I started judging dogs in 1961, I never enter a show ring to begin an assignment without thinking back to what the late, great judge Alva Rosenberg told me when we discussed my apprentice judging under his watchful eyes. His most significant observation I find still holds true for me today—that a judge's first and most lasting impression of a dog's temperament and bearing will be made the moment it walks into the ring.

It has always been a source of amazement to me the way so many exhibitors ruin that important first impression of their dog before the judge. So many are guilty of dragging their dogs along behind them, squeezing through the ringside crowds and snapping at people to get out of their way, just to arrive in the ring with a dog whose feet have been stepped on by people pushing to get closer to ringside, and whose coat has been ruined by food and cigarette ashes. After all this, the dog is expected to turn on its charm once inside the ring, fascinate the crowds, captivate the judge, and bring home the silverware and ribbons! All this on a day that invariably is either too hot or too cold—or too rainy—not to mention the hours of standing rigidly on a crate, being sprayed in the face and all over their

bodies with a grooming substance that doesn't smell or taste too good, and then brushed and trimmed until dry to their handler's satisfaction. Add this to the lengthy bath and grooming session the day before the show, and the bumpy ride to the show grounds, and, well, Alva Rosenberg had a point! Any dog that can strut into the ring after what it regards as a forty-eight-hour torture treatment *does* have to have an excellent disposition and a regal bearing. How fortunate we are that so many of our flashy little Maltese do have such marvelous temperaments in spite of our grooming rituals!

There is no reason an exhibitor cannot allow sufficient time to get to ringside with a few minutes to spare, in order to wait calmly somewhere near the entrance to the ring. They need only walk directly ahead of the dog, politely asking the people along the way to step aside with a simple statement to the effect that there is a "dog coming through." It works. I have seen spectators promptly step aside, not only to oblige this simple request when politely stated, but also to observe the beauty of the show dog passing by. Those who prefer to carry their dogs, and know how to do it without disturbing the coat, can make the same request for the same result.

159

Ch. Bar None Popeye winning the group at the prestigious Beverly Hills Kennel Club in California. Bred and owned by Michele Perlmutter, Ghent, New York.

The short waiting period at ringside also allows time for the dog to gain his footing and perspective, and gives the exhibitor time to get his armband on securely so it won't drop down the arm and onto the dog's head during the first sprint around the ring. These few spare moments will also allow a great deal of the "nervousness" that travels down the lead to your dog to disappear as the realization occurs to you that you have arrived at your class on time and you and your dog can both relax.

ENTERING THE RING

When the ring steward calls out the numbers for your class, there is no need for you to try to be first in the ring. There is no prize for being first. If you are new at the game, you would do well to get behind a more experienced exhibitor or professional handler where you can observe and perhaps learn something about ring behavior. The judges will be well aware of your presence in the ring when they make a small dot or a small check mark in their judge's book as you enter. The judges must also mark all

absentees before starting to evaluate the class, so you can be sure no one will be overlooked as they "count noses."

Simply enter the ring as quickly and calmly as possible with your dog on a loose lead, and at the first opportunity make sure you show your armband to the judge. Then take a position in the line-up already forming in the ring (usually at the opposite side from the judge's table). Set your dog up in the show pose so that once the judge has checked in all the dogs in the class, he will have an immediate impression of the outline of your dog in show stance.

The judge will then go up and down the line of dogs in order to compare one outline with another, while getting an idea of the symmetry and balance of each profile. This is the time when you should see that your dog maintains the show stance. Don't be nervously brushing your dog, constantly adjusting his feet, tilting his head, and primping his tail. All of this should have been done while the judge was walking down the line with his eyes on the other dogs in the class.

160

By the time the judge gets to your dog, it should be standing as still as a statue, with your hands off it if at all possible. Far too many exhibitors handle show dogs as if they were puppets with strings attached to all the moving parts. They are constantly pushing them in place, prodding them to a desired angle for the judge to see, placing the head and tail and feet according to their idea of perfection. More often than not, their fingers are covering the dog's muzzle or they are employing their thumbs to straighten out a topline, or using a finger to tilt a tail to the proper angle. Repeatedly moving a dog's feet tends to make the judge believe the dog can't stand correctly by itself. If a dog is standing incorrectly, the judge might assume that it just happened to be standing incorrectly at that moment, and that the exhibitor couldn't imagine such a thing and therefore never noticed it!

Fussing over a dog only calls attention to the fact that the exhibitor either has to do a lot to make the dog look good, or is a rank amateur and is nervously mis-handling the dog. A free,

natural stance, even when a little "off base," is still more appealing to the judge than a dog presented with all four feet barely touching the ground. All Maltese are beautiful on their own, and unnecessary handling can only be regarded as a distraction, not as indulgence on the part of the exhibitor. Do not get the mistaken idea that if the judge thinks you are working hard with your dog you deserve to win.

MOVE THEM OUT

Once the judge has compared the outlines (or profiles) of each dog, he will ask the exhibitors to move the dogs around the ring so that he might observe the dogs in action. This usually means two complete circles of the ring, depending on the size of the ring and the number of dogs competing in it. This is the time when the judge must determine whether the dog is moving properly or if it is limping or lame. The judge will check out the dog for proper gait and observe if the dog is moving freely on its own—not strung up on the end of a lead.

Ch. Su-Le's Roadrunner takes to the ring in big time Group competition at the 1973 Battle Creek Kennel Club show.

Be careful not to hamper your dog in any way in the limited time and space you have to show the judge how your dog moves. This means gaiting on a loose lead. Move next to your dog at a safe distance to the side so that you do not step on it going around corners or pull it off balance on turns. You must also keep in mind that you should not get too close to the dog ahead of you and that you must keep far enough ahead of the dog behind you so that your dog doesn't get spooked—or that you don't break the gait.

Once the judge has had the time to observe each dog in motion, the signal will be given to one person to stop at a specific spot in the ring, forming the line-up for closer inspection of each dog individually. At the judge's discretion, the individual evaluation may be done either in place or on a small table placed in the ring. Whether the judge chooses to evaluate each dog on the ground or on a table, the judge must go over the dog completely in order to evaluate it in accordance with the standard for the breed.

JUDGING THE MALTESE

As the judge approaches your dog, he will get his first close look at the expression. The judge will want to see the dark eye, will check the stop, the muzzle, the occiput, ear leather and set, and the head in its entirety for excellence. During this examination, the exhibitor must make sure the dog remains perfectly still and in correct

Petit Point Poker Chip, bred and owned by Susan M. Sandlin, The Original Petit Point kennels in Alexandria, Virginia.

Ten-month-old Ch. Villa Malta's Misha Lee was shown five times and finished with four majors. Owned by Bill Wright; bred by Marge Rozik.

show stance. Since the dangers of the various virus infections and contagious diseases that can be passed from dog to dog at the shows has been made known to us, it is hoped the judge will ask that you show your dog's bite. It is permissible, however, for the judge to open the dog's mouth to check out the bite, especially if the judge has reason to believe there is a fault. The judge will also evaluate the head from straight on as well as in profile.

Next, the neck and shoulders will be checked. The judge will lift up the ears to see just how long the neck really is and how well placed the shoulders are. Shoulders play an important part in the proper placement of the front legs and pasterns. Running his hands down the front leg, the judge will go all the way to the foot, picking it up and checking the foot pads and nails, and paying particular notice to whether the dog puts its foot down correctly in place when released.

The judge will check the brisket and the tuck-up as well as the topline. At this point, with his hands going over the dog, the judge can determine the proper texture of the coat, the profusion of feathering, and the general weight of the dog. Tail length and carriage are to be considered as well. Judging the hindquarters should prove the dog's legs are sturdy and well placed and strong enough to provide the strength for proper gait and movement.

Once the judge has gone over the dog completely, he will usually take a step or two away from the dog to give it a final over-all view, keeping a complete picture of it in his mind to make the comparison with the dog he has judged just before and will judge after yours. This is the time you must still keep your dog "on his toes," so that when the judge glances ahead or behind, your dog is not sitting down, chasing butterflies, or lifting his leg on the number markers. Remember, training is done at home—*performance* is required in the show ring at all times.

Ch. Russ Ann Bonus Baby ("Beep") is owned by Anna Mae Hardy of Floral City, Florida. Missy Yuhl photo.

Ch. Pen San September Song is pictured winning a four-point major and on to Best of Breed at the 1970 Portland show. Breeder-owner is Gloria Busselman of Richland, Washington.

INDIVIDUAL GAITING

Once the judge has gone over each dog individually, he will go to the end of the ring and ask each handler to gait his dog. It is important at this point to pay strict attention to the judge's instructions as to how this is to be done. Some judges require the "T" formation, others the half-triangle. Further observation of your dog may bring a request for you to repeat the pattern, especially if your dog did not show well during the first trip. It is important that you hear whether the judge wants you to repeat the entire exercise or merely to gait your dog "down and back" this time.

When each dog has been gaited, the judge will want a last look at all of them lined up together before making his final decisions. Usually the procedure will be to once again present the left side of your dog as the judge weaves in and out of the line to check once more the fronts or rears or other individual points of comparison. Some dogs may be asked to gait a third time, or to gait side by side with one of the other dogs should the judge want to "break a tie" as to which dog is the better mover. Because such deciding factors cannot be predicted or anticipated, it is necessary for the handler to always be ready to oblige once the request is given by the judge.

After the decisions are made, the judge will point to his four placements and those four will set their dogs up in front of the designated number markers on the side of the ring. Be ready at this point to show the numbers on your armband so that the judge can mark his judge's book. The judge then will present the winners with the appropriate color ribbons and any trophies won, and you may leave the ring.

Ch. Fantasyland Betty Lou was a three-point major on the way to championship. Owned by Madonna Garber; bred, handled, and co-owned by Carole M. Baldwin.

Contrary to popular opinion, it is not necessary or even correct to thank the judge for the ribbon. It is to be assumed that the dog *deserved* the ribbon or the judge would not have awarded it. Handing you the ribbon is part of the procedure and does not warrant a thank-you. The club, not the judge, is responsible for the donation of the trophies. It is not called for that the exhibitor speak to the judge, but if the win is significant enough so that you feel compelled to say *something,* a simple and not overly exuberant "I'm so pleased that you like my dog," or something similar is still more than is necessary.

The "thank-you" for the ribbon has on occasion become what some exhibitors like to think of as a "weapon." At ringside you can sometimes hear words to the effect that, "I didn't even thank him for that rotten red ribbon!" As if the judge had even noticed! However, it *is* expected that you take with you from the ring a ribbon of *any color.* To throw it on the ground or leave it behind in the ring so that the steward is obliged to call you back into the ring for the judge to hand it to you again is most unsportsman-like. You must play the game according to the rules. Your entry fee is to obtain the opinion of your dog by the judge. You must take the opinion and behave accordingly. If you do not like it, do not give them another entry, but you owe the judge the courtesy of respect for that title.

After this judging procedure is followed in the five classes for dogs, and Winners Dog and Reserve Winners Dog have been determined, the bitches are judged in this same manner. After Winners Bitch and Reserve Winners Bitch awards have been made, the Best of Breed judging follows. Class procedures here are discussed elsewhere in this chapter. Once the judge has completed his assignment and signed his judge's book, it is permissible to request any photographs that you may wish to have taken of your wins. At this time it is also permissible to ask the judge his motives in his judging of *your* dog. If you wish to, it should be done in a polite and calm manner. It must be remembered that the judge is not going to make comparisons rating one dog against another, but can, if he chooses, give a brief explanation as to how he evaluated your dog.

It is helpful to remember that "no one wins them all." You will win some and lose some no matter how good your dog is. Judges are human and, while no one is perfect, they have earned the title of "judge" for some mighty good reasons. Try to recall that this is a sport and it should be fun—tomorrow is another day.

A winner in the 1970s for Gloria Busselman is Pen San Magician, pictured here with judge Marjorie Siebern.

Ch. Marimack Happy Holly (on the left) wins Best of Breed while Marimack Hokey Pokey takes Best of Winners at a 1976 show. Both are owned and bred by Mary P. McKinnon, Marimack Kennels, Milton, Florida.

THE GAMES PEOPLE PLAY

If you are new to the game of dog-show exhibiting, there are a few things you should know about, such as how to protect yourself and your dog so that you do not get too discouraged and disillusioned right at the start.

There may be an occasion where your dog is winning a great deal and jealousy will arise from others competing in the ring with you. It has been known that some of these bad sports will try to get between you and the judge so the judge cannot see your dog at his best. Others may try stepping on your dog, breaking his gait so that he cannot be adequately judged, bringing bitches in season into the ring, throwing bait around to distract your dog, and so on. Needless to say, most judges are aware of these nasty tricks people play and will not tolerate them. Just be on your guard. Do not leave your dog alone or leave it in the care of others. Thefts have been known at dog shows, as well as poisoning and physical abuse.

CHILDREN IN THE SHOW RING

No one is more approving than I of children learning to love and to care for animals. It is beautiful to see a child and an animal sharing com-

plete rapport and companionship or performing as a team in the show ring. Those of us who have been around dog shows for any length of time have all been witness to some remarkable performances by children and their dogs. Junior Showmanship is one example; dogs caring for or standing guard over babies and infants is another example.

If a child shows the natural desire to exhibit a dog after having attended handling classes where they are taught how to properly show a dog, they must also be taught ring procedure. It is not fair to expect other exhibitors to show patience while a judge or the steward informs the child where to stand, or waits for the child exhibitor to gait the dog several times before it is done in the formation requested. Lack of knowledge or repeated requests delay the judging, look bad to the ringside crowds, and certainly don't make the dog look good.

If necessary, parents might stay after the dog-show judging and actually train the child in an empty ring. Parents should also sit ringside with the children to explain the judging procedures to them so they will know what to expect when they enter the ring. Many match show appearances should precede any appearance in a point show ring also.

A boy and his dog, both bred and loved by Anthony and Kathy DiGiacomo, Kathan Maltese, Fair Lawn, New Jersey.

165

BAITING

No matter how one feels about baiting a dog in the ring, we must acknowledge that almost everyone at one time or another has been guilty of it. Certain breeds are particularly responsive to it, while others show little or no interest with so much going on all around them.

There is no denying that baiting can be an aid to basic training. But in the show ring some judges consider it an indication that the training of the dog for the show ring is not yet complete. It becomes obvious to the judge that the dog still needs an incentive to respond to what other dogs are doing in the name of performance and showmanship.

Frequently, squeaky toys will work as well. Using conversation and pet nicknames in trying to encourage the dog is equally inappropriate.

DOUBLE-HANDLING

Double-handling is both distracting and frowned upon by the American Kennel Club. Nonetheless, some owners go to all sorts of ridiculous lengths to get their apathetic dogs to perform in the ring. They hide behind trees or posts at ringside or may lurk behind the ringside crowd until the exact moment when the judge is looking at or gaiting their dog, and then pop out in full view perhaps emitting some familiar whistle or noise, or wave of a hat, or whatever, in hopes that the dog will suddenly become alert and express a bit of animation.

Ch. Pen San Winsong of Ethridge, bred and owned by Gloria Busselman of Richland, Washington.

Don't be guilty of double-handling. The day may come when you finally have a great show dog, but the reputation of an owner guilty of double-handling lives on forever! You'll be accused of the same shady practices and your new show dog is apt to suffer for it.

JUDGING ON THE TABLE

Most Maltese judges will require that you place your dog on a table in the ring, so that they may go over your dog thoroughly without having to bend over or stoop down. You must watch for the judge to indicate this and be ready to place your dog on the table facing the judge as he or she approaches. As the judge goes over your dog—which you have set up in show stance—be prepared to move around the table so that the judge will get to see your dog from every angle.

At times the judge may require you to place your dog on the table with another dog, if the judge is trying to make a comparison between two choices being considered for placement. You also must be alert to this suggestion and place your dog in show stance at a safe distance from the other dog, thus allowing the judge to once again go over each dog individually, at close quarters.

At outdoor shows you will find that judges will want to see the dogs at least once on the table. Since dogs likely will be required to gait in the grass at outdoor shows (which may obliterate the chance of effectively evaluating the gait), the table examination becomes all the more important to the judge in making a final decision.

Japanese Ch. A-S Gloria's Snow French Dancer, an eight-month-old male Maltese owned by Akira Shinohara of Osaka, Japan. The sire was American Ch. Joanne-Chen's Shikar Dancer ex Ch. Joanne-Chen's Aga-Lynn Dancer.

APPLAUSE, APPLAUSE!

Another "put-on" by some of our less secure exhibitors is the practice of bringing their own cheering section to applaud vigorously every time the judge happens to cast an eye on their dog.

The judge is concentrating on what he is doing and will not pay attention to this or will not be influenced by the cliques set up by those trying to push their dogs to a win, supposedly by popular approval. The most justified occasions for applause are during a Parade of Champions, during the gaiting of an entire Specialty Best of Breed Class, or during the judging awards for Stud Dog, Brood Bitch, and Veterans Class. At these thrilling moments the tribute of spontaneous applause—and the many tears—are understandable and well received, but to try to prompt a win or stir up interest in a particular dog during the normal course of class judging is amateurish.

If you have ever observed this practice, you will notice that the dogs being applauded are sometimes the poorest specimens whose owners seem to subconsciously realize they cannot win under normal conditions.

Martin's Hoppel-Cid, whelped in 1981 and owner-handled by Marjorie Martin, Columbus, Ohio.

The lovely Ch. Encore's Faberge, bred and owned by William Bissell of Las Vegas, Nevada. Al-Dor, Vicbrita, and the illustrious Villa Malta are all behind Faberge's pedigree.

SINS WHEN SHOWING A MALTESE

1. DON'T forget to exercise your dog before entering the ring. Do it before grooming if you are afraid the dog will get wet or dirty after grooming is completed.

2. DON'T be late for your class; avoid entering the ring with you and your dog both in a nervous state.

3. DON'T drag the dog around the ring on a tight lead and destroy the proud carriage.

4. DON'T alter the appearance of your Maltese by unnecessarily catching hairs up in rubber bands or bows. If your Maltese isn't show-worthy in its natural state, don't show it.

5. DON'T talk to the judge in the ring, but do watch the judge closely and follow instructions. Don't talk to people at ringside or to others who are competing with you in the ring.

6. DON'T strike or in any way abuse your dog—especially not in the ring. The time for training and discipline is at home or in a class and not in front of the judge or the public.

7. DON'T be a bad loser. Win or lose, be a good sport. You can't win them all, so if you win today, be gracious; if you lose, be happy for the exhibitor who won today. Your turn may come tomorrow.

8. DON'T shove your dog in a crate or leave it on the bench and forget about him until it's time to go home. A drink of water or something to eat and a little companionship will go a long way.

Ch. Martin's Michael-Cid, whelped in 1978 and the chief stud force at Marjorie Martin's Kennel in Columbus, Ohio. Sired by Ch. Maltacello El-Cid; bred, owned, and photographed by Marjorie Martin.

CHAPTER TEN

Breeding Your Maltese

Martin's Samuel-Cid, pictured at eighteen months of age, is owned by Monika Moser. Sired by Ch. Martin's Michael-Cid, his breeder was Marjorie Martin.

Let us assume the time has come for your dog to be bred, and you have decided you are in a position to enjoy producing a litter of puppies that you hope will make a contribution to the breed. The bitch you purchased is sound, her temperament is excellent and she is a most worthy representative of the breed.

You have a calendar and have counted off the ten days since the first day of red staining, and have determined the tenth to fourteenth day, which will more than likely be the best days for the actual mating. You have additionally counted off sixty to sixty-five days before the puppies are likely to be born to make sure everything necessary for their arrival will be in good order by that time.

From the moment the idea of having a litter occurred to you, your thoughts should have been given to the correct selection of a proper stud. Here again, the novice would do well to seek advice on analyzing pedigrees and tracing bloodlines for the best breedings. As soon as the bitch is in season and you see color (or staining) and a swelling of the vulva, it is time to notify the owner of the stud you selected and make appointments for the breedings. There are several pertinent questions you will want to ask the stud owners after having decided upon the pedigree. The owners, naturally, will also have a few questions they wish to ask you. These questions will concern your bitch's bloodlines, health, age, and how many previous litters she's had, if any.

THE POWER IN PEDIGREES

Someone in the dog fancy once remarked that the definition of a show prospect puppy is one third the pedigree, one third what you see, and one third what you *hope* it will be! Well, no matter how you break down your qualifying fractions, we all quite agree that good breeding is essential if you have any plans at all for a show career for your dog. Many breeders will buy on pedigree alone, counting largely on what they themselves can do with the puppy by way of feeding, conditioning, and training. Needless to say, that very important piece of paper commonly referred to as the "pedigree" is mighty reassuring to a breeder or buyer new at the game, or to one who has a breeding program in mind and is trying to establish his own bloodline.

One of the most fascinating aspects of tracing pedigrees is the way the names of the really great dogs of the past keep appearing in the pedigrees of the great dogs of today—positive proof of the strong influence of heredity and witness to a great deal of truth in the statement that great dogs frequently reproduce themselves, though not necessarily in appearance only.

To the novice buyer or one who is perhaps merely switching to another breed and sees only a frolicking, leggy, squirming bundle of energy in a fur coat, a pedigree can mean everything! To those of us who believe in heredity, a pedigree is more like an insurance policy—so always read it carefully and take heed.

169

For the even more serious breeder of today who wishes to make a further study of bloodlines in relation to his breeding program, the American Kennel Club library stud books can and should be consulted.

THE HEALTH OF THE BREEDING STOCK

Some of your first questions should concern whether the stud has already proved himself by siring a normal healthy litter. Also inquire as to whether the owners have had a sperm count made to determine just exactly how fertile or potent the stud is. Determine for yourself whether the dog has two normal testicles.

When considering your bitch for this mating, you must take into consideration a few important points that lead to a successful breeding. You and the owner of the stud will want to recall whether she has had normal heat cycles, whether there were too many runts in the litter, and whether a Caesarean section was ever necessary. Has she ever had a vaginal infection? Could she take care of her puppies by herself, or was there a milk shortage? How many surviving puppies were there from the litter, and what did they grow up to be in comparison to the requirements of the breed standard?

Don't buy a bitch that has problems in heat and has never had a live litter. Don't be afraid, however, to buy a healthy maiden bitch, since

Japanese Best in Show winner Ch. A-S Gloria's Snow Samanser, Maltese bitch owned by Yoshimichi Tanaka of Japan. The sire was American Ch. Joanne-Chen's Shikar Dancer ex Ch. Joanne-Chen's Aga Lynn Dancer.

170

chances are, if she is healthy and from good stock, she will be a healthy producer. Don't buy a monorchid male, and certainly not a cryptorchid. If there is any doubt in your mind about his potency, get a sperm count from the veterinarian. Older dogs that have been good producers and are for sale are usually not too hard to find at good established kennels. If they are not too old and have sired quality show puppies, they can give you some excellent show stock from which to establish your own breeding lines.

WHEN TO BREED A GROWN BITCH

The best advice used to be not until her second heat. Today with our new scientific knowledge, we have become acutely aware of such things as hip dysplasia, juvenile cataracts, and other congenital diseases. The best advice now seems to be aimed at not breeding your dogs before two years of age, when both the bitch and the sire have been examined by qualified veterinarians and declared—in writing—to be free and clear of these conditions.

THE DAY OF THE MATING

Now that you have decided upon the proper male and female combination to produce what you hope will be—according to the pedigrees—a fine litter of puppies, it is time to set the date. You have selected the two days (with a one day lapse in between) that you feel are best for the breeding, and you call the owner of the stud. The bitch always goes to the stud, unless, of course, there are extenuating circumstances. You set the date and the time and arrive with the bitch *and* the money.

Standard procedure is payment of a stud fee at the time of the first breeding, if there is a tie. For the stud fee, you are entitled to two breedings with ties. Contracts may be written up with specific conditions on breeding terms, of course, but this is general procedure. Often a breeder will take the pick of a litter to protect and maintain his bloodlines; this can be especially desirable if he needs an outcross for his breeding program or if he wishes to continue his own bloodlines if he sold you the bitch to start with, and this mating will continue his line-breeding program. This should all be worked out ahead of time and written and signed before the two dogs are bred. Remember that the payment of the stud fee is for the services of the stud—not for a guarantee of a litter of puppies. This is why it is

Ch. March'en Lady Bug Dancer with two of her babies whelped in 1980 and sired by Ch. March'en Top Hat Dancer.

so important to make sure you are using a proven stud. Bear in mind also that the American Kennel Club will not register a litter of puppies sired by a male that is under eight months of age. In the case of an older dog, they will not register a litter sired by a dog over twelve years of age, unless there is a witness to the breeding in the form of a veterinarian or other responsible person.

Many studs over twelve years of age are still fertile and capable of producing puppies, but if you do not witness the breeding there is always the danger of a "substitute" stud being used to produce a litter. This brings up the subject of sending your bitch away to be bred if you cannot accompany her.

The disadvantages of sending a bitch away to be bred are numerous. First of all, she will not be herself in a strange place, so she'll be difficult to handle. Transportation, if she goes by air (while reasonably safe), is still a traumatic experience. There is always the danger of her being put off at the wrong airport, not being fed or watered properly, etc. Some bitches get so upset that they go out of season and the trip—which may prove expensive, especially on top of a substantial stud fee—will have been for nothing.

If at all possible, accompany your bitch so that the experience is as comfortable for her as it can be. In other words, make sure, before setting this kind of schedule for a breeding, that there is no stud in the area that might be as good for her as the one that is far away. Don't sacrifice the proper breeding for convenience, since bloodlines are so important, but put the safety of the bitch above all else. There is always a risk in traveling, since dogs are considered cargo on a plane.

HOW MUCH DOES THE STUD FEE COST?

The stud fee will vary considerably—the better the bloodlines, the more winning the dog does at shows, the higher the fee. Stud service from a top winning dog could run $500.00 and up. Here again, there may be exceptions. Some breeders will take part cash and then, say, third pick of the litter. The fee can be arranged by a private contract rather than the traditional procedure we have described.

Here again, it is wise to get the details of the payment of the stud fee in writing to avoid trouble.

American and Canadian Ch. March'en Top Hat Dancer, bred, owned, and handled by Marcia Hostetler to this win under judge Joe Gregory. The sire was Ch. Joanne-Chen's Square Dancer ex March'en Bali Dancer. Marcia Hostetler's March'en Maltese are located in Des Moines, Iowa.

Two adorable Maltese puppies bred by Gail Hennessey, Chelsea Maltese, Wappingers Falls, New York.

THE ACTUAL MATING

It is always advisable to muzzle the bitch. A terrified bitch may fear-bite the stud, or even one of the people involved, and the wild or maiden bitch may snap or attack the stud to the point where he may become discouraged and lose interest in the breeding. Muzzling can be done with a lady's stocking tied around the muzzle with a half knot, crossed under the chin and knotted at the back of the neck. There is enough "give" in the stocking for her to breathe or salivate freely, and yet not open her jaws far enough to bite. Place her in front of her owner, who holds onto her collar and talks to her and calms her as much as possible.

If the male will not mount on his own initiative, it may be necessary for the owner to assist in lifting him onto the bitch, perhaps even in guiding him to the proper place. Usually, the tie is accomplished once the male gets the idea. The owner should remain close at hand, however, to make sure the tie is not broken before an adequate

breeding has been completed. After a while the stud may get bored, and try to break away. This could prove injurious.

We must stress at this point that while some bitches carry on physically, and vocally, during the tie, there is no way the bitch can be hurt. However, a stud can be seriously or even permanently damaged by a bad breeding. Therefore, the owner of the bitch must be reminded that she must not be alarmed by any commotion. All concentration should be devoted to the stud and a successful and properly executed service.

Many people believe that breeding dogs is simply a matter of placing two dogs, a male and a female, in close proximity, and letting nature take its course. While often this is true, you cannot count on it. Sometimes it is hard work, and in the case of valuable stock, it is essential to supervise to be sure of the safety factor, especially if one or both of the dogs are inexperienced. If the owners are also inexperienced, it may not take place at all.

172

ARTIFICIAL INSEMINATION

Breeding by means of artificial insemination is usually unsuccessful, unless under a veterinarian's supervision, and can lead to an infection for the bitch and discomfort for the dog. The American Kennel Club requires a veterinarian's certificate to register puppies from such a breeding. Although the practice has been used for over two decades, it now offers new promise, since research has been conducted to make it a more feasible procedure for the future.

There now exists a frozen semen concept that has been tested and found successful. The study, headed by Dr. Stephen W.J. Seager, M.V.B., an instructor at the University of Oregon Medical School, has the financial support of the American Kennel Club, indicating that organization's interest in the work. The study is being monitored by the Morris Animal Foundation of Denver, Colorado.

Dr. Seager announced in 1970 that he had been able to preserve dog semen and to produce litters with the stored semen. The possibilities of selective world-wide breedings by this method are exciting. Imagine simply mailing a vial of semen to the bitch! The perfection of line-breeding by storing semen without the threat of death interrupting the breeding program is exciting also.

As it stands today, the technique for artificial insemination requires the depositing of semen (taken directly from the dog) into the bitch's vagina, past the cervix and into the uterus by syringe. The correct temperature of the semen is vital, and there is no guarantee of success. The storage method, if successfully adopted, will present a new era in the field of purebred dogs.

Two-week-old Maltese puppies bred by Delores Halley of Blue Grass, Iowa.

A typical, typey Maltese puppy bred at Fantasyland Kennels in California.

THE GESTATION PERIOD

Once the breeding has taken place successfully, the seemingly endless waiting period of about sixty-three days begins. For the first ten days after the breeding, you do absolutely nothing for the bitch—just spin dreams about the delights you will share with the family when the puppies arrive.

Around the tenth day, it is time to begin supplementing the diet of the bitch with vitamins and calcium. We strongly recommend that you take her to your veterinarian for a list of the proper or perhaps necessary supplements and the correct amounts of each for your particular bitch. Guesses, which may lead to excesses or insufficiencies, can ruin a litter. For the price of a visit to your veterinarian, you will be confident that you are feeding properly.

The bitch should be free of worms, of course, and if there is any doubt in your mind, she should be wormed now, before the third week of pregnancy. Your veterinarian will advise you on the necessity of this and proper dosage as well.

PROBING FOR PUPPIES

Far too many breeders are overanxious about whether the breeding "took" and are inclined to feel for puppies or persuade a veterinarian to radiograph or x-ray their bitches to confirm it. Unless there is reason to doubt the normalcy of a pregnancy, this is risky. Certainly sixty-three days is not too long to wait, and why risk endangering the litter by probing with your inexperienced hands? Few bitches give no evidence of being in whelp, and there is no need to prove it for yourself by trying to count puppies.

ALERTING YOUR VETERINARIAN

At least a week before the puppies are due, you should telephone your veterinarian and notify him that you expect the litter and give him the date. This way he can make sure that there will be someone available to help, should there be any problems during the whelping. Most veterinarians today have answering services and alternative vets on call when they themselves are not available. Some veterinarians suggest that you call them when the bitch starts labor so that they may further plan their time, should they be needed. Discuss this matter with your veterinarian when you first take the bitch to him for her diet instructions, and establish the method that will best fit in with his schedule.

DO YOU NEED A VETERINARIAN IN ATTENDANCE?

Even if this is your first litter, I would advise that you go through the experience of whelping without panicking and calling desperately for the veterinarian. Most animal births are accomplished without complications, and you should call for assistance only if you run into trouble.

When having her puppies, your bitch will appreciate as little interference and as few strangers around as possible. A quiet place, with

Outdoor playpen for Marcia Hostetler's Maltese trio.

174

her nest, a single familiar face, and her own instincts are all that is necessary for nature to take its course. An audience of curious children squealing and questioning, other family pets nosing around, or strange adults, should be avoided. Many a bitch that has been distracted in this way has been known to devour her young. This can be the horrible result of intrusion into the bitch's privacy. There are other ways of teaching children the miracle of birth, and there will be plenty of time later for the whole family to enjoy the puppies. Let them be born under proper and considerate circumstances.

LABOR

Some litters—many first litters—do not run the full term of sixty-three days. So, at least a week before the puppies are actually due, and at the time you alert your veterinarian as to their expected arrival, start observing the bitch for signs of the commencement of labor. This will manifest itself in the form of ripples running down the sides of her body that will come as a revelation to her as well. It is most noticeable when she is lying on her side—and she will be sleeping a great deal as the arrival date comes closer. If she is sitting or walking about, she will perhaps sit down quickly or squat peculiarly. As the ripples become more frequent, birth time is drawing near, and you will be wise not to leave her. Usually within twenty-four hours before whelping she will stop eating, and as much as a week before she will begin digging a nest. The bitch should be given something resembling a whelping box with layers of newspaper (black and white only) to make her nest. She will dig more and more as birth approaches, and this is the time to begin making your promise to stop interfering unless your help is specifically required. Some bitches whimper and others are silent, but whimpering does not necessarily indicate trouble.

THE ARRIVAL OF THE PUPPIES

The sudden gush of green fluid from the bitch indicates that the water or fluid surrounding the puppies has "broken" and they are about to start down the canal and come into the world. When the water breaks, birth of the first puppy is imminent. The first puppies are usually born within minutes to a half hour of each other, but a couple of hours between the later ones is not uncommon. If you notice the bitch straining con-

A darling puppy from Vera Rebbin's brood in Aurora, Ohio.

stantly without producing a puppy, or if a puppy remains partially in and partially out for too long, it is cause for concern. Breech births (puppies born feet first instead of head first) can often cause delay or hold things up, and this is often a problem that requires veterinarian assistance.

FEEDING THE BITCH BETWEEN BIRTHS

Usually the bitch will not be interested in food for about twenty-four hours before the arrival of the puppies, and perhaps as long as two or three days after their arrival. The placenta that she cleans up after each puppy is high in food value and will be more than ample to sustain her. This is nature's way of allowing the mother to feed herself and her babies without having to leave the nest and hunt for food during the first crucial days. In the wild, the mother always cleans up all traces of birth so as not to attract other animals to her newborn babies.

However, there are those of us who believe in making food available should the mother feel the need to restore her strength during or after delivery—especially if she whelps a large litter. Raw chopped meat, beef bouillon, and milk are all acceptable and may be placed near the whelping box during the first two or three days. After that, the mother will begin to put the babies on a sort of schedule. She will leave the whelping box at frequent intervals, take longer exercise periods and begin to take interest in other things. This is where the fun begins for you. Now the babies are no longer soggy little pinkish blobs. They begin to crawl around and squeal and hum and grow before your very eyes!

It is at this time, if all has gone normally, that the family can be introduced gradually and great praise and affection given to the mother.

BREECH BIRTHS

Puppies normally are delivered head first; however, some are presented feet first or in other abnormal positions, and this is referred to as a "breech birth." Assistance is often necessary to get the puppy out of the canal, and great care must be taken not to injure the puppy or the dam.

Aid can be given by grasping the puppy with a piece of turkish toweling and pulling gently during the dam's contractions. Be careful not to squeeze the puppy too hard; merely try to ease it out by moving it gently back and forth. Because even this much delay in delivery may mean the puppy is drowning, do not wait for the bitch to remove the sac. Do it yourself by tearing the sac open to expose the face and head. Then cut the cord anywhere from one-half to three-quarters of an inch away from the navel. If the cord bleeds excessively, pinch the end of it with your fingers and count five. Repeat if necessary. Then pry open the mouth with your finger and hold the puppy upside down for a moment to drain any fluids from the lungs. Next, rub the puppy briskly with turkish or paper toweling.

Future champions bred and owned by Marcia Hostetler, March'en Maltese, Des Moines, Iowa. The two young hopefuls were sired by Ch. Joanne-Chen's Teddy Bear Dancer ex Joanne-Chen's Sheeba Dancer.

Petit Point Sugar Blues and Petit Point Sugar Daddy, two charming Petit Point puppies bred and owned by Susan M. Sandlin, The Original Petit Point kennels in Alexandria, Virginia.

If the litter is large, this assistance will help conserve the strength of the bitch and will probably be welcomed by her. However, it is best to allow her to take care of at least the first few herself to preserve the natural instinct and to provide the nutritive values obtained by her consumption of one or more of the afterbirths as nature intended.

DRY BIRTHS

Occasionally the sac will break before the delivery of a puppy and will be expelled while the puppy remains inside, thereby depriving the dam of the necessary lubrication to expel the puppy normally. Inserting vaseline or mineral oil via your finger will help the puppy pass down the birth canal. This is why it is essential that you be present during the whelping—so that you can count puppies and afterbirths and determine when and if assistance is needed.

THE TWENTY-FOUR HOUR CHECKUP

It is smart to have a veterinarian check the mother and her puppies within twenty-four hours after the last puppy is born. The veterinarian can check the puppies for cleft palates or umbilical hernia and may wish to give the dam—particularly if she is a show dog—an injection of Pituitin to make sure of the expulsion of all afterbirths and to tighten up the uterus. This can prevent a sagging belly after the puppies are weaned and the bitch is being readied for the show ring.

FALSE PREGNANCY

The disappointment of a false pregnancy is almost as bad for the owner as it is for the bitch. She goes through the gestation period with all the symptoms—swollen stomach, increased appetite, swollen nipples—even makes a nest when the time comes. You may even take an oath that you noticed the ripples on her body from the labor pains. Then, just as suddenly as you made up your mind that she was definitely going to have puppies, you will know that she definitely is not! She may walk around carrying a toy as if it were a puppy for a few days, but she will soon be back to normal and acting just as if nothing happened—and nothing did!

CAESAREAN SECTION

Should the whelping reach the point where there is complication, such as the bitch's not being capable of whelping the puppies herself, the "moment of truth" is upon you and a Caesarean section may be necessary. The bitch may be too small or too immature to expel the puppies herself, her cervix may fail to dilate enough to allow the young to come down the birth canal, there may be torsion of the uterus, a dead or monster puppy, a sideways puppy blocking the canal, or perhaps toxemia. A Caesarean section will be the only solution. No matter what the cause, get the bitch to the veterinarian immediately to insure your chances of saving the mother and/or the puppies.

Tiku of Khandese and Ch. Kaga of Khandese, photographed as young puppies at the home of Dr. and Mrs. Roger Brown, Omaha, Nebraska.

The Caesarean section operation (the name derived from the idea that Julius Caesar was delivered by this method) involves the removal of the unborn young from the uterus of the dam by surgical incision into the walls through the abdomen. The operation is performed when it has been determined that for some reason the puppies cannot be delivered normally. While modern surgical methods have made the operation itself reasonably safe, with the dam being perfectly capable of nursing the puppies shortly after the completion of the surgery, the chief danger lies in the ability to spark life into the puppies immediately upon their removal from the womb. If the mother dies, the time element is even more important in saving the young, since the oxygen supply ceases upon the death of the dam, and the difference between life and death is measured in seconds.

After surgery, when the bitch is home in her whelping box with the babies, she will probably nurse the young without distress. You must be sure that the sutures are kept clean and that no redness or swelling or ooze appears in the wound. Healing will take place naturally, and no salves or ointments should be applied unless prescribed by the veterinarian, for fear the puppies will get it into their systems. If there is any doubt, check the bitch for fever, restlessness (other than the natural concern for her young), or a lack of appetite.

EPISIOTOMY

Even though most dogs are generally easy whelpers, any number of reasons might occur to cause the bitch to have a difficult birth. Before automatically resorting to Caesarean section, many veterinarians are now trying the technique known as episiotomy.

Used rather frequently in human deliveries, episiotomy (pronounced *e-pease-e-ott-o-me*) is the cutting of the membrane between the rear opening of the vagina back almost to the opening of the anus. After delivery it is stitched together, and barring complications, heals easily, presenting no problem in future births.

SOCIALIZING YOUR PUPPY

The need for puppies to get out among other animals and people cannot be stressed enough. Kennel-reared dogs are subject to all sorts of idiosyncrasies and seldom make good house dogs or normal members of the world around them when they grow up.

Two Maltese puppies and a Chow puppy. All three were 6 weeks and 5 days old at the time of photographing. Bred and owned by Wendy Kobrzycki, Montgomery, Michigan.

The crucial age that determines the personality and general behavior patterns that will predominate during the rest of the dog's life are formed between the ages of three and ten weeks. This is particularly true from the twenty-first through the twenty-eighth day. It is essential that the puppy be socialized during this time by bringing him into family life as much as possible. Walking on floor surfaces, indoor and outdoor, should be experienced; handling by all members of the family and visitors is important; preliminary grooming gets him used to a lifelong necessity; light training, such as setting him up on tables, cleaning teeth and ears, and cutting nails, has to be started early if he is to become a show dog. The puppy should be exposed to car riding, shopping tours, a leash around its neck, children —your own and others—and in all possible ways, relationships with humans.

It is up to the breeder, of course, to protect the puppy from harm or injury during this initiation into the outside world. The benefits reaped from proper attention will pay off in the long run with a well-behaved, well-adjusted grown dog capable of becoming an integral part of a happy family.

REARING THE FAMILY

Needless to say, even with a small litter there will be certain considerations that must be adhered to in order to insure successful rearing of the puppies. For instance, the diet for the mother should be appropriately increased as the puppies grow and take more and more nourishment from her. During the first few days of rest while the bitch just looks over her puppies and regains her strength, she should be left pretty much alone. It is during these first days that she begins to put the puppies on a feeding schedule, and feels safe enough about them to leave the whelping box long enough to take a little extended exercise.

It is cruel, however, to try to keep the mother away from the puppies any longer than she wants to be because you feel she is being too attentive, or to give the neighbors a chance to peek in at the puppies. The mother should not have to worry about harm coming to her puppies for the first few weeks. The veterinary checkup will be enough of an experience for her to have to endure until she is more like herself once again.

The crucial period in a puppy's life occurs when the puppy is from twenty-one to twenty-eight days old, so all the time you can devote to it at this time will reap rewards later on in life. This is the age when several other important steps must be taken in a puppy's life. Weaning should start if it hasn't already, and it is the time to check for worms.

Happy Holly at six weeks of age, photographed in 1983 by owner Vera Rebbin, Aurora, Ohio.

"Oh, how I hate to get up in the morning ..." A young puppy in his sleeping box at Vera Rebbin's Sixpence Kennels.

EVALUATING THE LITTER

A show puppy prospect should be outgoing (probably the first one to fall out of the whelping box!), and all efforts should be made to socialize the puppy that appears to be the most shy. Once the puppies are about three weeks old, they can and should be handled a great deal by friends and members of the family.

During the third week they begin to try to walk instead of crawl, but they are unsteady on their feet. Tails are used for balancing, and the puppies begin to make sounds.

Exercise and grooming should be started at this time, with special care and consideration given to the diet. You will find that the dam will help you wean the puppies, leaving them alone more and more as she notices that they are eating well on their own. Begin by leaving them with her during the night for comfort and warmth; eventually when she shows less interest, keep them separated entirely.

By the time the fifth week arrives, you will already be in love with every member of the litter and desperately searching for reasons to keep them all. They recognize you—which really gets to you!—and they box and chew on each other, and try to eat your finger, and a million other captivating antics that are special with puppies. Their stomachs seem to be bottomless pits, and their weight will rise. At eight to ten weeks, the puppies will be weaned and ready to go.

SPAYING AND CASTRATING

A wise old philosopher once said, "Timing in life is everything!" No statement could apply more readily to the age-old question that every dog owner is faced with sooner or later . . . to spay or not to spay.

For the one-bitch pet owner, spaying is the most logical answer, for it solves many problems. The pet is usually not of top breeding quality, and therefore there is no great loss to the bloodline; it takes the pressure off the family if the dog runs free with children, and it certainly eliminates the problem of repeated litters of unwanted puppies or a backyard full of eager males twice a year.

But for the owner or breeder, the extra time and protection that must be afforded a purebred quality bitch can be most worthwhile—even if it is only until a single litter is produced after the first heat.

It is then not too late to spay; the progeny can perpetuate the bloodline, the bitch will have been fulfilled—though it is merely an old wives' tale that bitches should have at least one litter to be "normal"—and she may then be retired to her deserved role as family pet once again.

In the case of males, castration is seldom contemplated, which to me is highly regrettable. The owner of the male dog merely overlooks the dog's ability to populate an entire neighborhood, since he does not have the responsibility of rearing and disposing of the puppies. When you take into consideration all the many females the male dog can impregnate, it is almost more essential that the males rather than the females be taken out of circulation. The male dog will still be inclined to roam, but will be less frantic about leaving the grounds, and you will find that a lot of the *wanderlust* has left him.

Tennessa's Trinket of Weewyte, photographed at eight months of age. Bred and owned by Mrs. Kathy Blackard, Weewyte Maltese, Brooklyn, Connecticut.

Kissette weighs in when just six weeks old in March 1980. Owned by Vera Rebbin, Aurora, Ohio.

STERILIZING FOR HEALTH

When considering the problem of spaying or castrating, the first consideration after the population explosion should actually be the health of the dog or bitch. Males are frequently subject to urinary diseases, and sometimes castration is a help. Your veterinarian can best advise you on this problem. Another aspect to consider is the kennel dog that is no longer being used at stud. It is unfair to keep him in a kennel with females in heat when there is no chance for him to be used. There are other more personal considerations for both kennel and one-dog owners, but when making the decision, remember that it is final. You can always spay or castrate, but once the deed is done, there is no return.

A BREEDING WARNING

Raising a litter of puppies can be a wonderful experience for those who love dogs, especially if there are children in the family who also love animals. However, there is one very important consideration before thinking about having a litter. That is, is your bitch big enough? We are hearing more and more about "tea cup" Maltese, or pocket-size Maltese, which should not be bred at all—ever! While they are highly desirable among pet owners, they still require special care and frequently have a considerably shorter life span than the normal-size dogs.

If your little bitch is small she should not be bred. How small is small, you ask? Consult your veterinarian if you are not an experienced breeder, and let him decide if it would be too risky. Just remember, if she is too small and you breed her, you are apt to lose the puppies and the bitch. If the puppy bitch you bought grows up to be small, too small for breeding, keep her as your mascot, and buy another bitch. If you have a "tiny" in any of your litters, and you decide to sell it, make sure you explain to the buyer she is not to be bred. And to be sure she isn't—don't give the new owner any papers!

CULLING

Next to the importance of coat color in Maltese, perhaps the easiest way to start a heated debate is to discuss the merits of culling. Far too many breeders allow themselves to "play God" by evaluating and disposing of puppies, even though their experience in breeding dogs (or any animals) is practically nil.

Needless to say, many mistakes are made, and it is highly likely that over the years many valuable specimens have been lost because overzealous breeders, determined to breed the ideal dog, depended solely on their own judgment.

In explaining their attempts to save only the best puppies, some of the most ridiculous excuses are given for culling litters. If it is a large breed, they will cite monetary reasons, such as savings on food, or vet bills. Others will tell you they cull because the litter is too large.

Others go on to explain that culling also means less cleaning up after puppies, or that they will have fewer puppies to sell in a slow market. Actually the major consideration for culling should be a sort of "insurance" that the bitch is not over-taxed by feeding too many puppies, especially if she is to be bred again. Both bitch and breeder should be able to observe and enjoy the puppies individually and collectively.

Other legitimate reasons for culling may be consideration of breed disqualifications. Unacceptable breed colors or markings or structural faults are additional reasons given for culling. These faults should be checked out carefully before a decision to cull is reached.

Once the decision is made to cull, the next question should be, What is the "best" time? At birth? Within hours after birth? Two weeks? Two months? And what is the "proper" method of disposing of the unwanted puppies?

180

VETERINARY CONSIDERATIONS

Most breeders find they cannot depend on or expect the support of their veterinarians, if you ask them to put the "excess" puppies down. They will be quick to tell you that they are in business and dedicated to the preserving of life, not its termination. Some veterinarians will oblige rather than have the breeder do it, so they are sure it will be painless for the puppies. However, their attitude will more than likely be a suggestion to allow the puppies to live with spaying or neutering in the future as an alternative.

FOREIGN "CULLING"

In some foreign countries, culling is a government matter, and comes under the jurisdiction of the department of agriculture. However, the thought of a government or kennel club official coming to a breeder's home and culling a predetermined number of puppies from a litter without regard for quality or sex is abhorrent. Many of us would stop breeding before allowing ourselves and our bitches to be placed in such a position.

We have all heard of the Maltese puppy that was purchased in a pet shop and won a Best in Show. This is the living proof that "culling" is a talent few possess. Had the breeders of this puppy any inkling that it was show dog potential, they never would have parted with it.

Culling is not to be entered into lightly. Those breeders who dare to "play God" must remember that we are NOT God. . . only humans, and humans make mistakes. Mother Nature is actually the most stringent of all "cullers," and it is usually wise to leave culling up to her. It is also unwise to try to keep a struggling puppy alive. The risks of continued ill-health, retardation, or growth problems are frequently the result. The final decision should be determined by the survival of the fittest.

LOSING A PUPPY

There is great joy in planning, whelping, and raising a litter of puppies. We give so much of ourselves and hold such hopes and dreams for our little charges. And there is nothing like a litter of puppies to give us even more respect and closeness for our bitches in recognition of their efforts and care in bearing a litter.

Those of us who are fortunate enough to raise healthy puppies know all too well that sometimes, in spite of our devotion, something can go wrong. Sometimes we lose a puppy.

This lovely pen-and-ink drawing of Ch. Aennchen's Suni Dancer was rendered by Dr. Roger Brown of Omaha, Nebraska.

I was so deeply touched by a little poem (written by Fay Gold) which I came across in an old issue of the *Yorkshire Terrier Quarterly*, that I felt I wanted to include it in this book for all of us to share.

> *I*
> *Can never accept*
> *The fading of a*
> *New born*
> *Puppy*
>
> > *I*
> > *Waited*
> > *For this one a*
> > *Long time*
>
> *Gladly gave it*
> *All my time*
> *And all my*
> *Love*
>
> > *Just to*
> > *Keep it*
> > *Alive*
> > *And then*
> > *It slipped away*

Unfortunately, nature gives no guarantees, and we all may lose a puppy at some future time. It is never easy, but perhaps realizing that someone else feels as deeply about it as we do may help.

181

Six-week-old Nickolas, owned by Vera Rebbin of Aurora, Ohio.

CHAPTER ELEVEN

Buying Your Maltese Puppy

Beethoven, Bach, and Brahms, all with the Weewyte prefix of Mrs. Kathy Blackard's Maltese in Brooklyn, Connecticut. This charming trio was photographed at three months of age.

In searching for that special puppy, there are several paths that will lead you to a litter from which you may find the puppy of your choice. If you are uncertain as to where to find a reputable breeder, write to the breed club and ask for the names and addresses of members who have puppies for sale. If you live in the United States, you may obtain the address of a local club by contacting the American Kennel Club, 51 Madison Avenue, New York, N.Y. 10010. The classified ad listings in dog publications and the major newspapers may also lead you to that certain pup. The various dog magazines generally carry a monthly breed column which features information and news on the breed that may aid in your selection.

It is advisable that you become thoroughly acquainted with the breed prior to purchasing your puppy. Plan to attend a dog show or two in your area at which you may view purebred dogs of just about every breed at their best in the show ring. Even if you are not interested in purchasing a show-quality dog, you should be familiar with what the better specimens look like so that you will at least purchase a decent representative of the breed for the money. You can learn a lot from observing the show dogs in action in the ring, or in a public place where their personalities are clearly shown. The dog show catalogue is also a useful tool to put you in contact with the local kennels and breeders. Each dog that is entered in the show is listed along with the owner's name and address. If you

spot a dog that you think is a particularly fine and pleasing specimen, contact the owners and arrange to visit their kennel to see the type and color they are breeding and winning with at the shows. Exhibitors at the dog shows are usually more than delighted to talk to people interested in their dogs and the specific characteristics of their breed.

Once you've decided that the Maltese is the breed for you because you appreciate its exceptional beauty, personality, and intelligence, it is wise to thoroughly acquaint yourself by reading some background material on owning one. When you feel certain that this puppy will fit in with your family's way of life, it is time to start writing letters and making phone calls.

Some words of caution: don't choose a kennel simply because it is near your home, and don't buy the first "cute" puppy that romps around your legs or licks the end of your nose. All puppies are cute, and naturally some will appeal to you more than others. But don't let preferences sway your thinking. If you are buying your Maltese to be strictly a family pet, then preferences are permissible. If you are looking for a top-quality puppy for the show ring, you must evaluate clearly, choose wisely, and make the best possible choice. Whichever one you choose, you will quickly learn to love your Maltese puppy. A careful selection, rather than a "love at first sight" choice will save a disappointment later on.

183

A trio of twelve-week-old Maltese puppies owned by Vera Rebbin.

To get the broadest idea of what puppies are for sale and the going market prices, visit as many kennels as possible in your area and write to others farther away. With today's safe and rapid air flights on the major airlines, it is possible to purchase dogs from far-off places at nominal costs. While it is safest and wisest to first see the dog you are buying, there are enough reputable breeders and kennels to be found for you to take this step with a minimum of risk. In the long run, it can be well worth your while to obtain the exact dog or bloodline you desire.

It is customary for the purchaser to pay the shipping charges, and the airlines are most willing to supply flight information and prices upon request. Rental on the shipping crate, if the owner does not provide one for the dog, is nominal. While unfortunate incidents have occurred on the airlines in the transporting of animals by air, the major airlines are making improvements in safety measures and have reached the point of reasonable safety and cost. Barring unforeseen circumstances, the safe arrival of a dog you might buy can pretty much be assured if both seller and purchaser adhere to and follow up on even the most minute details from both ends.

WHAT TO LOOK FOR IN A MALTESE PUPPY

Anyone who has owned a Maltese as a puppy will agree that the most fascinating aspect of raising the pup is to witness the complete and extraordinary metamorphosis that occurs during its first year of maturing. Your puppy will undergo a marked change in appearance, and during this period you must also be aware of the puppy's personality, for there are certain qualities visible at this time that will generally make for a good adult dog. Of course, no one can guarantee nature, and the best puppy does not always grow up to be a great dog. However, even the novice breeder can learn to look for certain specifics that will help him to choose a promising puppy.

Should you decide to purchase a six- to eight-week old puppy, you are in store for all the cute antics that little pup may dream up for you! At this age, the puppy should be well on its way to being weaned, wormed, and ready to go out into the world with its responsible new owner. It is better not to buy a puppy that is less than six weeks old; it simply is not ready to leave its mother or the security of the other puppies. By eight to twelve weeks of age you will be able to notice much about the behavior and appearance of the dog. Maltese puppies are amazingly active and bouncy—as well they should be! The normal puppy should be alert, curious, and interested, especially about a stranger. However, if the puppy acts a little reserved or distant, don't necessarily construe these acts to be signs of fear or shyness. It might merely indicate that he hasn't quite made up his mind whether he likes you as yet! By the same token, though, he should not be openly fearful or terrified by a stranger—and especially should not show any fear of his owner!

These puppies, ranging from two to four months of age, were bred, owned, and photographed by Marjorie Martin.

In direct contrast, the puppy should not be ridiculously over-active either. The puppy that frantically bounds around the room and is never still is not especially desirable. And beware of the "spinners"! Spinners are the puppies or dogs that have become neurotic from being kept in cramped quarters or in crates, and that behave in an emotionally unstable manner when let loose in adequate space. When let out they run in circles and seemingly "go wild." Puppies with this kind of traumatic background seldom ever regain full composure or adjust to the big outside world. The puppy which has had the proper exercise and appropriate living quarters will have a normal, though spirited, outlook on life, and will do its utmost to win you over without having to go into a tailspin.

If the general behavior and appearance of the dog thus far appeal to you, it is time for you to observe him more closely for additional physical requirements. First of all, you cannot expect to find in the Maltese puppy all the coat he will bear upon maturity. That will come with time and good food, and will be additionally enhanced by the many wonderful grooming aids which can be found in pet shops today. Needless to say, the healthy puppy's coat should have a nice shine to it, and the more dense at this age, the better the coat will be when the dog reaches adulthood.

Look for clear, dark, sparkling eyes that are free of discharge. From the time the puppy's eyes open until the puppy is about three months old, the eyes might have a slight blue cast to them. The darker the blue, the better are the chances for a good dark eye in the adult dog.

It is important to check the bite. Even though the puppy will cut another complete set of teeth somewhere between four and seven months of age, there will already be some indication of how the final teeth will be positioned. Too much of an overshot bite (top teeth are positioned too far *over* the bottom teeth) or too much of an under-shot jaw (bottom teeth are positioned too far out *under* the top teeth) is undesirable as they are considered faults by the breed standard.

This one of Vera Rebbin's Maltese puppies was 12 weeks old in March, 1983.

Eight-year-old Anthony DiGiacomo with three-month-old Kathan's Johnny B Goode.

Correcting the bite on a Maltese can involve many generations of breeding. The tiny toy breeds are notorious for problems with their teeth. Baby teeth must be removed if they do not fall out on their own, or they could destroy the correct placement of the permanent teeth.

Removing stubborn teeth is usually a job for your veterinarian, as it requires the administration of some type of pain-killer. Maltese do not always take anesthesia well. A bad experience with an owner who wishes to pop them out with a thumb can make a dog hand shy as well as causing it pain.

It has become "fashionable" for owners to keep the teeth clean to start with, thus avoiding an accumulation of tartar on the teeth, and preventing a trip to the veterinarian. There are many ways to clean a dog's teeth. A baby toothbrush may be used with a mild solution of baking soda or a little salt. If the toothbrush is too rough, try using your finger, a wad of cotton, or a gauze bandage to rub over the surface of the teeth.

The best way to insure good teeth is still diet and exercising of the gums. Giving puppies something to chew on, such as a Nylabone® helps to clean their teeth and allow loose ones to fall out naturally.

186

Puppies usually have twenty-eight baby teeth. When these fall out and the jaw grows, they get forty-two permanent teeth. If all goes well, the dog will end up with either a level bite (all teeth matching each other), or a scissors bite (top teeth slightly extended over the lower teeth), both of which are acceptable in the breed. Bad bites occur when the top teeth extend too far out over the bottom teeth, and is referred to as a bad overbite; or when the teeth in the lower jaw extend too far out under the upper teeth, which is called an undershot bite.

Puppies take anything and almost everything into their mouths to chew on, and a lot of diseases and infections start or are introduced in the mouth. Brown-stained teeth, for instance, may indicate the puppy has had a past case of distemper, and the teeth will remain that way. This fact must be reckoned with if you have a show puppy in mind. The puppy's breath should be neither sour nor unpleasant. Bad breath can be a result of a poor mixture of food in the diet, or of eating meat of low quality, especially if fed raw. Some people say that the healthy puppy's breath should have a faint odor vaguely reminiscent of garlic. At any rate, a puppy should never be fed just table scraps, but should be raised on a well-balanced diet containing a good dry puppy chow and a good grade of fresh meat. Poor meat and too much cereal or fillers tend to make the puppy grow too fat. Puppies should be in good flesh, but not fat from the wrong kind of food.

A twelve-week old Maltese puppy owned by Vera Rebbin, Sixpence Kennels.

A typical Su-Le Maltese puppy.

Needless to say, the puppy should be clean. The breeder that shows a dirty puppy is one to steer away from. Look closely at the skin. Make sure it is not covered with insect bites or red, blotchy sores and dry scales. The vent area around the tail should not show evidences of diarrhea or inflammation. By the same token, the puppy's fur should not be matted with excretion or smell strongly of urine.

True enough, you can wipe dirty eyes, clean dirty ears, and give the puppy a bath when you get it home, but these things are all indications of how the puppy has been cared for during the important formative first months of its life, and can vitally influence its future health and development. There are many reputable breeders raising healthy puppies that have been reared in proper places and under the proper conditions in clean housing, so why take a chance on a series of veterinary bills and a questionable constitution?

MALE OR FEMALE?

The choice of sex in your puppy is also something that must be given serious thought before you buy. For the pet owner, the sex that would best suit the family life you enjoy would be the paramount choice to consider. For the breeder or exhibitor there are other vital considerations. If you are looking for a stud to establish a kennel, it is essential that you select a dog with both testicles evident, even at a tender age, and verified by a veterinarian before the sale is finalized if there is any doubt.

187

Canadian Ch. Four Halls Collector's Item, bred and owned by Glenna Fierheller of Vancouver, British Columbia, is shown here at just one year of age. The sire was American, Canadian and Bermudian Best in Show winner Ch. Artemas of Tissagables ex American and Canadian Best in Show Ch. Four Halls Conversation Piece.

The visibility of only one testicle, known as monorchidism, automatically disqualifies the dog from the show ring or from a breeding program, though monorchids are capable of siring. Additionally, it must be noted that monorchids frequently sire dogs with the same deficiency, and to introduce this into a bloodline knowingly is an unwritten sin in the fancy. Also, a monorchid can sire dogs that are completely sterile. Dog with undescended testes are called cryptorchids, and are sterile.

An additional consideration for the private owner in the male versus female decision is that with males there might be the problem of leglifting, and with females there is the inconvenience while they are in season. However, this need not be the problem it used to be—pet shops sell "pants" for both sexes, which help to control the situation.

THE PLANNED PARENTHOOD BEHIND YOUR PUPPY

Never be afraid to ask pertinent questions about the puppy, as well as questions about the sire and dam. Feel free to ask the breeder if you might see the dam; the purpose of your visit is to determine her general health and her appearance as a representative of the breed. Ask also to see the sire if the breeder is the owner. Ask what the puppy has been fed and should be fed after weaning. Ask to see the pedigree, and inquire if the litter or the individual puppies have been registered with the American Kennel Club, how many of the temporary and/or permanent inoculations the puppy has had, when and if the puppy has been wormed, and whether it has had any illness, disease, or infection.

You need not ask if the puppy is housebroken . . . it won't mean much. He may have gotten

188

the idea as to where "the place" is where he lives now, but he will need new training to learn where "the place" is in his new home! And you can't really expect too much from puppies at this age anyway. Housebreaking is entirely up to the new owner. We know puppies always eliminate when they first awaken, and sometimes dribble when they get excited. If friends and relatives are coming over to see the new puppy, make sure he is walked just before he greets them at the front door. This will help.

The normal time period for puppies (around three months of age) to eliminate is about every two or three hours. As the time draws near, either take the puppy out or indicate the newspaper for the same purpose. Housebreaking is never easy, but anticipation is about ninety per cent of solving the problem.

A reputable breeder will welcome any and all questions you might ask and will voluntarily offer additional information, if only to brag about the tedious and loving care he has given the litter. He will also sell a puppy on a twenty-four hour veterinary approval basis. This means you have a full day to get the puppy to a veterinarian of your choice to get his opinion on the general health of the puppy before you make a final decision. There should also be veterinary certificates and full particulars on the dates and types of inoculations the puppy has been given up to that time.

PUPPIES AND WORMS

Let us give further attention to the unhappy and very unpleasant subject of worms. Generally speaking, most puppies—even those raised in clean quarters—come into contact with worms early in life. The worms can be passed down from the mother before birth, or picked up during the puppies' first encounters with the earth or with their kennel facilities. To say that you must not buy a puppy because of an infestation of worms is nonsensical. You might be passing up a fine animal that can be freed of worms in one short treatment, although a heavy infestation of worms of any kind in a young dog is dangerous and debilitating.

The extent of the infection can be readily determined by a veterinarian, and you might take his word as to whether the future health and conformation of the dog has been damaged. He can prescribe the dosage and supply the medication at this time, and you will already have one of your problems solved.

VETERINARY INSPECTION

While your veterinarian is going over the puppy you have selected to purchase, you might just as well ask him for his opinion of it as a breed, as well as the facts about its general health. While few veterinarians can claim to be breed-conformation experts, they usually have a good eye for a worthy specimen, and can advise you where to go for further information. Perhaps your veterinarian could also recommend other breeders if you should want another opinion. The veterinarian can point out structural faults or organic problems that affect all breeds and can usually judge whether an animal has been abused or mishandled, and whether it is oversized or undersized.

I would like to emphasize here that it is only through this type of close cooperation between owners and veterinarians that we may expect to reap the harvest of modern research in the veterinary field.

Most reliable veterinarians are more than eager to learn about various breeds of purebred dogs, and we in turn must acknowledge and apply what they have proved through experience and research in their field. We may buy and breed the best dog in the world, but when disease strikes, we are only as safe as our veterinarian is capable—so let's keep him informed breed by breed, and dog by dog. The veterinarian may mean the difference between life and death!

Ch. Fantasyland Rebecca Lyn, pictured at three months of age, is owned by Marie White. Bred by Carole M. Baldwin of Novato, California, the sire was Ch. Fantasyland Bugalewey, M.M.A., ex Ch. Fantasyland Billy Jo, M.M.A.

THE CONDITIONS OF SALE

While it is customary to pay for the puppy before you take it away with you, you should be able to give the breeder a deposit if there is any doubt about the puppy's health. You might also (depending on local laws) postdate a check to cover the twenty-four hour veterinary approval. If you decide to take the puppy, the breeder is required to supply you with a pedigree along with the puppy's registration papers. He is also obliged to supply you with complete information about the inoculations and American Kennel Club instructions on how to transfer ownership of the puppy to your name.

Some breeders will offer buyers time payment plans for convenience if the price on a show dog is very high, or if deferred payments are the only way you can purchase the dog.

Joanne-Chen's Wakham Dancer, owned and handled by Randy Gemmill of Tacoma, Washington, and co-owned by Marcia Hostetler. Wakham is pictured here at nine months of age winning on the way to championship at the 1970 Whidby Island Kennel Club show. The sire was Ch. Mike Mars Joanne-Chen Dancer ex Joanne-Chen's Sheeba Dancer.

Eight-month old Chiffen, owned by Glenna Fierheller, photographed in 1981.

You will find most breeders cooperative if they believe you are sincere in your love for the puppy and that you will give it the proper home and the show ring career it deserves (if it is sold as a show quality specimen of the breed).

Also, if you purchase a show prospect and promise to show the dog, you definitely should show it! It is a waste to have a beautiful dog that deserves recognition in the show ring sitting at home as a family pet, and it is unfair to the breeder. This is especially true if the breeder offered you a reduced price because of the advertising his kennel and bloodlines would receive by your showing the dog in the ring. If you want a pet, buy a pet. Be honest about it, and let the breeder decide on this basis which is the best dog for you. Your conscience will be clear and you'll both be doing a real service to the breed.

BUYING A SHOW PUPPY

If you are positive about breeding and showing your Maltese, make this point clear so that the breeder will sell you the best possible puppy. If you are dealing with an established kennel, you will have to rely partially, if not entirely, on their choice, since they know their bloodlines and what they can expect from the breeding. They know how their stock develops, and it would be foolish of them to sell you a puppy that could not stand up as a show specimen representing their stock in the ring.

190

However, you must also realize that the breeder may be keeping the best puppy in the litter to show and breed himself. If this is the case, you might be wise to select the best puppy of the opposite sex so that the dogs will not be competing against one another in the show rings for their championship title.

Three of Mary Hohs' Maltese puppies that were featured on one of her Christmas cards.

Noodles and Bunny are pictured in 1968 with owner Cathy Lepetit of New Orleans, Louisiana.

THE COST OF BUYING ADULT STOCK

Prices for adult dogs fluctuate greatly. Some grown dogs are offered free of charge to good homes; others are put with owners on breeders' terms. But don't count on getting a "bargain" if it doesn't cost you anything! Good dogs are always in demand, and worthy studs or brood bitches are expensive. Prices for them can easily go up into the four-figure range. Take an expert with you if you intend to make this sort of investment. Just make sure the "expert" is free of professional jealousy and will offer an unprejudiced opinion. If you are reasonably familiar with the standard, and get the expert's opinion, you can usually come to a proper decision.

THE PURCHASE PRICE

Prices vary on all puppies, of course, but a good show prospect at six weeks to six months of age will usually sell for several hundred dollars. If the puppy is really outstanding, and the pedigree and parentage are also outstanding, the price will be even higher. Honest breeders, however, will all quote around the same figure, so price should not be a strong deciding factor in your choice. If you have any questions as to the current price range, a few telephone calls to different kennels will give you a good average. Reputable breeders will usually stand behind the health of their puppies should something drastically wrong develop, such as hip dysplasia. Their obligation to make an adjustment or replacement is usually honored. However, this must be agreed to in writing at the time of the purchase.

Ch. Lin-Lee's Maverick at ten months of age, wins at a 1980 show under judge Shirley Thomas. Owned by Linda and Lee Coleman, Lin-Lee Maltese, Finleyville, Pennsylvania.

This cute puppy is owned by the Sixpence Kennels of Vera Rebbin, Aurora, Ohio.

These two beauties are also from the kennels of Vera Rebbin, Aurora, Ohio.

Kissette, owned by Vera Rebbin of Aurora, Ohio. This photograph won a prize in the *Maltese Tales* photo contest.

Vera Rebbin's Butdon and her second litter. The size of these premature puppies can be compared to an average teacup next to them.

Litter of one-week-old puppies, owned, bred and photographed by Marjorie Martin, Martin's Maltese, Columbus, Ohio. These puppies, two males and two females, were sired by Martin's Hoppel-Cid.

Petit Point Queen of Hearts is enough to steal anyone's heart. Maltese puppy bred and owned by Susan M. Sandlin of Alexandria, Virginia.

Two darling Maltese are featured on the 1983 Christmas Card for Marjorie Martin's Maltese Kennel in Columbus, Ohio.

Vera Rebbin's Christmas puppy, appropriately named Happy Holly, was just six weeks old in this picture taken in early 1983.

Fantasyland Sno Rock Dream, photographed by his owner-breeder Carole M. Baldwin of Novato, California.

Six-month-old Wendy's Primrose Poet, photographed in May, 1981, bred by Marge Stuber and owned by Florence King of Cincinnati, Ohio.

Ch. Richelieu's Sassy Lizette, with daughter Patches, otherwise known as Ch. Louan's Apache Dancer, and puppy Louan's Apache Dream Baby. Three generations of Maltese at Elsie Burke's Louan Kennels in Farmington, Michigan.

Petit Point Berceuse, bred and owned by Susan M. Sandlin, is only one of the adorable Maltese puppies at the Original Petit Point Kennels in Alexandria, Virginia.

Opposite page: Jingles, Holly, and Nickolas photographed as a "basket of cheer" by their owner, Vera Rebbin.

Sharon Roberts and an adorable Mykiss puppy ready to go into the ring.

New Zealand Ch. Garegwen Shining Star with five of his puppies whelped in 1983. The breeder-owner is Mrs. N.C. Simpson, Carabelle Kennels, New Plymouth, New Zealand.

One of Gail Hennessey's puppies poses with a picture of kennelmate Kathan Blu Flower of Chelsea (enlarged on following page), perhaps dreaming about his own show ring career in the near future.

Ch. Kathan Blu Flower of Chelsea finishing for her championship. Bred and owned by Gail Hennessey; handled to this win by Terry Childs.

Seventeen-month-old American and Canadian Ch. Petit Point Sugar Blues, first homebred champion at Susan M. Sandlin's Original Petit Point Kennels in Alexandria, Virginia.

Ch. Su-Le's Atlantic Brent pictured at a 1981 show with owner and handler Kathy DiGiacomo. The sire was Ch. To The Victor of Eng ex Ch. Su-Le's Jacana. Judging was Anna Katherine Nicholas.

BEST OF
WINNERS
GREENWICH
KENNEL CLUB
1981
GILBERT PHOTO

American and Canadian Ch. Caramaya's Mister is an important breeding force for Diane Davis at her Windsong Maltese Kennels in Haines City, Florida.

American and Canadian Ch. Richelieu's Dennae, owner-handled by Elsie Burke, is one of the brood bitches at Louan's Maltese Kennels in Farmington, Michigan.

Samantha of Carabelle, pictured before one year of age. Bred and owned by Mrs. N.C. Simpson, Carabelle Maltese, New Plymouth, New Zealand.

Ch. Kathan's Bristol Stomp with owner, breeder, and handler Kathy DiGiacomo of Fair Lawn, New Jersey. "Bristol" is the dam of Kathan's Ragtime Cowboy Joe, who was undefeated at eight months of age for a total of ten points toward championship.

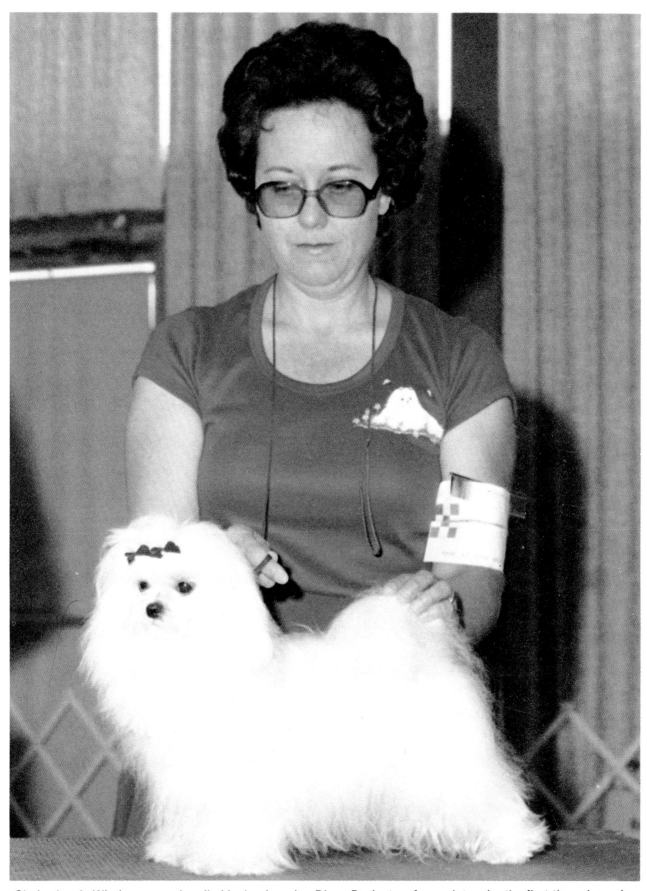

Ch. Luvlane's Windsong was handled by her breeder, Diane Davis, to a four-point major the first time shown in Open Class. Her owner is Sarah A. Slocum of Winter Haven, Florida. "Windy" became the thirty-second champion produced by American and Canadian Ch. Caramaya's Mister.

The joy of Christmas . . . a Maltese just like "Missy" Ch. Oak Ridge Melissa is owned by Linda and Lee Coleman of Lin-Lee's Maltese, Finleyville, Pennsylvania.

Martin's Golden Nugget on his first birthday. The sire was Ch. Su-Le's Golden Eagle. Breeder-owner-photographer was Marjorie Martin, Columbus, Ohio.

Ch. Russ Ann A Touch of Charm, wins at a 1979 show from Puppy Class under judge Joe Rowe. Owner-breeder-handled by Anna Mae Hardy, Floral City, Florida.

208

Ch. Gulfstream Dream Machine is co-owned by Mrs. H. H. Thies and Dorothy H. Hatley. The latter is the owner of the Jaydora Maltese, Trinity, North Carolina.

Ch. Sakhi of Khandese, owned by Mr. and Mrs. Don Derhammer. The breeders were Dr. Roger and Nancy Brown, Omaha, Nebraska.

Best in Show winner, Ch. Myis Sun Seeker, owned by Akira Shinohara of Osaka, Japan, is pictured winning in the United States under judge Anne Rogers Clark before his export to Japan.

MALTESE TOP PRODUCERS IN 1982

In May 1983 *Canine Chronicle* published a list of Top Producers in all breeds for the 1982 show season. No Maltese qualified for the all-breed category, but a male and a female Maltese qualified in the Toy Group.

The Maltese sire, Ch. Joanne-Chen Aennchen Show Biz was one of four dogs in sixth place on the list, all of which qualified by having sired seven champions during the year.

Ch. Forest Snowfire of Longbay qualified as one of several in fourth place as the dam of three champions.

Within the Maltese breed, sires producing three or more champions were the abovementioned "Show Biz" with seven champions. In second place with six champions each was Ch. Kathan's Sunshine Superman and Ch. To The Victor of Eng. There was also a double winner in the third spot with four champions each, Ch. Myis Sun Seeker and Ch. Oak Ridge Poppin Fresh. There were seven Top Producers for next position, each of which had produced three champions within the preceding year. They were Ch. Aennchen's Shiko Dancer, Ch. Gayla Joanne-Chen's Muskratluv, Ch. Maltas A Royal Miracle Match, Ch. Martin's Michael-Cid, Ch. Oak Ridge Country Charmer, Ch. Pegeen's Magic Touch, and Ch. Stan-Bar's Spark of Glory. Males needed three or more champions to qualify, while females were required to have only two.

210

The aforementioned Ch. Forest Snowfire of Longbay, with three, was first and qualified for the Toy Group. Within the breed a total of twenty-one bitches qualified with two champions each. They were Ch. Aennchen's Pompi Dancer, Ch. Al-Mar's Ray of Sunshine, Ch. Bianca's Holly Doll of Glenn, Cedarwood Satin Doll, Gayla's Somewhere My Love, Jo-L's Tarah of Darlene, Ch. Jular's Victoria, Mikael's Cookie, Ch. Moppet's Valdena, Ch. Myis Glory-Seer, Ch. Myis Ode to Glory, Oak Ridge Sand Pebble, Pashe's Sugar In The Morning, Peersun's Starbright, Ch. Su-Le's Phoebe, Sun Canyon Deville, Ch. Sunncrest Hey Look Me Over, Ch. Tennessa's Rampage, Ch. Tennessa's Valarie of Kathan, Ch. Windsong's Merry Mischief, and Ch. Windsong's Million Dollar Baby.

All positions bearing the same number of champion get are listed alphabetically.

TOP SIRES AND DAMS

Thanks to the compilations of Irene Phillips Schlintz, creator of the Phillips System, Maltese fanciers can boast of both a sire and dam in the category of Top-Producing Toy Sires and Dams. Number Seven in the ranks of Toy sires is Ch. To The Victor of Eng, who is credited with having produced 63 champions. Number Three in the Toy dams category is Ch. Su-Le's Jacana with 15 champions to her credit.

Ch. Cotterell's Luv of Tennessa, A Top-Producing Dam listed in the 1976 *Kennel Review* for having whelped ten champions. Owned by Annette S. Feldblum, Tennessa Maltese, Charlton, Massachusetts. Shafer photo.

Ch. Kathan's Johnny Reb, pictured winning at the age of ten months under judge Tom Baldwin, was sired by Ch. To The Victor of Eng ex Kathan's Tallahassee Lassie. Bred, owned, and handled by Kathy DiGiacomo of Fair Lawn, New Jersey.

Barbara Bergquist has compiled a list of Top-Producing Maltese, alphabetical by name, giving the total number of champions produced along with a notation as to any further honor of being the sire or dam of another top-producer.

TOP-PRODUCING DAMS (1965-1982)

Ch. Band G's Go Go Girl of Eng	3
Ch. Cotterell's Luv of Tennessa	10
Ch. Holli Ro Famous Fano O'Midhill	6
Ch. Inge of Windrift	7
Ch. Joanne-Chen Aga Lynn Dancer	5
Ch. Joanne-Chen Sweet Shi Dancer	5
Ch. Little Sheba of Cal Mar	3
Marie-Joanne-Chen's Kandikiss	4
Marleena of Al Mar	7
Mars Missy Too	3
Maryetta of Villa Malta	4
Nyssamead Tesspania	4
Ch. Russ Ann Petite Charmer	7
Ch. Su-Le's Jacana	*15
Sun Canyon Carmen	8
Sun Canyon Rena	7
Sun Canyon Sweet Marie	5
Twinkie Lee of Moderna	3
Ch. Windsong's Merry Mischief	5

*Includes one top producer.

TOP-PRODUCING SIRES (1965-1982)

Ch. Aennchen Shikar Dancer	29
Ch. Aennchen Siva Dancer	19
Ch. Bar None Hotrod Lincoln	11
Ch. C and M's Valentino of Midhill	12
Am., Can Ch. Caramaya's Mister	*29
Ch. Coeur de Lion	**13
Ch. Duncan's Kimberly	7
Ch. Eve-Ron's Snokist Cherub	8
Ch. Gayla's Piccolo Pete	7
Ch. Ha-Los' Mini Mite Dancer	13
Ch. Idar's King Midas	27
Ch. Joanne-Chen Aennchen Show Biz	9
Ch. Joanne-Chen Mino Maya Dancer	19
Ch. Joanne-Chen's Square Dancer	*14
Ch. Joanne-Chen's Sweet He Dancer	13
Ch. Kathan's Sunshine Superman	7
Ch. Myis Sun Seeker	11
Ch. Nyssamead Jonah of Tennessa	22
Ch. Oakridge Country Charmer	13
Ch. San Su Kee Star Edition	10
Ch. Stan-Bar's Spark of Glory	14
Ch. Su-Le's Bluebird	20
Ch. Tego Tu Tu of Almar	10
Ch. To The Victor of Eng	*63
Ch. Windrift's Sharazad	15

*Includes one top producer.
**Includes two top producers.

Ch. Inge of Winddrift was a Top Producer in 1977. Owned by Diane Davis of Haines City, Florida, her breeder was Vivian Edwards.

Feeding time at the Dil-Dal Kennels in Keyport, Washington.

212

CHAPTER TWELVE

Feeding and Nutrition

Butdon and her newborn puppy were photographed January 31, 1981. Owned and bred by Vera Rebbin, Sixpence Kennels, Aurora, Ohio.

FEEDING PUPPIES

There are many diets today for young puppies, including all sorts of products on the market for feeding the newborn, for supplementing the feeding of the young, and for adding "this or that" to diets, depending on what is lacking in the way of a complete diet.

When weaning puppies, it is necessary to put them on four meals a day, even while you are tapering off with the mother's milk. Feeding at six in the morning, noontime, six in the evening, and midnight is about the best schedule since it fits in with most human eating plans. Meals for the puppies can be prepared immediately before or after your own meals, without too much of a change in your own schedule.

6 A.M.

Two meat and two milk meals daily are best and should be served alternately, of course. Assuming the 6 A.M. feeding is a milk meal, the contents should be as follows: goat's milk is the very best milk to feed puppies, but is expensive and usually available only at drug stores, unless you live in farm country where it could be readily available fresh and less expensive. If goat's milk is not available, use evaporated milk (which can be changed to powdered milk later on) diluted as follows: two parts evaporated milk to one part water, mixed with raw egg yolk, honey, or Karo syrup, and sprinkled with high-protein baby cereal and some wheat germ. As the puppies mature, cottage cheese may be added or, at one of the two milk meals, it can be substituted for the cereal.

NOONTIME

A puppy chow that has been soaked in warm water or beef broth according to the time specified on the wrapper should be mixed with raw or simmered chopped meat in equal proportions with vitamin powder added.

6 P.M.

Repeat the milk meal—perhaps varying the type of cereal from wheat to oats, corn, or rice.

MIDNIGHT

Repeat the meat meal. If raw meat was fed at noon, the evening meal might be simmered.

Please note that specific proportions on this suggested diet are not given; however, it's safe to say that the most important ingredients are the milk and cereal, and the meat and puppy chow that forms the basis of the diet. Your veterinarian can advise on the portion sizes if there is any doubt in your mind as to how much to use.

If you notice that the puppies are cleaning their plates, you are perhaps not feeding enough to keep up with their rate of growth. Increase the amount at the next feeding. Observe them closely; puppies should each "have their fill," because growth is very rapid at this age. If they have not satisfied themselves, increase the amount so that they do not have to fight for the last morsel. They will not overeat if they know there is enough food available. Instinct will usually let them eat to suit their normal capacity.

If there is any doubt in your mind as to any ingredient you are feeding, ask yourself, "Would I give it to my own baby?" If the answer is no, then don't give it to your puppies. At this age, the comparison between puppies and human babies can be a good guide.

If there is any doubt in your mind, I repeat: ask your veterinarian to be sure.

Many puppies will regurgitate their food, perhaps a couple of times, before they manage to re-tain it. If they do bring up their food, allow them to eat it again, rather than clean it away. Sometimes additional saliva is necessary for them to digest it, and you do not want them to skip a meal just because it is an unpleasant sight for you to observe.

This same regurgitation process holds true sometimes with the bitch, who will bring up her own food for her puppies every now and then. This is a natural instinct on her part that stems from the days when dogs were giving birth in the wild. The only food the mother could provide at weaning time was too rough and indigestible for her puppies; therefore, she took it upon herself to predigest the food until it could be taken and retained by her young. Bitches today will sometimes resort to this, especially bitches that love having litters and have a strong maternal instinct. Some dams will help you wean their litters and even give up feeding entirely once they see you are taking over.

Dinner time at the Dil-Dal Kennels in Keyport, Washington, features American and Canadian Ch. Tutee Primrose Picca Dilly with her trio born in 1982.

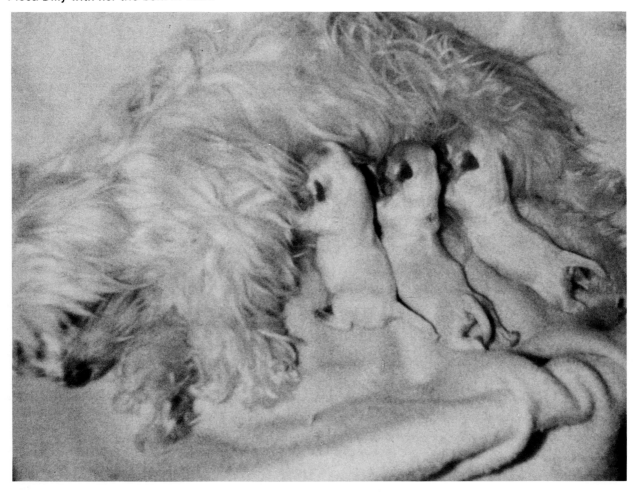

WEANING THE PUPPIES

When weaning the puppies, the mother is kept away from the little ones for longer and longer periods of time. This is done over a period of several days. At first she is separated from the puppies for several hours, then all day, leaving her with them only at night for comfort and warmth. This gradual separation aids in helping the mother's milk to dry up gradually, and she suffers less distress after feeding a litter.

If the mother continues to carry a great deal of milk with no signs of its tapering off, consult your veterinarian before she gets too uncomfortable. She may cut the puppies off from her supply of milk too abruptly if she is uncomfortable.

There are many opinions on the proper age to start weaning puppies. If you plan to start selling them between six and eight weeks, weaning should begin between two and three weeks of age. (Here again, each bitch will pose a different situation.) The size and weight of the litter should help determine the time, and your veterinarian will have an opinion as he determines the burden the bitch is carrying by the size of the litter and her general condition. If she is being pulled down by feeding a large litter, he may suggest that you start at two weeks. If she is glorying in her motherhood without any apparent taxing of her strength, he may suggest three to four weeks. You and he will be the best judges. But remember, there is no substitute that is as perfect as mother's milk—and the longer the puppies benefit from it, the better. Other food yes, but mother's milk first and foremost for the healthiest puppies.

ORPHANED PUPPIES

The ideal solution to feeding orphaned puppies is to be able to put them with another nursing dam who will take them on as her own. If this is not possible within your own kennel, or a kennel that you know of, it is up to you to care for and feed the puppies. Survival is possible but requires a great deal of time and effort on your part.

Your substitute formula must be precisely prepared, always served heated to body temperature, and refrigerated when not being fed. Esbilac, a vacuum-packed powder, with complete feeding instructions on the can, is excellent and about as close to mother's milk as you can get. If you can't get Esbilac, or until you do get Esbilac, there are two alternative formulas that you might use.

Mix one part boiled water with five parts of evaporated milk, and add one teaspoonful of dicalcium phosphate per quart of formula. Dicalcium phosphate can be secured at any drug store. If they have it in tablet form only, you can powder the tablets with the back part of a tablespoon. The other formula for newborn puppies is a combination of eight ounces of homogenized milk mixed well with two egg yolks.

You will need baby bottles with three-hole nipples. Sometimes doll bottles may be used for the newborn puppies, which should be fed at six-hour intervals. If they are consuming sufficient amounts, their stomachs should look full, or slightly enlarged, though never distended.

At two to three weeks, you can start adding Pablum or some other high protein baby cereal to the formula. Also, baby beef can be licked from your finger at this age, or added to the formula. At four weeks, the surviving puppies should be taken off the diet of Esbilac and put on a more substantial diet, such as wet puppy meal or chopped beef; however, Esbilac powder can still be mixed in with the food for additional nutrition. The baby foods of pureed meats in jars make for a smooth changeover also, and can be blended into the diet.

Petit Point Widget is pictured at ten weeks of age and weighing just eleven ounces. This orphan puppy, raised by Susan Sandlin, weighed just one ounce at birth.

A visit from the Easter bunny at Vera Rebbin's home in Aurora, Ohio.

HOW TO FEED THE NEWBORN PUPPIES

When the puppy is a newborn, remember that it is vitally important to keep the feeding procedure as close to the natural mother's routine as possible. The newborn puppy should be held in your lap in your hand in an almost upright position with the bottle at an angle to allow the entire nipple area to be full of the formula. Do not hold the bottle upright so the puppy's head has to reach straight up toward the ceiling. Do not let the puppy nurse too quickly or take in too much air and possibly get colic. Once in awhile take the bottle away and let him rest a moment and swallow several times. Before feeding, test the nipple to see that the fluid does not come out too quickly, or by the same token, too slowly, so that the puppy gets tired of feeding before he has had enough to eat.

When the puppy is a little older, you can place him on his stomach on a towel to eat, and even allow him to hold on to the bottle or to "come and get it" on his own. Since most puppies enjoy eating, this will be a good indication of how strong an appetite he has, and of his ability to consume the contents of the bottle.

It will be necessary to "burp" the puppy. Place a towel on your shoulder and put the puppy over the towel as if it were a human baby, patting and rubbing it gently. This will also encourage the puppy to defecate. At this time, you should observe for diarrhea or other intestinal disorders. The puppy should eliminate after each feeding with occasional eliminations between times as well. If the puppies do not eliminate on their own after each meal, massage their stomachs and under their tails gently until they do.

216

You must keep the puppies clean. Under no circumstances should fecal matter be allowed to collect on their skin or fur.

All this—plus your determination and perseverance—might save an entire litter of puppies that would otherwise have died without their real mother.

FEEDING THE ADULT DOG

The puppies' schedule of four meals a day should drop to three by six months and then to two by nine months; by the time the dog reaches one year of age, it is eating one meal a day.

The time when you feed the dog each day can be a matter of the dog's preference or your convenience, so long as once in every twenty-four hours the dog receives a meal that provides it with a complete, balanced diet. In addition, of course, fresh clean water should be available at all times.

There are many brands of dry food, kibbles, and biscuits on the market that are all of good quality. There are also many varieties of canned dog food that are of good quality and provide a balanced diet for your dog. But, for those breeders and exhibitors who show their dogs, additional care should be given to providing a few "extras" that enhance the good health and good appearance of show dogs.

Ch. Fantasyland Rock N Roll Star is pictured at ten months of age. Owned and photographed by Carole M. Baldwin of Novato, California.

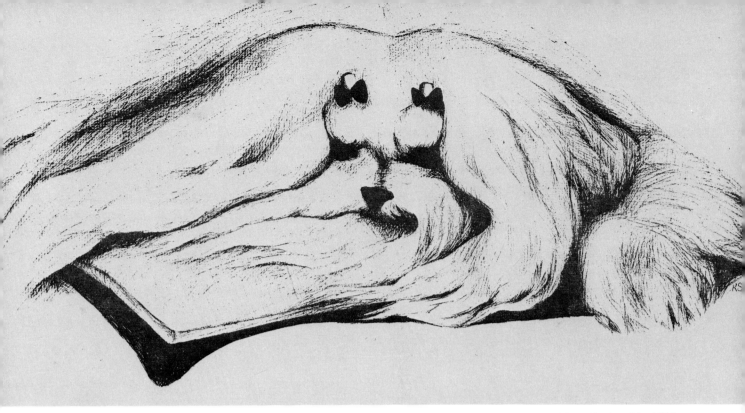

"Daydreaming" by Kathy Blackard of Brooklyn, Connecticut. This piece of art was done by Mrs. Blackard in 1982.

A good meal or kibble mixed with water or beef broth and raw meat is perhaps the best ration to provide. In cold weather, many breeders add suet or corn oil (or even olive or cooking oil) to the mixture, and others make use of the bacon fat after breakfast by pouring it over the dog's food.

Salting a dog's food in the summer helps replace the salt he "pants away" in the heat. Many breeders sprinkle the food with garlic powder to sweeten the dog's breath and prevent gas, especially in breeds that gulp or wolf their food and swallow a lot of air. I prefer garlic powder; the salt is too weak and the garlic clove is too strong.

There are those, of course, who cook very elaborately for their dogs, which is not necessary if a good meal and meat mixture is provided. Many prefer to add vegetables, rice, tomatoes, and so on, in with everything else they feed. As long as the extras do not throw the nutritional balance off, there is little harm, but no one thing should be fed to excess. Occasionally liver is given as a treat at home. Fish, which most veterinarians no longer recommend even for cats, is fed to puppies, but should not be given in excess of once a week. Always remember that no one food should be given as a total diet. Balance is most important; a 100 per cent meat diet can kill a dog.

THE ALL-MEAT DIET CONTROVERSY

In March of 1971, the National Research Council investigated a great stir in the dog fancy about the all-meat dog-feeding controversy. It was established that meat and meat by-products constitute a complete balanced diet for dogs only when it is further fortified.

Hazel's Bright Sunshine, owned and loved by Hazel Pierson, Stony Point, New York.

217

Therefore, a good dog chow or meal mixed with meat provides the perfect combination for a dog's diet. While the dry food is a complete diet in itself, the fresh meat additionally satisfies the dog's anatomically and physiologically meat-oriented appetite. While dogs are actually carnivores, it must be remembered that when they were feeding themselves in the wild, they ate almost the entire animal they captured, including its stomach contents. This provided some of the vitamins and minerals we must now add.

In the United States, the standard for diets that claims to be "complete and balanced" is set by the Subcommittee on Canine Nutrition of the National Research Council (NRC) of the National Academy of Sciences. This is the official agency for establishing the nutritional requirements of dog foods. Most foods sold for dogs and cats meet these requirements, and manufacturers are proud to say so on their labels, so look for this when you buy. Pet food labels must be approved by the Association of American Feed Control Officials (AAFCO) Pet Foods Committee. Both the Food and Drug Administration and the Federal Trade Commission of the AAFCO define the word "balanced" when referring to dog food as follows:

"Balanced is a term which may be applied to pet food having all known required nutrients in a proper amount and proportion based upon the recommendations of a recognized authority (The National Research Council is one) in the field of animal nutrition, for a given set of physiological animal requirements."

With this much care given to your dog's diet, there can be little reason for not having happy well-fed dogs in proper weight and proportions for the show ring.

A mounted specimen of the breed donated to The American Museum of Natural History in the 1890's by Mrs. Robert L. Seaman. Photo courtesy of the American Museum of Natural History.

OBESITY

As we mentioned before, there are many "perfect" diets for your dogs on the market today. When fed in proper proportions, they should keep your dogs in "full bloom." However, there are those owners who, more often than not, indulge their own appetites and are inclined to overfeed their dogs as well. A study in Great Britain in the early 1970's found that a major percentage of obese people also had obese dogs. The entire family was overfed and all suffered from the same condition.

Obesity in dogs is a direct result of the animal's being fed more food that he can properly "burn up" over a period of time, so it is stored as fat or fatty tissue in the body. Pet dogs are more inclined to become obese than show dogs or working dogs, but obesity also is a factor to be considered with the older dog since his exercise is curtailed.

A lack of "tuck up" on a dog, or not being able to feel the ribs, or great folds of fat that hang from the underside of the dog can all be considered as obesity. Genetic factors may enter into the picture, but usually the owner is at fault.

The life span of the obese dog is decreased on several counts. Excess weight puts undue stress on the heart as well as on the joints. The dog becomes a poor anesthetic risk and has less resistance to viral or bacterial infections. Treatment is seldom easy or completely effective, so emphasis should be placed on not letting your dog get fat in the first place!

Major Travis Haney exercises his Maltese dog in the rain while serving with the U.S. Air Force in Iran. Major and Mrs. Haney now live in Las Vegas, Nevada.

Joanne-Chen's Sheeba Dancer, 5½ pounds, was born in 1971. Her sire was Ch. Cla-Mal Sir Jumbie ex Aennchen's Sheeba Dancer.

GASTRIC TORSION

Gastric torsion, or bloat, sometimes referred to as "twisted stomach," has become more and more prevalent. Many dogs that in the past had been thought to die of blockage of the stomach or intestines because they had swallowed toys or other foreign objects, are now suspected of having been the victims of gastric torsion and the bloat that followed.

Though life can be saved by immediate surgery to untwist the organ, the rate of fatality is high. Symptoms of gastric torsion are unusual restlessness, excessive salivation, attempts to vomit, rapid respiration, pain, and the eventual bloating of the abdominal region.

To avoid the threat of gastric torsion, it is wise to keep your dog well exercised to be sure the body is functioning normally. Make sure that food and water are available for the dog at all times, thereby reducing the tendency to overeat. With self-service dry feeding, where the dog is able to eat intermittently during the day, there is not the urge to "stuff" at one time.

If you notice any of the symptoms of gastric torsion, call your veterinarian immediately. Death can result within a matter of hours!

A pastel portrait of Ch. Su-Le's Mynah II, rendered by artist James Fischer of Port Washington, New York.

CHAPTER THIRTEEN

The Blight of Parasites

Ch. Aennchen's Suni Dancer, bred by Mr. and Mrs. J. P. Antonelli and owned by Dr. and Mrs. Roger Brown of Omaha, Nebraska.

Anyone who has ever spent hours peering intently at their dog's warm, pink stomach waiting for a flea to appear will readily understand why I call this chapter the "blight of parasites." It is that dreaded onslaught of the pesky flea that heralds the subsequent arrival of worms.

If you have seen even one flea scoot across that vulnerable expanse of skin, you can be sure there are more lurking on other areas of your dog. They seldom travel alone. So, it is now an established fact that *la puce*, as the French refer to the flea, has set up housekeeping on your dog! It is going to demand a great deal of your time before you manage to evict them—probably just temporarily at that—no matter which species your dog is harboring.

Fleas are not always choosy about their host, but chances are your dog has what is commonly known as *Ctenocephalides canis*, the dog flea. If you are a lover of cats also, your dog might even be playing host to a few *Ctenocephalides felis*, the cat flea, or vice versa. The only thing you can be really sure of is that your dog is supporting an entire community of them, all hungry and sexually oriented, and you are going to have to be persistent in your campaign to get rid of them.

One of the chief reasons fleas are so difficult to catch is that what they lack in beauty and eyesight (they are blind at birth, throughout infan-

cy, and see very poorly if at all during adulthood), they make up for in their fantastic ability to jump and scurry about.

Modern research has provided a panacea in the form of flea sprays, dips, collars, and tags which can be successful to varying degrees. However, there are those who still swear by the good old-fashioned methods of removing them by hand, which can be a challenge to your sanity as well as your dexterity.

Since the fleas' conformation (they are built like envelopes, long and flat), with their spiny skeletal system on the outside of their bodies, is specifically provided for slithering through forests of hair, they are given a distinct advantage to start with. Two antennae on the head select the best spot for digging, and then two mandibles penetrate the skin and hit a blood vessel. It is also at this moment that the flea brings into play his spiny contours to prop himself against surrounding hairs to avoid being scratched off as he puts the bite on your dog. A small projecting tube is then lowered into the hole to draw out blood and another tube pumps saliva into the wound; this prevents the blood from clotting and allows the flea to drink freely. Simultaneously, your dog jumps into the air and gets one of those back legs into action, scratching endlessly and in vain.

If you should be so lucky as to catch an itinerant flea as it mistakenly shortcuts across your dog's stomach, the best hunting grounds in the world are actually in the deep fur all along the dog's back from neck to tail. However, the flea, like every other creature on earth, must have water, so several times during its residency it will make its way to the moister areas of your dog's anatomy, such as the corners of the mouth, the eyes, or the genital parts. This is when the flea collars and tags are useful. Their fumes prevent fleas from passing the neck to get to the head of your dog.

Your dog can usually support several generations of fleas, if it doesn't scratch itself to death or go out of its mind with the itching in the interim. The propagation of the flea is insured by the strong mating instinct and well-judged decision of the female flea as to the best time to deposit her eggs. She has the rare capacity to store semen until the time is right to lay the eggs after some previous brief encounter with a passing member of the opposite sex.

When that time comes for her to lay, she does so without so much as a backward glance and moves on. The dog shakes the eggs off during a normal day's wandering, and they remain on the ground until hatched and the baby fleas are ready to jump back onto a passing dog. If any of the eggs have remained on the original dog, chances are that in scratching an adult flea, he will help the baby fleas emerge from their shells.

Larval fleas are small and resemble slender maggots; they begin their lives eating their own egg shells until the dog comes along and offers them a return to the world of adult fleas, whose excrement provides the predigested blood pellets they must have to thrive. They cannot survive on fresh blood, nor are they capable at this tender age of digging for it themselves.

After a couple of weeks of this freeloading, the baby flea makes his own cocoon and becomes a pupa. This stage lasts long enough for the larval flea to grow legs, mandibles, and sharp spines, and to flatten out and in general become identifiable as the commonly known and obnoxious *Ctenocephalides canis*. The process can take several weeks or several months, depending on weather conditions, heat, and moisture, but generally three weeks is all that is required to enable the flea to start gnawing your dog in its own right.

And so the life-cycle of the flea is renewed and begun again. If you don't have plans to stem the tide, you will certainly see a population explosion that will make the human one resemble an endangered species. Getting rid of fleas can be accomplished by the aforementioned spraying of the dog, or the flea collars and tags, but air, sunshine and a good shaking out of beds, bedding, carpets, and cushions, certainly must be undertaken to get rid of the eggs or larvae lying around the premises.

Should you be lucky enough to get hold of a flea, you must squeeze it to death (which isn't easy), or break it in two with a sharp, strong fingernail (which also isn't easy), or you must release it *underwater* in the toilet bowl and flush immediately. This prospect is only slightly easier.

There are those dog owners, however, who are much more philosophical about the flea, since, like the cockroach, it has been around since the beginning of the world. For instance, that old-time philosopher, David Harum, has been much quoted with his remark, "A reasonable amount of fleas is good for a dog. They keep him from broodin' on bein' a dog." We would rather agree with John Donne who, in his *Devotions*, reveals that, "The flea, though he kill none, he does all the harm he can." This is especially true if your dog is a show dog! If the scratching doesn't ruin the coat, the inevitable infestation of parasites left by the fleas will!

We readily see that dogs can be afflicted by both internal and external parasites. The external parasites are known as the aforementioned fleas, plus ticks and lice; while all of these are bothersome, they can be treated. However, the internal parasites, or worms of various kinds, are usually well-entrenched before discovery, and more substantial means of ridding the dog of them completely are required.

INTERNAL PARASITES

The most common worms are the round worms. These, like many other worms, are carried and spread by the flea and go through a cycle within the dog host. They are excreted in egg or larval form and passed on to other dogs in this manner.

Worm medicine should be prescribed by a veterinarian, and dogs should be checked for worms at least twice a year—or every three months if there is a known epidemic in your area— and during the summer months when fleas are plentiful.

222

Major types of worms are hookworms, whipworms, tapeworms (the only non-round worms on this list), ascarids (the "typical" round worms), heartworms, kidney, and lung worms. Each can be peculiar to a part of the country, or may be carried by a dog from one area to another. Kidney and lung worms are fortunately quite rare; the others are not. Some symptoms for worms are vomiting intermittently, eating grass, lack of pep, bloated stomach, rubbing the tail along the ground, loss of weight, dull coat, anemia and pale gums, eye discharge, or unexplained nervousness and irritability. A dog with worms will usually eat twice as much as he normally would.

Never worm a sick dog or a pregnant bitch after the first two weeks she has been bred, and never worm a constipated dog—it will retain the strong medicine within the body for too long a time.

HOW TO TEST FOR WORMS

Worms can kill your dog if the infestation is severe enough. Even light infestations of worms can debilitate a dog to the point where he is more susceptible to other serious diseases that can kill.

Today's medication for worming is relatively safe and mild, and worming is no longer the traumatic experience for either the dog or owner that it used to be. Great care must be given, however, to the proper administration of the drugs. Correct dosage is a "must," and clean quarters are essential to rid your kennel of these parasites. It is almost impossible to find an animal that is completely free of parasites, so we must consider worming as a necessary evil.

However mild today's medicines may be, it is inadvisable to worm a dog unnecessarily. There are simple tests to determine the presence of worms, and this chapter is designed to help you learn how to administer these tests yourself.

All that is needed by way of equipment is a microscope with 100X power. These can be purchased in the toy department of a department or regular toy store for a few dollars. The basic, least expensive sets come with the necessary glass slides and attachments.

After the dog has defecated, take an applicator stick, a toothpick with a flat end, or even an old-fashioned wooden matchstick and gouge off a piece of the stool about the size of a small pea. Have one of the glass slides ready with a large drop of water on it. Mix the two together until you have a cloudy film over a large area of the slide. This smear should be covered with another slide or a cover slip—though it is possible to obtain readings with just the one open slide. Place your slide under the microscope and prepare to focus in on it. To read the slide you will find that your eye should follow a certain pattern. Start at the top and read from left to right, then right back to the left and then left over to the right side once again until you have looked at every portion of the slide from the top left to the bottom right side.

Make sure that your smear is not too thick or watery or the reading will be too dark and confused to make proper identification. If you decide you would rather not make your own fecal examinations, but would prefer to have the veterinarian do it, the proper way to present a segment of the stool is as follows:

After the dog has defecated, a portion of the stool, say a square inch from different sections of it, should be placed in a glass jar or plastic container and labeled with the dog's name and address of the owner. If the sample cannot be examined within three or four hours after passage, it should be refrigerated. Your opinion as to what variety of worms you suspect is sometimes helpful to the veterinarian, and may be noted on the label of the jar you submit to him for the examination.

Checking for worms on a regular basis is advisable not only for the welfare of the dog but for the protection of your family, since most worms are transmissible, under certain circumstances, to humans.

Villa Malta's Topsy and Villa Malta's Missey are owned by Rita and Charlie Gilbert.

223

Ch. Brown's Joni Dancer, bred and owned by Dr. and Mrs. Roger Brown, Bel Air Animal Clinic, Omaha, Nebraska.

224

CHAPTER FOURTEEN

Your Dog, Your Veterinarian, and You

Angela Dahl and Beau in a tender moment.

The purpose of this chapter is to explain why you should never attempt to be your own veterinarian. Quite the contrary, we urge emphatically that you establish a good liaison with a reputable veterinarian who will help you maintain happy, healthy dogs. Our purpose is to bring you up-to-date on the discoveries made in modern canine medicine, and to help you work with your veterinarian by applying these new developments to your own animals.

We have provided here "thumbnail" histories of many of the most common types of diseases your dog is apt to come in contact with during his lifetime. We feel that if you know a little something about the diseases and how to recognize their symptoms, your chances of catching them in the preliminary stages will help you and your veterinarian effect a cure before a serious condition develops.

Today's dog owner is a realistic, intelligent person who learns more and more about his dog —inside and out—so that he can care for and enjoy the animal to the fullest. He uses technical terms for parts of the anatomy, has a fleeting knowledge of the miracles of surgery, and is fully prepared to administer clinical care for his animals at home. This chapter is designed for study and/or reference, and we hope you will use it to full advantage.

We repeat, we do *not* advocate your playing "doctor." This includes administering medication without veterinary supervision, or even doing your own inoculations. General knowledge of diseases, their symptoms, and side effects will assist you in diagnosing diseases for your veterinarian. He does not expect you to be an expert, but will appreciate your efforts in getting a sick dog to him before it is too late.

ASPIRIN: A DANGER

There is a common joke about doctors telling their patients, when they telephone with a complaint, to take an aspirin, go to bed and let him know how things are in the morning. Unfortunately, that is exactly the way it turns out with a lot of dog owners who think aspirins are cure-alls, and who give them to their dogs indiscriminately. They finally call the veterinarian when the dog has an unfavorable reaction.

Aspirin is not a panacea for everything—certainly not for every dog. In an experiment, fatalities in cats treated with aspirin in one laboratory alone numbered ten out of thirteen within a two-week period. Dogs' tolerance was somewhat better, as to actual fatalities, but there was considerable evidence of ulceration on the stomach linings in varying degrees when necropsy was performed.

This playful Maltese begging for a treat or attention belongs to Kathy DiGiacomo of Fair Lawn, New Jersey.

Aspirin has been held in the past to be almost as effective for dogs as for people when given for many of the everyday aches and pains. The fact remains, however, that medication of any kind should be administered only after veterinary consultation and a specific dosage suitable to the condition is recommended.

While aspirin is chiefly effective in reducing fever, relieving minor pains, and cutting down on inflammation, the acid has been proven harmful to the stomach when given in strong doses. Only your veterinarian is qualified to determine what the dosage is or whether it should be administered to your particular dog at all.

WHAT THE THERMOMETER CAN TELL YOU

You will notice in reading this chapter dealing with the diseases of dogs that practically everything a dog might contract in the way of sickness has basically the same set of symptoms: loss of appetite, diarrhea, dull eyes, dull coat, warm and/or runny nose, and *fever!*

Therefore, it is most advisable to have a thermometer on hand for checking temperature. There are several inexpensive metal rectal-type thermometers that are accurate, and safer than the glass variety that can be broken. This may happen either by dropping it, or perhaps by its breaking off in the dog because of improper insertion, or an aggravated condition with the dog that makes him violently resist the injection of the thermometer.

Whatever type you use, it should first be sterilized with alcohol and then lubricated with petroleum jelly to make the insertion as easy as possible.

The normal temperature for a dog is 101.5 degrees Fahrenheit, as compared to the human 98.6 degrees. Excitement as well as illness can cause this to vary a degree or two, but any sudden or extensive rise in body temperature must be considered as cause for alarm. Your first indication will be that your dog feels unduly "warm," and this is the time to take the temperature, *not* when the dog becomes very ill or manifests additional serious symptoms.

COPROPHAGY

Perhaps the most unpleasant of all phases of dog breeding is to come up with a dog that takes to eating stool. This practice, which is referred to politely as coprophagy, is one of the unsolved mysteries in the dog world. There simply is no confirmed explanation as to why some dogs do it.

However, there are several logical theories, all or any of which may be the cause. Some people cite nutritional deficiencies; others say that dogs that are inclined to gulp their food (which passes through them not entirely digested) find it still partially palatable. There is another theory that the preservatives used in some meat are responsible for an appealing odor that remains through the digestive process. Then again, poor quality meat can be so tough and unchewable that dogs swallow it whole and it passes through them in large undigested chunks.

There are others who believe the habit is strictly psychological, the result of a nervous condition or insecurity. Others believe the dog cleans up after itself because it is afraid of being punished as it was when it made a mistake on the carpet as a puppy. Some people claim boredom is the reason, or even spite. Others will tell you a dog does not want its personal odor on the premises for fear of attracting other hostile animals to itself or its home.

226

The most logical of all explanations, and the one veterinarians are inclined to accept, is that it is a deficiency of dietary enzymes. Too much dry food can be bad, and many veterinarians suggest trying meat tenderizers, monosodium glutamate, or garlic powder, all of which give the stool a bad odor and discourage the dog. Yeast or certain vitamins or a complete change of diet are even more often suggested. By the time you try each of the above you will probably discover that the dog has outgrown the habit anyway. However, the condition cannot be ignored.

There is no set length of time that the problem persists, and the only real cure is to walk the dog on leash, morning and night, and after every meal. In other words, set up a definite eating and exercising schedule before coprophagy is an established pattern.

MASTURBATION

A source of embarrassment to many dog owners, masturbation can be eliminated with a minimum of training.

The dog that is constantly breeding anything and everything, including the leg of the piano or perhaps the leg of your favorite guest, can be broken of the habit by stopping its cause.

The over-sexed dog—if truly that is what he is —which will never be used for breeding can be castrated. The kennel stud dog can be broken of the habit by removing any furniture from his quarters or by keeping him on leash and on verbal command when he is around people or in the house, where he might be tempted to breed pillows, people, etc.

Hormone imbalance may be another cause and your veterinarian may advise injections. Exercise can be of tremendous help. Keeping the dog's mind occupied by physical play when he is around people will also help relieve the situation.

Females might indulge in sexual abnormalities like masturbation during their heat cycle, or again, because of a hormone imbalance. But if they behave this way because of a more serious problem, a hysterectomy may be indicated.

A sharp "no!" command when you can anticipate the act, or a sharp "no!" when caught in the act will deter most dogs if you are consistent in your correction. Hitting or other physical abuse will only confuse a dog.

Two Maltese beauties from Barbara Bergquist's Su-Le Kennels in New Boston, Michigan.

RABIES

The greatest fear in the dog fancy today is still the great fear it has always been—rabies.

What has always held true about this dreadful disease still holds true today. The only way rabies can be contracted is through the saliva of a rabid dog entering the bloodstream of another animal or person. There is, of course, the Pasteur treatment for rabies which is very effective.

It should be administered immediately if there is any question of exposure. There was of late the incident of a little boy, who survived being bitten by a rabid bat. Even more than dogs being found to be rabid, we now know that the biggest carriers are bats, skunks, foxes, rabbits, and other warmblooded animals that pass it from one to another since they do not have the benefit of inoculation. Dogs that run free should be inoculated for protection against these animals. For city or house dogs that never leave their owner's side, it may not be as necessary.

For many years, Great Britain (because it is an island and because of the country's strictly enforced six-month quarantine) was entirely free of rabies. But in 1969, a British officer brought back his dog from foreign duty and the dog was found to have the disease soon after being released from quarantine. There was a great uproar about it, with Britain killing off wild and domestic animals in a great scare campaign, but the quarantine is once again down to six months, and things seem to have returned to a normal, sensible attitude.

Health departments in rural towns usually provide rabies inoculations free of charge. If your dog is outdoors a great deal, or exposed to other animals that are, you might wish to call the town hall and get information on the program in your area. One cannot be too cautious about this dread disease. While the number of cases diminishes each year, there are still thousands being reported.

Portrait study of Ch. Aennchen's Sitar Dancer, bred by the Joseph Antonellis of Waldwick, New Jersey.

Rabies is caused by a neurotropic virus which can be found in the saliva, brain, and sometimes the blood of the afficted warmblooded animal. The incubation period is usually two weeks or as long as six months, which means you can be exposed to it without any visible symptoms. As we have said, while there is still no known cure, it can be controlled.

You can help effect this control by reporting animal bites, educating the public to the dangers and symptoms, and prevention of it, so that we may reduce the fatalities.

There are two kinds of rabies; one form is called "furious" and the other is referred to as "dumb." The mad dog goes through several stages of the disease. His disposition and behavior change radically and suddenly; he becomes irritable and vicious. The eating habits alter, and he rejects food for things like stones and sticks; he becomes exhausted and drools saliva out of his mouth constantly. He may hide in corners, look glassy-eyed and suspicious, bite at the air as he races around snarling and attacking with his tongue hanging out. At this point paralysis sets in, starting at the throat so that he can no longer drink water though he desires it desperately; hence, the term hydrophobia is given. He begins to stagger and eventually convulse, and death is imminent.

In "dumb" rabies, paralysis is swift; the dog seeks dark, sheltered places and is abnormally quiet. Paralysis starts with the jaws, spreads down the body, and death is quick. Contact by humans or other animals with the drool from either of these types of rabies on open skin can produce the fatal disease, so extreme haste and proper diagnosis is essential. In other words, you do not have to be bitten by a rabid dog to have the virus enter your system. An open wound or cut that comes in touch with the saliva is all that is needed.

The incubation and degree of infection can vary. You usually contract the disease faster if the wound is near the head, since the virus travels to the brain through the spinal cord. The deeper the wound, the more saliva is injected into the body, and the more serious the infection. So, if bitten by a dog under any circumstances—or any warmblooded animal for that matter—immediately wash out the wound with soap and water, bleed it profusely, and see your doctor as soon as possible.

Also, be sure to keep track of the animal that bit, if at all possible. When rabies is suspected,

Ch. Russ Ann Mr. Pip wins Best of Breed at a recent show. "Pipen" belongs to breeder-handler Anna Mae Hardy, Floral City, Florida.

the public health officer will need to send the animal's head away to be analyzed. If it is found to be rabies free, you will not need to undergo treatment. Otherwise, your doctor may advise that you have the Pasteur treatment, which is extremely painful. It is rather simple, however, to have the veterinarian examine a dog for rabies without having the dog sent away for positive diagnosis of the disease. A ten-day quarantine is usually all that is necessary for everyone's peace of mind.

Rabies is no respecter of age, sex, or geographical location. It is found all over the world from North Pole to South Pole, and has nothing to do with the old wives' tale of dogs going mad in the hot summer months. True, there is an increase in reported cases during summer, but only because that is the time of the year for animals to roam free in good weather and during the mating season when the battle of the sexes is taking place. Inoculation and a keen eye for symptoms and bites on our dogs and other pets will help control the disease until the cure is found.

229

Ch. Aennchen's Sitar Dancer is pictured winning Best in Show from the classes at the 1968 Staten Island Kennel Club Show under judge Frank Landgraf.

VACCINATIONS

If you are to raise a puppy, or a litter of puppies, successfully, you must adhere to a realistic and strict schedule of vaccinations. Many puppyhood diseases can be fatal—all of them are debilitating. According to the latest statistics, ninety-eight per cent of all puppies are being inoculated after twelve weeks of age against the dread distemper, hepatitis, and leptospirosis, and manage to escape these horrible infections. Orphaned puppies should be vaccinated every two weeks until the age of twelve weeks. Distemper and hepatitis live virus vaccines should be used, since the puppies are not protected with the colostrum normally supplied to them through the mother's milk. Puppies weaned at six to seven weeks should also be inoculated repeatedly because they will no longer be receiving mother's milk. While not all will receive protection from the serum at this early age, it should be given and they should be vaccinated once again at both nine and twelve weeks of age.

Leptospirosis vaccination should be given at four months of age with thought given to booster shots if the disease is known in the area, or in the case of show dogs which are exposed on a regular basis to many dogs from far and wide. While animal boosters are in order for distemper and hepatitis, every two or three years is sufficient for leptospirosis, unless there is an outbreak in your immediate area.

Strict observance of such a vaccination schedule will not only keep your dog free of these debilitating diseases, but will prevent an epidemic in your kennel, or in your locality, or to the dogs that are competing at the shows.

SNAKEBITE

As field trials and hunts and the like become more and more popular with dog enthusiasts, the incident of snakebite becomes more of a likelihood. Dogs that are kept outdoors in runs, or dogs that work the fields and roam on large estates are also likely victims.

230

Most veterinarians carry snakebite serum, and snakebite kits are sold to dog owners for just such a purpose. To catch a snakebite in time might mean the difference between life and death, and whether your area is populated with snakes or not, it behooves you to know what to do in case it happens to you or your dog.

Your primary concern should be to get to a doctor or veterinarian immediately. The victim should be kept as quiet as possible (excitement or activity spreads the venom through the body more quickly), and if possible the wound should be bled enough to clean it out before applying a tourniquet, if the bite is severe.

First of all, it must be determined if the bite is from a poisonous or non-poisonous snake. If the bite carries two horseshoe-shaped pinpoints of a double row of teeth, the bite can be assumed to be non-poisonous. If the bite leaves two punctures or holes—the result of the two fangs carrying venom—the bite is definitely poisonous.

Recently, physicians have come up with an added help in the case of snakebite. A first aid treatment referred to as "hypothermia," which is the application of ice to the wound to lower body temperature to a point where the venom spreads less quickly, minimizes swelling, helps prevent infection, and has some influence on numbing the pain. If ice is not readily available, the bite may be soaked in ice-cold water. But even more urgent is the need to get the victim to a hospital or a veterinarian for additional treatment.

Ch. Duncans Nicholas takes Best in Show at the 1971 Columbia, South Carolina, show under judge Melbourne Downing. Handled by Betty Mundie for owner Muriel Calhoun of Hampstead, North Carolina. Earl Graham photo.

EMERGENCIES

No matter how well you run your kennel or keep an eye on an individual dog, there will almost invariably be some emergency at some time that will require quick treatment until you get the animal to the veterinarian. The first and most important thing to remember is to keep calm! You will think more clearly, and your animal will need to know he can depend on you to take care of him. However, he will be frightened and you must beware of fear-biting. Therefore, do not shower him with kisses and endearments at this time, no matter how sympathetic you feel. Comfort him reassuringly, but keep your wits about you. Before getting him to the veterinarian, try to alleviate the pain and the shock.

If you can take even a minor step in this direction it will be a help toward the final cure. Listed here are a few of the emergencies that might occur, and what you can do *after* you have called the vet and told him you are coming.

BURNS

If you have been so foolish as to not turn your pot handles toward the back of the stove—for your children's sake as well as your dog's—and the dog is burned, apply ice or ice-cold water and treat for shock. Electrical or chemical burns are treated the same, but with an acid or alkali burn use, respectively, a bicarbonate of soda and a vinegar solution. Check the advisability of covering the burn when you call the veterinarian.

Snowfire's Legacy is owned by Jeanne L. McGuckin of the Bec Chon Kennels in Houston, Texas.

232

DROWNING

Most animals love the water but sometimes get in "over their heads." Should your dog take in too much water, hold him upside down and open his mouth so that water can empty from the lungs, then apply artificial respiration or mouth-to-mouth resuscitation. With a large dog, hang the head over a step or off the end of a table while you hoist the rear end in the air by the back feet. Then treat for shock by covering him with a blanket, administering a stimulant such as coffee with sugar, and soothing him with your voice and hands.

FITS AND CONVULSIONS

Prevent the dog from thrashing about and injuring himself, cover with a blanket, and hold down until you can get him to the veterinarian.

FROSTBITE

There is no excuse for an animal getting frostbite if you are "on your toes" and care for the animal; however, should frostbite set in, thaw out the affected area slowly by massaging with a circular motion and stimulation.

HEART ATTACK

Be sure the animal keeps breathing by applying artificial respiration. A mild stimulant may be used, and give him plenty of air. Treat for shock as well, and get him to the veterinarian quickly.

SHOCK

Shock is a state of circulatory collapse that can be induced by a severe accident, loss of blood, heart failure, or any injury to the nervous system. Until you can get the dog to the veterinarian, keep him warm by covering him with a blanket, and administer a mild stimulant such as coffee or tea with sugar. Try to keep the dog quiet until the appropriate medication can be prescribed. Relapse is not uncommon, so the dog must be observed carefully for several days after initial shock.

SUFFOCATION

Administer artificial respiration and treat for shock with plenty of air.

SUN STROKE

Cooling the dog off immediately is essential. Ice packs, submersion in ice water, and plenty of cool air are needed.

WOUNDS

Open wounds or cuts that produce bleeding must be treated with hydrogen peroxide, and tourniquets should be used if bleeding is excessive. Also, shock treatment must be given, and the animal must be kept warm.

THE FIRST AID KIT

It would be sheer folly to try to operate a kennel or to keep a dog without providing for certain emergencies that are bound to crop up when there are active dogs around. Just as you would provide a first aid kit for people, you should also provide a first aid kit for the animals on the premises.

The first aid kit should contain the following items:

> BFI or other medicated powder
> jar of petroleum jelly
> cotton swabs
> bandage—1" gauze
> adhesive tape
> bandaids
> cotton gauze or cotton balls
> boric acid powder

A trip to your veterinarian is always safest, but there are certain preliminaries for cuts and bruises of a minor nature that you can take care of yourself.

Cuts, for instance, should be washed out and medicated powder should be applied with a bandage. The lighter the bandage the better, so that the most air possible can reach the wound. Cotton-swabs can be used for removing debris from the eyes, after which a mild solution of boric acid wash can be applied. As for sores, use dry powder on wet sores, and petroleum jelly on dry sores. Use cotton for washing out wounds and drying them.

A particular caution must be given here on bandaging. Make sure that the bandage is not too tight to hamper the dog's circulation. Also, make sure the bandage is applied correctly so that the dog does not bite at it trying to remove it. A great deal of damage can be done to a wound by a dog tearing at a bandage to get it off. If you notice the dog is starting to bite at it, do it over or put something on the bandage that smells and tastes bad to him. Make sure, however, that the solution does not soak through the bandage and enter the wound. Sometimes, if it is a leg wound, a sock or stocking slipped on the dog's leg will cover the bandage edges and will also keep it clean.

Ghost Moon White Lightning is owned by Delores Halley of Blue Grass, Iowa. The sire was Caramaya's Sweet Pea Dancer ex Standee's Heidi Snow Glo.

HOW NOT TO POISON YOUR DOG

Ever since the appearance of Rachel Carson's book *Silent Spring*, people have been asking, "Just how dangerous are chemicals?" In the animal fancy where disinfectants, room deodorants, parasitic sprays, solutions, and aerosols are so widely used, the question has taken on even more meaning. Veterinarians are beginning to ask, "What kind of disinfectant do you use?" "Have you any fruit trees that have been sprayed recently?" When animals are brought into their offices in a toxic condition, or for unexplained death, or when entire litters of puppies die mysteriously, there is good reason to ask such questions.

The popular practice of protecting animals against parasites has given way to their being exposed to an alarming number of commercial products, some of which are dangerous to their very lives. Even flea collars can be dangerous, especially if they get wet or somehow touch the genital regions or eyes. While some products are much more poisonous than others, great care must be taken that they be applied in proportion to the size of the dog and the area to be covered. Many a dog has been taken to the vet with an unusual skin problem that was a direct result of having been bathed with a detergent rather than a proper shampoo. Certain products that are safe for dogs may be fatal for cats. Extreme care must be taken to read all ingredients and instructions carefully before using the products on any animal.

American Ch. Joanne-Chen's Shikar Dancer is now owned by Akira Shinohara of Osaka, Japan.

The same caution must be given to outdoor chemicals. Dog owners must question the use of fertilizers on their lawns. Lime, for instance, can be harmful to a dog's feet. The unleashed dog that covers the neighborhood on his daily rounds is open to all sorts of tree and lawn sprays and insecticides that may prove harmful to him, if not as a poison, then as a producer of an allergy.

There are numerous products found around the house that can be lethal, such as rat poison, boric acid, hand soap, detergents, car anti-freeze, and insecticides. These are all available in the house or garage and can be tipped over easily and consumed. Many puppy fatalities are reported as a result of puppies eating mothballs. All poisons should be placed on high shelves out of the reach of *both* children and animals.

Perhaps the most readily available of all household poisons are plants. Household plants are almost all poisonous, even if taken in small quantities. Some of the most dangerous are the elephant ear, the narcissus bulb, any kind of ivy leaves, burning bush leaves, the jimson weed, the dumb cane weed, mock orange fruit, castor beans, Scottish broom seeds, the root or seed of the plant called "four o'clock," cyclamen, pimpernel, lily of the valley, the stem of the sweet pea, rhododendrons of any kind, spider lily bulbs, bayonet root, foxglove leaves, tulip bulbs, monkshood roots, azalea, wisteria, poinsettia leaves, mistletoe, hemlock, locoweed, and arrowglove. In all, there are over 500 poisonous plants in the United States. Peach, elderberry, and cherry trees can cause cyanide poisoning if the

bark is consumed. Rhubarb leaves, either raw or cooked, can cause death or violent convulsions. Check out your closets, fields, and grounds around your home, and especially the dog runs, to see what should be eliminated to remove the danger to your dogs.

SYMPTOMS OF POISONING

Be on the lookout for vomiting, hard or labored breathing, whimpering, stomach cramps, and trembling as a prelude to convulsions. Any delay in a visit to your veterinarian can mean death. Take along the bottle or package or a sample of the plant you suspect to be the cause to help the veterinarian determine the correct antidote.

The most common type of poisoning, which accounts for nearly one-fourth of all animal victims, is staphylococcic—infested food. Salmonella ranks third. These can be avoided by serving fresh food and not letting it lie around in hot weather.

There are also many insect poisonings caused by animals eating cockroaches, spiders, flies, butterflies, etc. Toads and some frogs give off a fluid that can make a dog foam at the mouth—and even kill him—if he bites just a little too hard!

Some misguided dog owners think it is "cute" to let their dogs enjoy a cocktail with them before dinner. There can be serious effects resulting from encouraging a dog to drink— sneezing fits, injuries as a result of intoxication, and heart stoppage are just a few. Whiskey for medicinal purposes, or beer for brood bitches should be administered only on the advice of your veterinarian.

There have been cases of severe damage and death when dogs have emptied ash trays and eaten cigarettes, resulting in nicotine poisoning. Leaving a dog alone all day in a house where there are cigarettes available on a coffee table is asking for trouble. Needless to say, the same applies to marijuana. The narcotic addict who takes his dog along with him on "a trip" does not deserve to have a dog. All the ghastly side effects are as possible for the dog as for the addict, and for a person to submit an animal to this indignity is indeed despicable. Don't think it doesn't happen. Unfortunately, in all our major cities the practice is becoming more and more a problem for the veterinarian.

Be on the alert and remember that in the case of any type of poisoning, the best treatment is prevention.

Sir Gerie Hamrun's Dhuli Dancer, photographed in 1971, was bred by Marcia Hostetler.

THE CURSE OF ALLERGY

The heartbreak of a child being forced to give up a beloved pet because he is suddenly found to be allergic to it is a sad but true story. Many families claim to be unable to have dogs at all; others seem to be able only to enjoy them on a restricted basis. Many children know animals only through occasional visits to a friend's house or the zoo.

While modern veterinary science has produced some brilliant allergists, the field is still working on a solution for those who suffer from exposure to their pets. There is no permanent cure as yet.

Over the last quarter of a century there have been many attempts at a permanent cure, but none has proven successful because the treatment was needed too frequently, or was too expensive to maintain over extended periods.

However, we find that most people who are allergic to their animals are also allergic to a variety of other things as well. By eliminating the other irritants, and by taking medication given for the control of allergies in general, many are able to keep pets on a restricted basis. This may necessitate the dog's living outside the house, being groomed at a professional grooming parlor instead of by the owner, or merely being kept out of the bedroom at night. A discussion of this "balance" factor with your medical and veterinary doctors may give new hope to those willing to try.

A paper presented by Mathilde M. Gould, M.D., a New York allergist, before the American Academy of Allergists in the 1960's, and reported in the September-October 1964 issue of the *National Humane Review* magazine, offered new hope to those who are allergic, by a method referred to as hyposensitization. You may wish to write to the magazine and request the article for discussion of your individual problem with your medical and veterinary doctors.

Surely, since the sixties, there have been additional advances in the field of allergy since so many people—and animals—are affected in so many ways.

Firecracker Teddy Bear is owned by Marcia Hostetler.

235

ALLERGIES IN DOGS

It used to be that you recognized an allergy in your dog when he scratched out his coat and developed a large patch of raw skin, or sneezed himself almost to death on certain occasions. A trip to the veterinarian involved endless discussion as to why it might be, and an almost equally endless "hit and miss" cure of various salves and lotions with the hope that one of them would work. Many times the condition would correct itself before a definite cure was effected.

However, during the 1970s, through preliminary findings at the University of Pennsylvania Veterinary School, there evolved a diagnosis for allergies that eliminated the need for skin sensitivity tests. It is called RAST, and is a radio-allergosobant test performed with a blood serum sample. It is not even necessary in all cases for the veterinarian to see the dog.

A cellulose disc laced with a suspected allergen is placed in the serum, and if the dog is allergic to that particular allergen, the serum will contain a specific antibody that adheres to the allergen on the disc. The disc is placed in a radioactively "labeled" antiserum that is attracted to that particular antibody. The antiserum binds with the antibody and can be detected with a radiation counter.

Furthermore, the scientists at the University of Pennsylvania also found that the RAST test has shown to be a more accurate diagnostic tool than skin testing because it measures the degree, and not merely the presence, of allergic reactions.

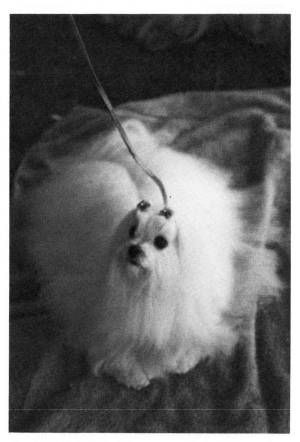

A magnificent profuse coat is displayed by American and Canadian Ch. Lin-Lee's Marquis, owned by Linda and Lee Coleman, Lin-Lee Maltese, Finleyville, Pennsylvania.

The first Easter for Darlin' was in 1982. Owned by Vera Rebbin, Sixpence Kennels, Aurora, Ohio.

DO ALL DOGS CHEW?

Chewing is the best possible method of cutting teeth and exercising gums. Every puppy goes through this teething process, and it can be destructive if the puppy uses shoes or table corners or rugs instead of the proper items. All dogs should have a Nylabone® available for chewing, not only to teethe on, but also for inducing growth of the permanent teeth, to assure normal jaw development, and to settle the permanent teeth solidly in the jaws. Chewing on a Nylabone® also has a cleaning effect and serves as a "massage" for the gums, keeping down the formation of tartar that erodes tooth enamel.

When you see a puppy pick up an object to chew, immediately remove it from his mouth with a sharp "No!" and replace the object with a Nylabone® Puppies take anything and everything into their mouths so they should be provided with several Nylabones to prevent damage to the household. This same Nylabone® eliminates the need for the kind of "bone" which may chip your dog's mouth or stomach or intestinal walls. Cooked bones, soft enough to be powdered and added to the food, are also permissible if you have the patience to prepare them, but Nylabone® serves all the purposes of bones for chewing that your dog may require, so why take a chance on meat bones?

Electrical cords and wires of any kind present a special danger that must be eliminated during puppyhood, and glass dishes that can be broken and played with are also hazardous.

The answer to the question about whether all dogs chew is an emphatic *yes*, and the answer is even more emphatic in the case of puppies.

SOME REASONS FOR CHEWING

Chewing can also be a form of frustration or nervousness. Dogs sometimes chew for spite if owners leave them alone too long or too often. Bitches will sometimes chew if their puppies are taken away from them too soon; insecure puppies often chew thinking they're nursing. Puppies that chew wool, blankets, carpet corners, or certain other types of materials may have a nutritional deficiency or something lacking in their diet. Perhaps the articles have been near something that tastes good and they have retained the odor of food.

The act of chewing has no connection with particular breeds or ages. So we repeat, it is up to you to be on guard at all times until the need —or habit—passes.

Puppies and young dogs need something with resistance to chew on while their teeth and jaws are developing—for cutting the puppy teeth, to induce growth of the permanent teeth under the puppy teeth, to assist in getting rid of the puppy teeth at the proper time, to help the permanent teeth through the gums, to assure normal jaw development, and to settle the permanent teeth solidly in the jaws. The adult dog's desire to chew stems from the instinct for tooth cleaning effect, gum massage, and jaw exercise—plus the need for an outlet for periodic doggie tensions. Unlike many other dog bones on the market today, Nylabone® does not splinter or fall apart; it will last indefinitely and as it is used it frills, becoming a doggie toothbrush that cleans teeth and massages gums.

237

Ch. Kathan's Cinderella Sunshine was sired by Ch. Su-Le's Bluebird ex Ch. Su-Le's Sun Bittern. "Cindi" is co-owned by Jerri Walters and breeder-handler Kathy DiGiacomo.

HIP DYSPLASIA

Hip dysplasia, or HD, is one of the most widely discussed of all animal afflictions, since it has appeared in varying degrees in just about every breed of dog. True, the larger breeds seem most susceptible, but it has hit the small breeds and is beginning to be recognized in cats as well.

While HD in man has been recorded as far back as 370 B.C., HD in dogs was more than likely referred to as rheumatism until veterinary research came into the picture. In 1935, Dr. Otto Schales, at Angell Memorial Hospital in Boston, wrote a paper on hip dysplasia and classified the four degrees of dysplasia of the hip joints as follows:

Grade 1—slight (poor fit between ball socket)
Grade 2—moderate (moderate but obvious shallowness of the socket)
Grade 3—severe (socket quite flat)
Grade 4—very severe (complete displacement of head of femur at early age)

HD is an incurable, hereditary, though not congenital disease of the hip sockets. It is transmitted as a dominant trait with irregular manifestations. Puppies appear normal at birth but the constant wearing away of the socket means the animal moves more and more on muscle, thereby presenting a lameness, a difficulty in getting up, and severe pain in advanced cases.

The degree of severity can be determined around six months of age, but its presence can be noticed from two months of age. The problem is determined by x-ray, and if pain is present it can be relieved temporarily by medication. Exercise should be avoided since motion encourages the wearing away of the bone surfaces.

Dogs with HD should not be shown or bred, if quality in the breed is to be maintained. It is essential to check a pedigree for dogs known to be dysplastic before breeding, since this disease can be dormant for many generations.

ELBOW DYSPLASIA

The same condition can also affect the elbow joints and is known as elbow dysplasia. This also causes lameness, and dogs so affected should not be used for breeding.

PATELLAR DYSPLASIA

Some of the smaller breeds of dogs suffer from patellar dysplasia, or dislocation of the knee. This can be treated surgically, but the surgery by no means abolishes the hereditary factor; therefore, these dogs should not be used for breeding.

All dogs—in any breed—should be x-rayed before being used for breeding. The x-ray should be read by a competent veterinarian, and the dog declared free and clear.

Japanese Best in Show winner A-S Gloria's Snow Gloria Dancer, bred and owned by Akira Shinohara of Osaka, Japan.

Ch. Su-Le's Mutton Bird, Winners Dog at the 1978 American Maltese Association Specialty held in Houston, Texas. Annette Lurton handled.

THE UNITED STATES REGISTRY

In the United States we have a central Hip Dysplasia Foundation, known as the OFA (Orthopedic Foundation for Animals). This HD control registry was formed in 1966. X-rays are sent to the Foundation for expert evaluation by qualified radiologists.

All you need do for complete information on getting an x-ray for your dog is to write to the Orthopedic Foundation for Animals at 817 Virginia Ave., Columbia, Missouri 65201, and request their dysplasia packet. There is no charge for this kit. It contains an envelope large enough to hold your x-ray film (which you will have taken by your own veterinarian), and a drawing showing how to position the dog properly for x-rays. There is also an application card for proper identification of the dog. Then, hopefully, your dog will be certified "normal." You will be given a registry number which you can put on his pedigree, use in your advertising, and rest assured that your breeding program is in good order.

All x-rays should be sent to the address above. Any other information you might wish to have may be requested from Mrs. Robert Bower, OFA, Route 1, Constantine, Missouri 49042.

We cannot urge strongly enough the importance of doing this. While it involves time and effort, the reward in the long run will more than pay for your trouble. To see the heartbreak of parents and children when their beloved dog has to be put to sleep because of severe hip dysplasia as the result of bad breeding is a sad experience. Don't let this happen to you or to those who will purchase your puppies!

Additionally, we should mention that there is a method of palpation to determine the extent of affliction. This can be painful if the animal is not properly prepared for the examination. There have also been attempts to replace the animal's femur and socket. This is not only expensive, but the percentage of success is small.

For those who refuse to put their dog down, there is a new surgical technique that can relieve pain but in no way constitutes a cure. This technique involves the severing of the pectinius muscle which for some unknown reason brings relief from pain over a period of many months—even up to two years. Two veterinary colleges in the United States are performing this operation at the present time. However, the owner must also give permission to "de-sex" the dogs at the time of the muscle severance.

HD PROGRAM IN GREAT BRITAIN

The British Veterinary Association (BVA) has made an attempt to control the spread of HD by appointing a panel of members of their profession who have made a special study of the disease to read x-rays. Dogs over one year of age may be x-rayed and certified as free. Forms are completed in triplicate to verify the tests. One copy remains with the panel, one copy is for the owner's veterinarian, and one for the owner. A record is also sent to the British Kennel Club for those wishing to check on a particular dog for breeding purposes.

GERIATRICS

If you originally purchased good healthy stock and cared for your dog throughout his life, there is no reason why you cannot expect your dog to live to a ripe old age. With research and the remarkable foods produced for dogs, especially in this past decade or so, his chances of longevity have increased considerably. If you have cared for him well, your dog will be a sheer delight in his old age, just as he was while in his prime.

Ch. Martin's Chanel-Cid, handled during her show ring career by Barbara Alderman for breeder-owner Marjorie Martin, Columbus, Ohio.

We can assume you have fed him properly if he is not too fat. If there has been no great illness, then you will find that very little additional care and attention are needed to keep him well. Exercise is still essential, as is proper food, booster shots, and tender loving care.

Even if a heart condition develops, there is still no reason to believe your dog cannot live to an old age. A diet may be necessary, along with medication and limited exercise, to keep the condition under control. In the case of deafness, or partial blindness, additional care must be taken to protect the dog, but neither infirmity will in any way shorten his life. Prolonged exposure to temperature variances; overeating; excessive exercise; lack of sleep; or being housed with younger, more active dogs, may take an unnecessary toll of the dog's energies and induce serious trouble. Good judgment, periodic veterinary checkups, and individual attention will keep your dog with you for many added years.

When discussing geriatrics, the question of when a dog becomes old or aged usually is asked. We have all heard the old saying that one year of a dog's life is equal to seven years in a human. This theory is strictly a matter of opinion, and must remain so, since so many outside factors enter into how quickly each individual dog "ages." Recently, a new chart was devised that is more realistically equivalent:

DOG	HUMAN
6 months	10 years
1 year	15 years
2 years	24 years
3 years	28 years
4 years	32 years
5 years	36 years
6 years	40 years
7 years	44 years
8 years	48 years
9 years	52 years
10 years	56 years
15 years	76 years
21 years	100 years

It must be remembered that such things as serious illnesses, poor food and housing, general neglect, and poor beginnings as puppies will take their toll of a dog's general health and age him more quickly than a dog that has led a normal, healthy life. Let your veterinarian help you determine an age bracket for your dog in his later years.

While good care should prolong your dog's life, there are several "old age" disorders to watch for no matter how well he may be doing. The tendency toward obesity is the most common, but constipation is another. Aging teeth and a slowing down of the digestive processes may hinder digestion and cause constipation, just as any major change in diet can bring on diarrhea. There is also the possibility of loss or impairment of hearing or eyesight which will also tend to make the dog wary and distrustful. Other behavioral changes may result as well, such as crankiness, loss of patience, and lack of interest; these are the most obvious changes. Other ailments may manifest themselves in the form of rheumatism, arthritis, tumors and warts, heart disease, kidney infections, male prostatism, and female disorders. Of course, all these require a veterinarian's checking the degree of seriousness and proper treatment.

DOG INSURANCE

Much has been said for and against canine insurance, and much more will be said before this kind of protection for a dog becomes universal and/or practical. There has been talk of establishing a Blue Cross-type plan similar to the one now existing for humans. However, the best insurance for your dog is *you*! Nothing compensates for tender, loving care. Like the insurance policies for humans, there will be a lot of fine print in the contracts revealing that the dog is not covered after all. These limited conditions usually make the acquisition of dog insurance expensive and virtually worthless.

Blanket coverage policies for kennels or establishments that board or groom dogs can be an advantage, especially in transporting dogs to and from their premises. For the one-dog owner, however, whose dog is a constant companion, the cost for limited coverage is not necessary.

IN THE EVENT OF YOUR DEATH

This is a morbid thought perhaps, but ask yourself the question, "If death were to strike at this moment, what would become of my dogs?"

Perhaps you are fortunate enough to have a relative, child, spouse, or friend who would take over immediately, if only on a temporary basis. Perhaps you have already left instructions in your last will and testament for your pet's housing, as well as a stipend for its care.

Provide definite instructions before a disaster occurs or your dogs are carted off to the pound to be destroyed, or stolen by commercially inclined neighbors with "resale" in mind. It is a simple thing to instruct your lawyer about your wishes in the event of sickness or death. Leave instructions as to feeding and care, posted on your kennel room or kitchen bulletin board, or wherever your kennel records are kept. Also, tell several people what you are doing and why. If you prefer to keep such instructions private, merely place them in sealed envelopes in a known place with directions that they are to be opened only in the event of your death.

KEEPING RECORDS

Whether you have one dog or a kennel full of them, it is wise to keep written records. It takes only a few moments to record dates of inoculations, trips to the vet, tests for worms, etc. It can avoid confusion or mistakes such as having your dog not covered by immunization if too much time elapses between shots because you have to guess at the date of the last shot.

In an emergency, these records may prove their value if your veterinarian cannot be reached and you have to call on another, or if you move and have no case history on your dog for the new veterinarian.

"Lover," is a little dog taken in by Vera Rebbin when the owner died. Vera decided to train the dog, in the woman's memory, at her Aurora Companion Dog Training School in Ohio.

Angela Dahl with Sir Romeo of Alegha, her 4-H club Maltese that won top honors at both county and state levels. Angela was with the 4-H dog club for ten years before enrolling at the University of Puget Sound in Washington.

CHAPTER FIFTEEN

Pursuing a Career in Dogs

Exercise pen outside the motor home of the Dil-Dal Kennels as they run the dog show circuit. Dil-Dal Kennels are owned by Rita Dahl of Keyport, Washington.

One of the biggest joys for those of us who love dogs is to see someone we know or someone in our family grow up in the fancy and go on to enjoy the sport of dogs in later life. Many dog lovers, in addition to leaving codicils in their wills, are providing in other ways for veterinary scholarships for deserving youngsters who wish to make their association with dogs their profession.

Unfortunately, many children who have this earnest desire are not always able to afford the expense of an education that will take them through veterinary school, and they are not eligible for scholarships. In the 1960s, during my tenure as editor of *Popular Dogs* magazine, I am happy to say I had something to do with the publicizing of college courses, whereby those who could not go all the way to a veterinary degree could earn an Animal Science degree and thus still serve the fancy in a significant way. The Animal Science courses cost less than half of what it would take to become a veterinarian, and those achieving these titles have become a tremendous assistance to the veterinarian.

We all have experienced the more and more crowded waiting rooms at the veterinary offices, and are aware of the demands on the doctor's time, not just for office hours, but for his research, consultation, surgery, and other expertise. The tremendous increase in the number of dogs and cats and other domestic animals, both in cities and the suburbs, has resulted in an almost overwhelming consumption of veterinarians' time.

Until recently, most veterinary assistance was made up of kennel men or women who were restricted to services more properly classified as office maintenance, rather than actual veterinary aid. Needless to say, their part in the operation of a veterinary office is both essential and appreciated, as are the endless details and volumes of paperwork capably handled by office secretaries and receptionists. However, still more of a veterinarian's duties could be handled by properly trained semi-professionals.

With exactly this additional service in mind, many colleges are now conducting two-year courses in animal science for the training of such para-professionals, thereby opening a new field for animal technologists. The time saved by the assistance of these trained technicians, who now relieve the veterinarians of the more mechanical chores and allow them additional time for diagnosing and general servicing of their clients, will be beneficial to all involved.

"Delhi Tech," the State University Agricultural and Technical College at Delhi, New York, was one of the first to offer the required courses for this degree. Now, many other institutions of learning are offering comparable courses at the college level. Entry requirements are usually that each applicant must be a graduate of an approved high school or have taken the State University admissions examination. In addition, each applicant for the Animal Science Technology program must have some previous credits in mathematics and science, with chemistry an important part of the science background.

243

"Two for the Show."—a limited edition of Kathy Blackard's artistry.

The program at Delhi was a new educational venture dedicated to the training of competent technicians for employment in the biochemical field, and has been generously supported by a five-year grant, designated as a "Pilot Development Program in Animal Science." This grant provided both personal and scientific equipment with obvious good results when it was done originally pursuant to a contract with the United States Department of Health, Education, and Welfare. Delhi is a unit of the State University of New York and is accredited by the Middle States Association of Colleges and Secondary Schools. The campus provides offices, laboratories, and animal quarters, and is equipped with modern instruments to train technicians in laboratory animal care, physiology, pathology, microbiology, anesthesia, X-ray, and germ-free techniques. Sizable animal colonies are maintained in air-conditioned quarters: animals housed include mice, rats, hamsters, guinea pigs, gerbils, and rabbits, as well as dogs and cats.

First-year students are given such courses as livestock production, dairy food science, general, organic and biological chemistry, mammalian anatomy, histology and physiology, pathogenic microbiology, and quantitative and instrumental analysis, to name a few. Second year students matriculate in general pathology, animal parasitology, animal care and anesthesia, introductory psychology, animal breeding, animal nutrition, hematology and urinalysis, radiology, genetics, food sanitation and meat inspection, histological techniques, animal laboratory practices, and axenic techniques. These, of course, may be supplemented by electives that prepare the student for contact with the public in the administration of these duties. Such recommended electives include public speaking, botany, animal reproduction, and other related subjects.

In addition to Delhi, one of the first to offer this program was the State University of Maine. Part of their program offered some practical training for the students at the Animal Medical Center in New York City. Often after this initial "in the field" experience, the students could perform professionally, immediately upon entering a veterinarian's employ, as personnel to do laboratory tests, x-rays, blood work, fecal examinations, and general animal care. After the courses at college, they were equipped to perform all of the following procedures as para-professionals:

* Recording of vital information relative to a case. This would include such information as the client's name, address, telephone number, and other facts pertinent to the visit. The case history would include the breed, age of animal, its sex, temperature, etc.

* Preparation of the animal for surgery.
* Preparation of equipment and medicaments to be used in surgery.
* Preparation of medicaments for dispensing to clients on prescription of the attending veterinarian.
* Administration and application of certain medicines.
* Administration of colonic irrigations.
* Application or changing of wound dressings.
* Cleaning of kennels, exercise runs, and kitchen utensils.
* Preparation of food and the feeding of patients.
* Explanation to clients on the handling and restraint of their pets, including needs for exercise, house training, and elementary obedience training.
* First-aid treatment for hemorrhage, including the proper use of tourniquets.
* Preservation of blood, urine, and pathologic material for the purpose of laboratory examination.
* General care and supervision of the hospital or clinic patients to insure their comfort. Nail trimming and grooming of patients.

Credits are necessary, of course, to qualify for this program. Many courses of study include biology, zoology, anatomy, genetics, and animal diseases, and along with the abovementioned courses, the fields of client and public relations are touched upon, as well as a general study of the veterinary medical profession.

By the mid-seventies there were a reported 30,000 veterinarians practicing in the United States. It is estimated that within the following decade more than twice that number will be needed to take proper care of the domestic animal population in this country. While veterinarians are graduated from twenty-two accredited veterinary colleges in this country and Canada, recent figures released by the Veterinary Medical Society inform us that only one out of every seven applicants is admitted to these colleges. It becomes more and more obvious that the para-professional person will be needed to back up the doctor.

Students having the desire and qualifications to become veterinarians, however, may suffer financial restrictions that preclude their education and licensing as full-fledged veterinarians. The Animal Science Technologist with an Associate degree in Applied Science may very well become the answer as a profession in an area close to their actual desire.

Their assistance in the pharmaceutical field, where drug concerns deal with laboratory animals, covers another wide area for trained assistants. The career opportunities are varied and reach into job opportunities in medical centers, research institutions, and government health agencies; at present, the demand for graduates far exceeds the current supply of trained personnel.

All dressed up and no place to go is Vera Rebbin's Maltese named Rebbeau.

245

As to financial remuneration, beginning yearly salaries are relatively low and estimated costs of basic college expenses relatively high, but the latter include tuition, room and board, college fees, essential textbooks, and limited personal expenses. These personal expenses, of course, will vary with individual students, as well as their other expenses, though the costs are about half of those involved in becoming a full-fledged veterinarian.

High school graduates with a sincere affection and regard for animals and a desire to work with veterinarians and perform such clinical duties as mentioned above will find they fit in especially well.

Those interested in pursuing a career of this nature might obtain the most current list of accredited colleges and universities offering these programs by consulting the American Veterinary Medical College, 600 S. Michigan Avenue, Chicago, Illinois 60605.

As the popularity of this profession increased, additional attention was given to the list of services, and the degrees to which one could aspire was expanded. There are para-professionals with Associate of Science degrees, and some colleges and universities have extended the courses to four years' duration which lead to Bachelor of Science degrees.

Ch. Kathan's Chantilly Lace, owned by Phyllis Schwartz and bred by Kathy DiGiacomo, was sired by Ch. Su-Le's Bluebird ex Angie Baby.

Joanne-Chen's Mini Maid Dancer is pictured cut down to show excellent conformation. This four pound four ounce bitch was the dam of Ch. March'en Martini Dancer, Ch. March'en Bali Dancer, Ch. March'en Ripple Dancer, and Canadian Ch. March'en Daiquiri Dancer.

At the University of Minnesota Technical College, a two year course offers a degree of Associate in Applied Science after the successful completion of 108 credit hours. This Animal Health Technology course prepares the students for future careers in the following fields:
* Laboratory Animal Technician (Junior)
* Experimental Animal Technician
* Clinical Laboratory Animal Assistant
* Laboratory Animal Assistant in Radiology
* Laboratory Animal Research Assistant
* Small Animal Technician (General)
* Small Animal Veterinarian's Assistant
* Small Animal Veterinarian's Receptionist
* Animal Hospital Technician
* Zoo Technician
* Large Animal Technician (General)
* Large Animal Veterinarian's Receptionist
* Large Animal Clinic Assistant
* Meat Animal Inspection Technician

PART-TIME KENNEL WORK
Youngsters who do not wish to go on to become veterinarians or animal technicians can get valuable experience and extra money by working part-time after school and on weekends, or full-time during summer vacations, in a veterinarian's office. The exposure to animals and office procedure will be time well spent.

Kennel help is also an area that is wide open for retired men and women. They are able to help out in many areas where they can learn and stay active, and most of the work allows them to set their own pace.

PROFESSIONAL HANDLING

For those who wish to participate in the sport of dogs and whose interests or abilities do not center around the clinical aspects of the fancy, there is yet another avenue of involvement.

For those who excel in the show ring, who enjoy being in the limelight and putting their dogs through their paces, a career in professional handling may be the answer. Handling may include a weekend of showing a few dogs for special clients, or it may be a full-time career that can also include boarding, training, conditioning, breeding, and showing dogs for several clients.

Depending on how deep is your interest, the issue can be solved by a lot of preliminary consideration before it becomes necessary to make a

Oak Ridge Ciara wins at a 1981 show with handler Sandy Tremont. Bred by Carol and Thomas Neth, her owner is Gail Hennessey, Chelsea Maltese, Wappingers Falls, New York.

Ch. Viceroy Kathan Honeycomb finishes for her championship with breeder-handler Kathy DiGiacomo. Co-breeder was Claudia Grunstra; owner is Laura Ford.

decision. The first move would be to have a long, serious talk with a successful professional handler to learn the pros and cons of such a profession. Watching handlers in action from ringside as they perform their duties can be revealing. A visit to their kennels for an on-the-spot revelation of the behind-the-scenes responsibilities is essential. Working for them full or part-time would be the best way of all to resolve any doubt you might have.

Professional handling is not all glamour in the show ring. There is plenty of "dirty work" behind the scenes twenty-four hours of every day. You must have the necessary ability and patience for this work, as well as the ability and patience to deal with the *clients*—the dog owners who value their animals above almost anything else and would expect a great deal from you in the way of care and handling.

247

Ch. Brown's Joni Dancer, bred and owned by Dr. Roger and Nancy Brown of Omaha, Nebraska.

DOG TRAINING

Like the professional handler, the professional dog trainer has a most responsible job. You need not only to be thoroughly familiar with the correct and successful methods of training a dog, but must also have the ability to communicate with dogs. True, it is very rewarding work, but training for the show ring, obedience, or guard dog work must be performed exactly right for successful results, and to maintain a good business reputation.

Training schools are quite the vogue nowadays, with all of them claiming success. Careful investigation should be made before enrolling a dog, and even more careful investigation should be made of their methods and of their actual successes before becoming associated with them.

GROOMING PARLORS

If you do not wish the twenty-four-hour a day job that is required by a professional handler or professional trainer, but still love working with and caring for dogs, there is always the very profitable grooming business. Poodles started the ball rolling for the swanky, plush grooming establishments that sprang up all over the major cities, many of which seem to be doing very well. Here again, handling dogs and the public well is necessary for a successful operation, in addition to skill in the actual grooming of dogs of all breeds.

While shops flourish in the cities, some of the suburban areas are now featuring mobile units which by appointment will visit your home with a completely equipped shop on wheels, and will groom your dog right in your own driveway.

American and Canadian Ch. Su-Le's Martin is owned by Barbara Bergquist of New Boston, Michigan.

Joanne-Chen's Gay Dancer, C.D., bred by Joanne Hesse and owned and handled by Tracy Brown. Gay Dancer won her title in just six months' time when nine years of age with her teenage owner.

THE PET SHOP

Part-time or full-time work in a pet shop can help you make up your mind rather quickly as to whether you would like to have a shop of your own. For those who love animals and are concerned with their care and feeding, the pet shop can be a profitable and satisfying association. Supplies that are available for sale in these shops are almost limitless, and a nice living can be garnered from pet supplies if the location and population of the city you choose warrant it.

DOG JUDGING

There are also those whose professions, age, or health prevent them from owning, breeding, or showing dogs, and who turn to judging at dog shows after their active years in the show ring are no longer possible. Breeder-judges make a valuable contribution to the fancy by judging in accordance with their years of experience in the fancy, and the assignments are enjoyable. Judging requires experience, a good eye for dogs, and an appreciation of a good animal.

Ch. Su-Le's Jonina, Best in Show winner, with handler A. Lurton. Owned by Barbara Bergquist of New Boston, Michigan.

Ch. Joanne-Chen's Sheeta Dancer pictured winning under judge Byron Elder with owner-handler Mrs. Roger Brown of Omaha, Nebraska.

Ch. Brown's Saci Dancer, bred by Dr. and Mrs. Roger Brown and owned and handled by Mrs. Don Derhammer to this win under the late judge Joseph Faigel.

Ch. Fantasyland Dream Baby, pictured winning Best of Winners and Best of Opposite Sex under judge Len Carey. Dream Baby is co-owned by Candace Mathes and breeder-handler Carole M. Baldwin.

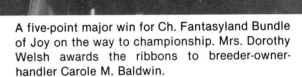
A five-point major win for Ch. Fantasyland Bundle of Joy on the way to championship. Mrs. Dorothy Welsh awards the ribbons to breeder-owner-handler Carole M. Baldwin.

Ch. Fantasyland Fame D Cedarwood is shown winning Best of Breed from the classes, over Specials, for a four-point major under judge Joseph Gregory. Bred and handled by Carole M. Baldwin, Fame is owned by Grace Varga.

Ch. Fantasyland Fresh As A Daisy winning the Best of Breed award from the classes over Specials under judge Langdon Skarda at the Golden Gate Kennel Club. Breeder-owner-handler Carole M. Baldwin, Novato, California.

251

Future champion Fantasyland Richelieu Charm, was bred, owned, and photographed by Carole M. Baldwin, Novato, California.

One of the beautiful little Maltese at the home of Dr. and Mrs. Roger Brown, Omaha, Nebraska.

Ch. Fantasyland Cedarwood D Brat seemed to be expressing an opinion when photographed by owner-breeder Carole M. Baldwin.

Ch. Maree's Tu-Grand Kandi-Kane, a male Maltese owned by Nancy H. Shapland, was winner of eleven all-breed Bests in Show. Kandi is also winner of 47 Group Firsts and was a Quaker Oats Award recipient.

These three Villa Malta champions are owned by Joy and Ed Woodard, Gresham, Oregon.

(Above) Ch. March'en Lady Bug Dancer, bred and owned by Marcia Hostetler of Des Moines, Iowa. (Below) Ch. March'en Love Bug Dancer in a photograph taken by Olan Mills for owner Marcia Hostetler.

Ch. Bar None Buckaneer, one of Michele Perlmutter's favorite show dogs, after 22 years in the breed. Her Bar None Kennels are located in Ghent, New York.

(Above) "Houdini," more formally known as Ch. Su-Le's Great Egret, and (below) Ch. Su-Le's Nightengale. Both are owned by Mrs. Barbara Bergquist of the Su-Le Kennels in New Boston, Michigan.

(Above) Japanese Ch. A-S Gloria's Snow Mars Dancer, owned by Akira Shinohara, and (below) Japanese Ch. A-S Gloria's Snow Electa Dancer, owned by Umeko Yamaga.

American Ch. Joanne-Chen's Sweet He Dancer, famous show dog exported from the United States to Japan for owner Akira Shinohara of Osaka, Japan.

Best in Show winner Ch. Joanne-Chen's Maja Dancer, owned and handled by Jo Ann Dinsmore of Arlington Heights, Illinois.

American and Canadian Ch. Joanne-Chen's Wakham Dancer, pictured in full coat at thirteen months of age, was bred by Marcia Hostetler and is co-owned by her and Randy Gemmill.

American and Canadian Ch. Four Halls Dancing Master and American and Canadian Ch. Four Halls Dancing Mistress, the first homebreds at Glenna Fierheller's kennel in Vancouver, British Columbia.

Ch. Aennchen's Stela Dancer, bred and owned by Nicholas Cutillo of New York City.

(Above) Carabelle First Edition, pictured at thirteen months of age, and (below) the Australian import and New Zealand Ch. Whiteglory Dreamtime. Both are owned by the Carabelle Kennels in New Zealand.

Ch. Villa Malta's Jeronamoe is owned by Marge Rozik who now has the Villa Malta Kennels, Belle Vernon, Pennsylvania.

One of the first ladies of the obedience world, Mary Lee Whiting, was honored with the first Gaines Fido award in obedience. The statuette was presented by A. Steve Willett, Director of Gaines Professional Services, before a crowd of hundreds of obedience people at the banquet marking the Gaines Obedience Classic, November 1980, in Denver, Colorado. The inscription cites Mary Lee for "outstanding contributions to the advancement of obedience training and competition." She is also an American Kennel Club approved judge for all obedience classes and was a member of the A.K.C. Obedience Advisory Committee. She is owner and trainer at her Canine College in Minneapolis.

CHAPTER SIXTEEN

The Maltese in Obedience

Martin's Plico Puff, U.D., poses with her dumbbell during an obedience trial with owner-trainer Mary R. Mills of Jacksonville, Florida. Puff earned her title in 1978.

Dog shows and conformation classes had a big head start on obedience. It was not until 1933 that the first obedience tests were held. Mrs. Helene Whitehouse Walker inaugurated these initial all-breed obedience tests that she brought from England. Obedience training and tests for dogs were an immediate success from the moment those first 150 spectators saw the dogs go through their paces. Mrs. Walker and Blanche Saunders, her kennelmaid at that time, were responsible for the staging of the first four obedience tests held in the United States.

Mrs. Walker also was instrumental in getting the American Kennel Club to recognize and even sponsor obedience trials at shows, and her discussions with Charles T. Inglee (then the vice president of the A.K.C.) ultimately led to their acceptance. In 1935 she wrote the first published booklet on the subject—called simply "Obedience Tests." These tests were eventually incorporated into the rules of the A.K.C. obedience requirements in March of 1936. It later developed into a 22-page booklet that served as a manual for judges, handlers, and the show-giving clubs. The larger version was called "Regulations and Standards for Obedience Test Field Trials."

Mrs. Walker, Josef Weber (another well-known dog trainer), and Miss Saunders added certain refinements and basic procedures and exercises, and these were published in the April 1936 issue of the *American Kennel Gazette*.

THE FIRST A.K.C. OBEDIENCE TRIAL

On June 13 of that same year, the North Westchester Kennel Club held the first American Kennel Club licensed obedience test in conjunction with their all-breed show. There were twelve entries for judge Mrs. Wheeler H. Page. The exercises for Novice and Open classes remain virtually unchanged today, half a century later. Only Tracking Dog, Tracking Dog Excellent and championships have been added in the intervening years.

By June of 1939 the A.K.C. realized that obedience was here to stay and saw the need for an advisory committee. One was established and chaired by Donald Fordyce with enthusiastic members from all parts of the country willing to serve on it. George Foley of Pennsylvania was on the board. He was one of the most important of all men in the fancy, being superintendent of most of the dog shows on the Eastern seaboard. Mrs. Radcliff Farley, also of Pennsylvania, was on the committee with Miss Aurelia Tremaine of Massachusetts, Mrs. Bryant Godsell of California, Mrs. W. L. McCannon of Massachusetts, Samuel Blick of Maryland, and Frank Grant of Ohio—as well as Mrs. Walker and Josef Weber.

A little of the emphasis on dog obedience was diverted with the outbreak of World War II, when talk switched to the topic of having dogs serve in defense of their country. As soon as peace was declared, however, interest in obedience reached new heights.

Ch. Gulfstream Treasure, U.D., wins another first place in Utility Class—this one in 1976 under judge Lucy Neeb. Owner-trainer is Mary Lou Porlick of Miami, Florida.

In 1946, the American Kennel Club called for another obedience advisory committee, this time headed by John C. Neff. The committee included Blanche Saunders, Clarence Pfaffenberger, Theodore Kapnek, L. Wilson Davis, Howard P. Claussen, Elliot Blackiston, Oscar Franzen, and Clyde Henderson. Under their leadership, the regulations were even more standardized than before, and there was the addition of requirements for the Tracking Dog title.

GROWTH OF OBEDIENCE

In 1971 an obedience department was established at the American Kennel Club offices to keep pace with the growth of the sport and for constant review and guidance of show-giving clubs. Judge Richard H. D'Ambrisi was the director until his untimely death in 1973, at which time his duties were assumed by James E. Dearinger along with his two special consultants, L. Wilson Davis for tracking and Reverend Thomas O'Connor for handicapped handlers.

The members of this 1973 committee were Thomas Knott of Maryland, Edward Anderson of Pennsylvania, Jack Ward of Virginia, Lucy Neeb of Louisiana, William Phillips of California, James Falkner of Texas, Mary Lee Whiting of Minnesota, and Robert Self of Illinois (co-publisher of the important *Front and Finish* obedience newspaper).

While the committee functions continuously, meetings of the board are tentatively held every other year—unless a specific function or obedience question comes up, in which case a special meeting is called.

During the 1975 session, the committee held discussions on several old and new aspects of the obedience world. In addition to their own ever-increasing responsibilities to the fancy, they discussed seminars and educational symposiums, the licensing of tracking clubs, a booklet with suggested guidelines for obedience judges, Schutzhund training, and the aspects of a Utility Excellent Class degree.

Through the efforts of succeeding advisory committee members, the future of the sport has been assured, as well as continuing emphasis on the working abilities for which dogs were originally bred. Obedience work also provides the opportunity for novices to train and handle their dogs in an atmosphere that offers maximum pleasure and accomplishment at minimum expense, which is precisely what Mrs. Walker had intended.

When the advisory committee met in December 1980, many familiar names were among those listed as attending and continuing to serve the obedience exhibitors. James E. Dearinger, James Falkner, Rev. Thomas O'Connor, Robert Self, John Ward, Howard Cross, Helen Phillips, Samuel Kodis, George S. Pugh, Thomas Knott, and Mrs. Esme Treen were present and accounted for.

As we look back on a half a century of obedience trials, we can only surmise that the pioneers—Mrs. Helene Whitehouse Walker and Blanche Saunders—would be proud of the progress made in the obedience rings.

THE OBEDIENCE RATING SYSTEMS

Just as the Phillips System mushroomed out of the world of show dogs, it was almost inevitable that a "system" or "systems" to measure successes of obedience dogs would become a reality.

By 1974, Nancy Shuman and Lynn Frosch had established the "Shuman System" of recording the top ten all-breed obedience dogs in the country. They also listed the top four in every breed if each dog had accumulated a total of 50 points or more according to their requirements. Points were accrued based on qualifying scores of 170 and up.

These three Tracking Maltese are Dazzlyn Sir Frost, U.D.T., Canadian C.D.X., T.D.; Joy's Mr. Feather, American and Canadian U.D.T.X.; and Joy's Mr. Puff of Eng, T.D. Photographed after a session in the obedience ring the day Feather finished for his American T.D.X. in Michigan. Photo courtesy of Betty Drobac.

No Maltese qualified for All-Breed Top Ten or Toy Breed Top Ten. However, four Maltese did qualify in the breed ratings. First was Cee Gee's Wee Willie Winkle, U.D., owned by K. M. Froemming. Second was Belle Towers Caballero, C.D.X., owned by K. B. Morgan and R. R. Forcier. Third was Primrose Chip O Dillon, C.D.X., owned by M. Folley; and fourth was E. J. Bennett's McIverns Buttons.

OBEDIENCE WINNERS

Front and Finish published the list of Top Ten Obedience Dogs, as compiled by Kent Delaney. Under his system, dogs are rated in a manner different from the Shuman System.

In the Delaney System, points are awarded for High in Trial or for class placements only, based on results published in the *American Kennel Gazette*. High in Trial winners get a single point for each dog in competition. First place in the class earns a point for each dog competing in that class. Second place in the class earns a point for each dog in the class less one. Third dog place in the class earns a point less two, and fourth place earns a point for each dog less three.

1975

In 1975 no Maltese placed in the all-breed Top Ten or in the Toy Group Top Ten. But there was a full measure of ten Maltese in the breed finals.

First was Caijes Razzle Dazzle Darling, owned by J. and C. Pressman; second was Lizaras Promises Promises, owned by E. Walker; third was Misty Marion, C.D., owned by B. and F. Johnson; fourth was Alexus Van Rensselaer, owned by Mr. and Mrs. J. Van Collins; fifth was L. and R. Roach's R and B's Kriss Kringle; sixth was their R and B's Little Sonny Boy, C.D.; and seventh was Diamond Jim, owned by C. Lepetit. Eight was the previous year's first place winner under the Shuman System, K. Froemmings' Wee Willie Winkle, U.D.; ninth was Martin's Plico Puff, owned by Mrs. M. Mills; and tenth was C. Kollander's Joys Mr. Feather.

Martin's Plico Puff, U.D., goes over the jump during an obedience exercise at a 1978 trial. Owned and trained by Mary R. Mills, Jacksonville, Florida.

Mary Lou Porlick's Ch. Gulfstream Treasure, U.D., flies over a utility bar jump.

1976

Eight breed winners came through in the Delaney System this year. In first place was Liberated Lady Love, owned by L. Smith. Following that leader were, in order: Sun Canyon Bojangles Cobi, owned by Mr. and Mrs. G. Nagasawa; G. Latigo's Joanne-Chen's Apollo Dancer, C.D.; R and B's Kriss Kringle, owned by L. and R. Roach; Ch. Gulfstream Treasure, C.D.X., owned by M. Porlick; Ch. Akinbaks Thunder Clooud, C.D., owned by G. Rankin; the Roach's R and B's Little Sonny Boy; and Macho Mio, C.D.X., owned by L. McCarty.

In the Shuman System for 1976, there were four finalists in breed competition. Robert and LaVonne Roach's R and B's Little Sonny Boy and Kriss Kringle were Number One and Number Two respectively, and it was noted that they both also had earned their Canadian C.D. titles. Number Three and Number Four became a tie between Ch. Akinbaks Thunder Cloud, owned by G. Rankin, and L. M. McCarty's Macho Mio, U.D.

1977

There was a repeat of the Shuman System rankings for the Roach's dogs, except this time it was Kriss Kringle's turn to take the Number One position with Sonny Boy designated as Number Two. Third place went to C. Kollander's Joys Mr. Feather, and there was a tie for

fourth place between Dazzlyn Sir Frost, owned by E. W. Droback, and Wya Constant Joy O Yap Yap, owned by M. and E. Wyckoff.

1978

The winners for 1978 under the Delaney System were a full ten in number—and with the exception of two of the dogs, all were new to the finals. First place went to J. Lewis's Nat and Joans Sugar Cookie. Second was Ginger Jake, C.D., owned by F. Maciejewski; third was Julies Ruffian, owned by A. Bissonnette; and fourth was Jules Foolish Pleasure, C.D., owned by K. Jones. Number Five was a tie between K. Froemming's Cee Gees Wee Willie Winkle, U.D., and the Mills' Martin's Plico Puff. The Number Seven spot was also a tie between Ch. Gulfstream Treasure, C.D.X., and Jerell's Easy Temptation, owned by L. Grantham. Number Nine was the Roach's R and B's Kriss Kringle, C.D.X.; and Number Ten was Bennetts Salty Peanut, C.D., owned by E. Bennett.

The Roachs' R and B's Kriss Kringle made it to the Number One spot again in the Shuman System for 1978. The Number Two spot went to M. L. Porlick's Ch. Gulfstream Gen of C and M; Number Three was C. Kollander's Joys Mr. Feather, U.D.T., and there was a tie for Number Four between J. Lewis' Nat and Joans Sugar Cookie and E. Bennett's Bennetts Salty Peanut.

Three beautiful obedience Maltese owned by LaVonne Roach of Omaha, Nebraska. Sonny, Bounce, and Kriss are seen in this lovely portrait.

1979

The Delaney System Top Ten this year actually was a Top Twelve, since three dogs tied for the Number Ten position. Number One was Isbells Scoot A Round, owned by K. and S. Isbell; Number Two was R and B's Little Sonny, C.D.X., and Number Three was V. Taylor's Bonny Prince Charley. Numbers Four through Nine went to Millicent Ann McMillan, owned by S. McMillan; Clarween Serena of Joga, owned by Mrs. G. Hall; Ch. Joanne-Chen's Apollo Dancer, C.D.X., owned by G. Latigo; F. Maciejewski's Ch. Ginger Jake, C.D.X.; T. William's Kamios English Muffin, C.D.; and D. Utterback's Diamond Tiki of Mar Jos. The three tying for Number Ten were D. Darrow's Fantasyland He Sno Bug, S. Gill's Gills Pappuccion of Julars, and J. Lewis's Nat and Joans Sugar Cookie, C.D.

The 1979 Shuman System featured all repeaters from previous years. Number One was R and B's Little Sonny Boy, U.D.; Number Two was Ginger Jake; Number Three was Nat and Joans Sugar Cookie; and Number Four was Ch. Joanne-Chen's Apollo Dancer. This was the year that Sonny Boy made his U.D. title.

1980

By the 1980s there were still no Maltese which made it into the All-Breed Top Ten or the Top Ten Toy Group. We had nine in the breed finals, however, with the Number One spot going to F. Maciejewski's Ch. Ginger Jake, C.D.X.

A new name became Number Two in N. Jones' Tibit Tabau Beaser. Number Three was J. Richmond's Beau Garcon; Number Four was the Bissonettes' Julies Ruffian, C.D.X.; and Number Five was L. Ostermeyer's Max Million Snowcloud. It was a tie for Number Six between D. Utterback's Diamond Tiki of Mar Jos and S. Hunter's Kims Delight. Number Eight was P. Knight's Marshall Mac Cloud. There was another tie for the final two positions with S. Gill's Gills Pappuccino of Julars and Mrs. H. Thies's Ch. Rustwick Dorbets Dream.

THE DECADE OF THE NINETEEN EIGHTIES

By the eighties, it was obvious that many of our little Maltese were going to continue in obedience rings and that more titles and competitions were going to be made available for them. To keep current on today's leaders, refer to the Maltese obedience scores published in *Yorkie Tales* magazine.

Brown's Dandi Sno Dancer, C.D.X., one of the leading obedience dogs in the breed, is owned by Dennis and Pam Brown of Lincoln, Nebraska.

BREED OBEDIENCE ACHIEVEMENTS

During the decade from 1972 to 1982, several Maltese distinguished themselves by earning obedience titles that very few years before might have been considered out of the reach of our little dogs. Following is a year-by-year listing which includes the number of Maltese that competed for obedience titles and the number of obedience titles awarded. Thanks to Pamela Brown of Lincoln, Nebraska, we have the final statistics from 1972 through 1982, and it is an impressive list indeed.

Year	Number of Maltese	Titles Earned
1972	20	9 CD, 1 CDX
1973	18	10 CD, 2 CDX
1974	23	16 CD, 2 CDX, 1 UD, 1 TD
1975	24	11 CD, 7 CDX, 1 TD
1976	25	13 CD, 3 CDX, 2 UD, 1 Can. TDX
1977	32	14 CD, 2 CDX, 2 UD
1978	24	4 CD, 7 CDX, 2 UD
1979	29	11 CD, 3 CDX, 1 UD, 1 TD
1980	26	11 CD, 1 CDX, 2 UD, 1 Can. CD
1981	31	13 CD, 6 CDX, 4 UD
1982	22	12 CD, 4 CDX, 1 UD

MALTESE OBEDIENCE FIRSTS

While records are made to be broken, it is always interesting to be able to look back on the successes achieved by those dogs that went down in breed history as accomplishing "famous firsts." We are happy to report that several Maltese dogs fit into this category and we pay tribute to them here.

Accomplishment	Dog's Name	Owner
1st C.D.X.	Ch. Tristan of Villa Malta	
1st U.D.	Luce's Miss Lucy of Villa Malta	B. Carlquist
2nd U.D.	Muff of Buckeye Circle	Ida Marsland
3rd U.D.	Whispering Pines Sweet Jill	Inez Funk
4th U.D.	Caress of Winddrift	B. Carlquist
1st Ch. U.D.	Ch. Gulfstream Treasure	Mary Porlick
1st T.D.	Joy's Mr. Feather	C. Kollander
2nd T.D.	Dazzlyn Sir Frost	E. Drobac
1st U.D.T.	Joy's Mr. Feather	C. Kollander
1st High in Trial	Muff of Buckeye Circle, U.D.	
2nd High in Trial	Caje's Razzle Dazzle Darling	C. Pressman
Most titles	Joy's Mr. Feather, Am. U.D.T., Can. C.D.X., T.D.X.	

Betty Drobac's many-titled obedience dog, Dazzlyn Sir Frost, U.D.T. and Canadian C.D.X., T.D. Frostie was thirteen years old in 1983 and still in good health. Portrait by Olan Mills.

BREED CHAMPIONS WITH OBEDIENCE TITLES

Following is an alphabetical listing of the Maltese that earned obedience titles in addition to championships garnered in the show ring. It is likely that additional Maltese have received such dual awards after the date of this writing.

Ch. Aennchen's Good Time Electa, C.D.
Ch. Akinbak's Thunder Cloud, C.D.X.
Ch. Al-Dor Randy, C.D.
Ch. Bacco of Villa Malta, C.D.
Ch. Cari Joanne-Chen's White Radar, C.D.
Ch. Cozy Vista Springtime, C.D.
Ch. The Feather King, C.D.
Ch. Folklore True Blue Lou, C.D.
Ch. Gigi, C.D.X.
Ch. Ginger Jake, U.D.
Ch. Good Time Princess Chila, C.D.
Ch. Gulfstream Chalk One Up, C.D.
Ch. Gulfstream Dream, C.D.
Ch. Gulfstream Gem of C & M, C.D.X.
Ch. Gulfstream Treasure, U.D.
Ch. Jerell's Daisy Mae of Al Mar, C.D.X.
Ch. Jerell's Quite a Charmer, C.D.
Ch. Joanne-Chen's Apollo Dancer, C.D.X.
Ch. Moppet Dominique, C.D.
Ch. Moppet Starshine, C.D.
Ch. Rustwick Dorbets Dream, C.D.
Ch. Schapio of Villa Malta, C.D.
Ch. Shabudi of Kismet, C.D.
Ch. Sir Soni Rava Reveille, C.D.
Ch. Sonny Morning Reveille, C.D.
Ch. Tristan of Villa Malta, C.D.X.
Ch. Valettas Princess Norma, C.D.
Ch. Whispers Jana, C.D.

Ch. Gulfstream Dream, C.D., performing the figure 8 in Novice B class. Owned and trained by Mary Lou Porlick, one of the staunchest of Maltese obedience trainers.

Ch. Gulfstream Treasure, U.D., retrieving over the high jump. Owned and trained by Mary Lou Porlick of Miami, Florida.

THE DOG OBEDIENCE CLASSICS

In March 1976 the Gaines Dog Research Center, located in White Plains, New York, began its sponsorship of the United States Dog Obedience Classic. Originally founded by the Illini Obedience Association in 1975, the first classic was held in Chicago.

Gaines' motive in the support of regional events and the Classic was to emphasize to dog owners, both present and future, the belief that an obedience-trained dog is a better citizen and an asset to any community. Their support was to offer rosettes, trophies, and plaques, as well as prize money for a series of regional competitions and for the Classic at the year's end. Prize money for the regional awards was almost $3000, while the Classic prize money was in excess of $5000. Each year the Classic is held in another region, where a local obedience club plays host to participants from all over the country.

By 1978, when the two-day Classic was held in Los Angeles at the Sports Arena, people from 23 states exhibited with an entry well over the 180-dog limit with dogs going through their paces in eight rings. The top winner earns the title of Super Dog and, along with other prizes and money, takes home the sterling silver dumbbell trophy.

The Gaines Dog Obedience Classic competition is open to all breeds and welcomes owners who qualify and enjoy the challenge of teamwork with their dogs.

THE GAINES DOG OBEDIENCE "FIDO"

In 1980 Gaines began yet another award of recognition in the dog fancy. They started to award a yearly "Fido" statue for outstanding achievement in the dog obedience field. Their first "Fido" was presented on November 22, 1980, at Denver, Colorado. It went to Mary Lee Whiting of Minneapolis, Minnesota.

"Marley" is an A.K.C. judge for all obedience classes and a member of the A.K.C. obedience advisory committee. She trains more than 250 dogs a week at her Canine College in Minneapolis and is a Cocker Spaniel breeder. She has also authored a book, *From Cradle to College—Raising Your Puppy.*

OTHER OBEDIENCE ACTIVITIES

For those interested in all aspects of the obedience sport, there are even more activities connected with dog training. To name just a few, there are Scent Dog Seminars, Hurdle Races, World Series of Dog Obedience in Canada, and the Association of Obedience Clubs and Judges. The best possible way to keep informed of activities on both national and local levels is by membership in kennel or obedience clubs. Also highly recommended is the reading of dog magazines and newspapers published by obedience enthusiasts.

Front and Finish, the dog trainer's newspaper, is perhaps the leading publication of the Delaney System. Current subscription rates can be obtained by writing to H. and S. Publications, Inc., 113 S. Arthur Avenue, Galesburg, Illinois 61401. A. J. Harler and Robert T. Self are co-editors of this most worthy and informative publication.

LATEST OBEDIENCE RULES AND REGULATIONS

The American Kennel Club publishes an Obedience Regulations booklet and offers it free of charge when single copies are requested. A modest price per copy is required if ordering in quantities for clubs and organizations.

UNDERSTANDING AN OBEDIENCE TRIAL

For those just getting into obedience work with their dogs, it is suggested that they obtain and read a booklet entitled "How to Understand and Enjoy an Obedience Trial," available free of charge from the Ralston Purina Company, Checkerboard Square, St. Louis, Missouri 63188.

TRAINING YOUR DOG

While the American Kennel Club will gladly send along booklets that include rules and regulations for competition at shows, you must be prepared to start "basic training" with your dog long before you start thinking about actually entering any obedience trials. There are few things in the world a dog would rather do than to please his master; therefore, obedience training—even the learning of his name—will be a pleasure for your dog. If taught correctly, it will certainly make him a much nicer animal for you to live with the rest of his life.

One of Sharon Roberts' Maltese puppies learns obedience training at a very early eage.

EARLY TRAINING AT HOME

Some breeders believe in starting a dog's training as early as two weeks of age. Repeating the puppy's name and encouraging the puppy to come when called is a good start—if you don't expect too much too soon. They also recommend placing a narrow ribbon around the puppy's neck to get him used to the feel of what will later be a leash. The puppy can play with it and learn the feel of the pull on his neck before he is actually expected to respond to it.

If you intend to show your puppy, there are other formalities you can observe as early as four weeks of age that will also minimize efforts when you start "real" training. One of the most important points is setting him up on a table in show stance. Make the training session short and sweet; make it a sort of game, but repeatedly place the puppy in a show stance and hold him that way, gently, meanwhile giving him lavish praise. After a couple of weeks of doing this a few times each day, you will find that your puppy takes to the idea of the "stand" and "stay" commands very readily.

The stand for examination at Vera Rebbin's Aurora Companion Dog Training School in Ohio.

WHEN TO START FORMAL TRAINING

Under normal conditions, official training should not start until the puppy is about six months of age. Most obedience trainers will not take puppies in their classes much before this age. As the puppy grows along the way, however, you should certainly get him used to his name, coming when he is called, and understanding the meanings of words like "no" and other basic commands. Repetition, patience, and "rewards" are the keys to success, since most dogs are not ready for a wide range of words in their rather limited attention span. If your dog is to be a show dog, it would be wise not to forget to concentrate on the "stand" and "stay" commands and to eliminate the "sit" command. You do not want a show dog to sit down in the ring!

THE REWARD METHOD

The only acceptable kind of training is the kindness and reward method which will build a strong bond between dog and master. Try to establish respect and attention, not a fear of punishment. Give each command, preceded by the dog's name, and make it "stick." Do not move on to another command or lesson until the first one is mastered. Train where there are no distractions at first, and never when the dog is tired, right after eating, or for too long a period of time. When his interest wanes, quit until another session later in the day. Two or three sessions a day with a bright dog, increasing the time from, say, five minutes to fifteen minutes might be just about right in the beginning. Each dog is different, and you must therefore set your own schedule according to your dog's ability.

WHAT YOU NEED TO START TRAINING

The soft nylon show leads available at all pet stores are best for early training. Later, perhaps, a choke chain can be used. Let the puppy play with the lead or even carry it around when you first put it on him. Too much pressure pulling at the end of it is likely to get him off to a bad start.

FORMAL SCHOOL TRAINING

The advertising pages of your telephone book may lead you to dog training schools or classes for official training, and you might best start making inquiries when the puppy is about four months of age. Then you will be ready for the start of the next training cycle. If you intend to show your dog, training will make him easier to handle in the show ring as well.

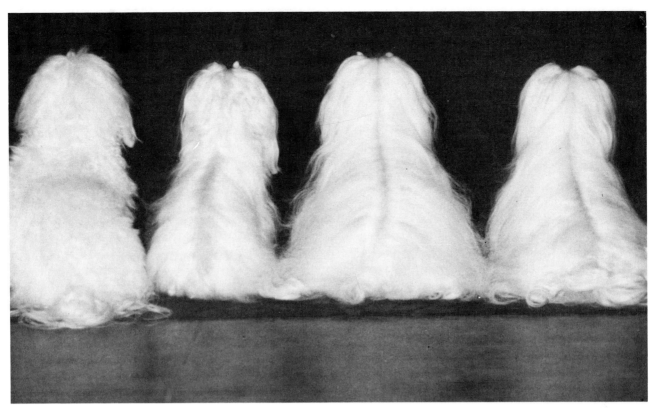

The long sit in one of Vera Rebbin's dog training classes in Aurora, Ohio.

OBEDIENCE DEGREES

There are several obedience titles recognized by the American Kennel Club that dogs may earn through a process of completed exercises in Novice, Open, and Utility classes, with 200 points representing a perfect score. After a dog has competed in Novice Class and has qualified with a score of at least 170 points or better three times, he has earned the right to have included the letters C.D. (for Companion Dog) after his name and is eligible to compete in Open Class competition to earn a Companion Dog Excellent degree, or C.D.X. title. Then, after qualifying in three shows for the Utility Dog degree, he may earn the right to use U.D. after his name. There are also Tracking Dog (T.D.) and Tracking Dog Excellent (T.D.X.) titles that may be earned.

OBEDIENCE TRIAL CHAMPIONSHIP TITLES

The Board of Directors of the American Kennel Club approved obedience trial championship titles in July 1977. Points for these titles are recorded only for those dogs that have earned the U.D. title. Any dog that has been awarded the title of Obedience Trial Champion may continue to compete. Dogs that complete require-

ments receive an Obedience Trial Championship Certificate from the American Kennel Club and are permitted the use of the letters "O.T. Ch." preceding their name.

There is great satisfaction for both owner and dog in working for these titles, and when considering such training for your little Maltese, you would do well to recall St. Mathilde's Prayer:

O, God,
Give unto me by grace
that obedience which thou hast
given to my little dog
by nature.

There are few things more beautiful to look at than a sparkling white Maltese floating around the show ring or diligently going through his paces to earn an obedience title.

HIGH OBEDIENCE TITLISTS

Pamela Brown for many years has been keeping records of our Maltese titlists and recording their progress. It is through her efforts and those of Mary Lou Porlick that we are able to pay tribute to our top obedience dogs in this chapter, and to tell you a little more about them than would appear on a list.

THE FIRST C.D.X. MALTESE

The first C.D.X. Maltese was Ch. Tristan of Villa Malta, owned by Blanche Carlquest (who, incidentally, also owned the fourth U.D. Maltese of record). It should be noted here that U.D. requirements were quite different in the early 1970s when Tristan made Maltese history by earning this title. Toys were virtually unable to earn the U.D. title, or perhaps he would have earned that title also.

The second Maltese to earn a C.D.X. title was Ch. Gulfstream Treasure, and this was accomplished in 1973. More complete records began to be kept for the breed around 1977, and in January of that year Ch. Joanne-Chen's Apollo Dancer became the third C.D.X. titlist. In October of 1977 Ch. Jerell's Daisy Mae of Al Mar was a C.D.X. In April and October of 1978 Ch. Gulfstream Gen of C & M and Ch. Ginger Jake had earned their titles.

Anna Mae Hardy, president of the American Maltese Association in 1977 appointed Pam Brown and Mary Lou Porlick as national obedience chairpersons for the organization, and information began to be recorded. Not very many Maltese owners were active—or even interested—in obedience in those days, so things were off to a slow start. It was only when Merrill Cohen judged both obedience and conformation at the Specialty in San Francisco that interest grew and now progress is being made, though as of this writing there are no Maltese Obedience Trial Champions—as yet! We have no doubt that there will be in the very near future.

We wish there were complete records of *all* C.D.X. and U.D. Maltese, but perhaps some of the earliest have been missed. As of now, we owe special congratulations to the following winners.

Breed Champions with C.D.X. Titles

Ch. Tristan of Villa Malta	Year unknown
Ch. Gulfstream Treasure	1973
Ch. Joanne-Chen's Apollo Dancer	1977
Ch. Jerell's Daisy Mae of Al Mar	1977
Ch. Gulfstream Gem of C & M	1978
Ch. Ginger Jake	1978

Breed Champions with U.D. Titles

Ch. Gulfstream Treasure	1977
Ch. Ginger Jake	1980

Ch. Gulfstream Treasure, U.D., and friend Lucy at the end of their workout in the obedience ring. The owner is Mary Lou Porlick, Miami, Florida.

Waiting for her turn in the obedience ring is "Lucy," owner-trained by Mary Lou Porlick.

C.D.X. MALTESE

Since 1977, when records began to be kept, the following Maltese were known to have finished their C.D.X. titles:

Ch. Akinbak's Thunder Cloud, owned by Gwen Rankin of Bloomfield, New Mexico, earned the title in 1976 with an average of 188.

Cotton's Snow White made it in 1981 with an average of 188, also, in Open A. Owned by K. Tofanelli and M. Cunningham of Phoenix, Arizona.

Gayla's Unchained Melody earned the title in 1981 with a 187 average and is owned by Shirley Perry of Garland, Texas.

Ch. Gulfstream Gem of C & M is owned by Mary Lou Porlick of Florida and achieved her title in 1978 with an average of 190. She is the dam of three champions and was shown in Specials class the same year she earned her C.D.X.

Isbells' Scoot-a-Round earned the C.D.X. in 1981 with an average of 190, and is owned by Ken and Susan Isbell of Oklahoma City, Ohio.

Ch. Jerell's Daisy Mae of Al-Mar made her title in October 1977 with an average of 185. She was also shown as a Special in 1978 while working toward the Utility degree.

Ch. Joanne-Chen's Apollo Dancer made her C.D.X. title in 1977 with an average of 188 in Open A that year. Owner is Gay Latigo of Pleasant Hill, California.

Jori Jolaine is owned by Susan Smith of Dallas, Texas, and made her C.D.X. in 1982. She also boasted a first place in Novice B out of thirty-one qualifiers.

Malako Orea made the C.D.X. list in 1980 with an average of 190 in Open. Owners are Barth and Connie Crana of Rochester, Minnesota.

Max Million Snowcloud, owned by Lavern Ostermeyer of Pacific Grove, California, earned the title in 1981 with a 185 average.

Pistol Pete earned his C.D.X. in 1977 with a 189 average and is owned by Ramona French of Oklahoma City, Oklahoma.

Wya Constant Joy O Yap Yap, with a 185 average, earned the title of C.D.X. very quickly in October 1977, the same year he earned his C.D. title.

As we progress from C.D.X. to the next highest plane in the obedience rings, we must make special mention of the Maltese bearing the R & B kennel name. Lavonne and Robert Roach of Omaha, Nebraska, owners of several Maltese obedience titlists, should receive special recognition for showing three obedience workers at the same approximate time.

R & B's Little Sonny Boy earned his C.D. in 1974, his C.D.X. in 1975, and his U.D. in 1979. In 1980 Sonny qualified six times in Open B (to average 185 plus) and twice in Utility (for an average of 179.25).

R & B's Kriss Kringle made C.D. in 1975 and C.D.X. in 1976 with an average of 189 plus and seven qualifying scores, and his U.D. in 1978.

Arev, C.D., waits for the command to release the dumbbell during an obedience training class. Owner-trainer is Vera Rebbin, Aurora Companion Dog Training School, Aurora, Ohio.

The Roach's R & B's More Bounce Per Ounce made his C.D. in 1977 and his C.D.X. in 1981 with an average of 185.

Other Utility Dog titlists in our breed are:

Beau Garcon is owned by Joan Richmond of Ballwin, Missouri. Beau made his C.D. title in 1980, C.D.X. in 1981, and U.D. in September 1981. This is an unusually short time to complete all three titles. He was the American Maltese Association High Open Awards winner for both 1980 (with an average of 194.5) and 1981 (with an average of 196.25).

Bennetts Salty Peanut, owned by Edna Bennett of Midvale, Utah, made his C.D. in 1977, C.D.X. in 1978, and U.D. in 1981.

Faith Ann Maciejewski's Ch. Ginger Jake earned his C.D. in 1977, C.D.X. in 1978 and U.D. in 1980 with an average of 190.7. Ginger Jake is undeniably one of the best working Maltese in the history of our breed and has demonstrated great consistency of good scores and in number of times qualifying. He was the American Maltese Association Top Dog of the Year in 1981, the year in which he was shown in Open B and Utility. He qualified seven times in Open for an average of 194, and six times in Utility to average 187.83. His highest single score was 197. He had *two combined scores:* one was 380½ and another was 385—out of a possible 400.

Muff of Buckeye Circle, owned by Bill and Ida Mae Marsland, earned her C.D. in 1963 before she was a year old. Her C.D.X. came along in 1965, and in 1967 she was a U.D. titlist—the second Maltese to earn the U.D. title in the United States. She also has her Canadian C.D., which she won in 1966, and her Canadian C.D.X. (1967) and her Canadian U.D. (1969). These Canadian titles were earned in ten consecutive trials. She is the first Maltese to be both an American Kennel Club and Canadian Kennel Club Utility Dog titlist. Muff won the *Dog World* magazine award in 1967 with scores of 195½ 198, and 196. She has other obedience titles as well, including that of being the first Maltese Highest Scoring in Trial, which she was at the 1968 Western Reserve Kennel Club show with a score of 199½. She is without doubt one of the most famous obedience Maltese in the breed and, certainly, in the bitch category.

Mary Lou Porlick of Miami, Florida, is also to be singled out as a top obedience trainer with several of her little dogs making names for themselves in the rings. Her Ch. Gulfstream Treasure earned the C.D. in 1971, C.D.X. in 1973, and U.D. in 1977. She was the American Maltese Association High Utility Awards winner the first year these awards were given. Her average for that year was 189. Treasure was retired in 1978.

Julie's Ruffian, owned by M. and M. Bissonnette of Oklahoma City, Oklahoma, earned his C.D. in 1976, C.D.X. in 1978, and U.D. in 1981. His average of 188.8 made him the American Maltese Association Highest Scoring Utility titlist for that year.

Macho Mio earned his C.D. in 1974, C.D.X. in 1975, and U.D. in 1976. He was the American Maltese Association Top Dog in 1977, the first year that award was presented.

One of the earliest U.D. titlists was Cee Gee's Wee Willie Winkle, who earned his title in 1974. In 1975 he averaged 192.5 when shown in Open B and Utility, and had a combined score of 385.

Martin's Plico Puff, owned by Mary Mills of Jacksonville, Florida, earned the C.D.X. in 1976 and the U.D. in 1978. In 1977, she was the American Maltese Association's Highest Average Utility Dog with an average of 183. Mary Mills also has another Maltese in obedience and works with the Jacksonville Drill Team. She had a C.D. title on her Martin's Plico-Twinkle Puff in 1981.

Nat and Joan's Sugar Cookie, U.D. is owned by Joan Lewis of Garland, Texas, and earned her C.D. in 1977, C.D.X. the following year, and U.D. in 1980.

THE GRAND OLD MAN OF OBEDIENCE

A truly remarkable little dog is Dazzlyn Sir Frost, owned by Betty Drobac of Okemos, Michigan. Frostie has more titles than you can shake a dumb-bell at, and include American and Canadian T.D., American and Canadian C.D.X., and American U.D.T. What is even more surprising is that he finished for his Utility Dog title at twelve years of age.

Frostie had earned his C.D.'s at the age of three, his T.D.'s at the age of five, and his American C.D.X. at the age of seven. At the age of eleven, when most dogs are retired to the good life at home, Frostie and Betty decided to go after the U.D. title. The U.D.T. came at age twelve. Frostie and Betty are to be congratulated on this most titled little Maltese!

Dazzlyn Sir Frost, U.D.T., Canadian C.D.X., T.D., is pictured winning first place in Obedience Open A under judge Corson Jones, on the Tar Heel circuit in 1977.

TRACKING TITLES

Dazzlyn Sir Frost, U.D.T., is owned by Elizabeth W. Drobac of Okemos, Missouri. Sir Frost earned his C.D. in 1974, his tracking title in 1975 (which, by the way, was only the second tracking title for a Maltese) and his C.D.X. in 1977 with an average of 191.833, making him the A.M.A. High Open Average for that year.

Carol Kollander of Lawron, Missouri, is owner of Joy's Mr. Feather, the *very first* Tracking Dog titlist. Feather won his C.D. in *1974* with an average of 187.5, and earned the T.D. title the same year. In 1975 he earned his C.D.X.,

and in 1977 the U.D. title followed with an average of 179. Carol Kollander's Joy's Mr. Puff of Eng is also a Tracking Dog, winning that title in 1979.

Considering the size of the Maltese and the earlier requirements for earning obedience titles and trial awards, we can all be duly proud of the accomplishments made by our little dogs. We can envision an even brighter future ahead as more and more fanciers are inspired by the impressive records set by these aforementioned winners. They and their owners and trainers are to be congratulated on their fine results and their leadership.

Photographed in 1983 are Arev, Darlin, Chevon. Kissette.   All belong to Vera Rebbin of Aurora, Ohio.

CHECK POINTS FOR OBEDIENCE COMPETITORS

* Do your training and have your lessons down pat before entering the ring.
* Don't expect more than your dog is ready or able to give. Obedience work is progressive, not all learned in the first few lessons.
* It's okay to be nervous, but try not to let your dog know it by over-handling or fidgeting.
* Do not punish your dog in or out of the ring. If the dog doesn't work well, it is probably your fault, not his.

* Pay attention to the judge and follow instructions exactly.
* Pay attention to your own dog and not to the competition.
* Don't forget to exercise your dog before entering the ring. He will work better and it will avoid an embarrassing mistake.
* Be a good loser. If you don't win today, you can try again another day.
* Have confidence in your dog's intelligence.
* If it isn't fun for you and your dog, stay out of the ring and try another sport.

272

Little Miss Ragamuffin III, C.D., proudly owned and trained by Elyse R. Fischer.

Arev, C.D., in the photograph Vera Rebbin uses to advertise her Aurora Companion Dog Training School in Aurora, Ohio.

Opposite page: Ch. Gayla's Vaya Con Dios, pictured here with handler Peggy Hogg, was bred by the late Shirley Hrabak and is owned by Diane Davis. "Vaya" became the last Champion offspring of the great Best in Show Ch. Joanne-Chen's Maya Dancer.

Gayla's Unchained Melody, U.D., a high titleholder owned by Shirley Perry of Garland, Texas.

Panda, Butdon, Kissette (partially hidden), Arev, and Rebbeau line up for this charming portrait taken by their owner Vera Rebbin of Aurora, Ohio.

Ch. Gulfstream Gem of C & M, owner-handled by Mary Lou Porlick of Miami, Florida, to this 1978 show win. "Lucy" was specialed during and after she earned her C.D.X. that same year.

Ch. Kathan's Elusive Butterfly, owned by Cheryl Sledge and co-owned by breeder-handler Kathy DiGiacomo. The sire was Ch. Kathan's Torquay of Toyland ex Ch. Su-Le's Winter Wren.

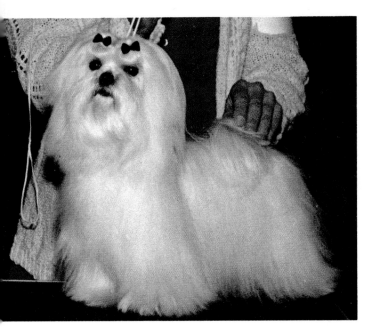

Ch. Sanibel Woofer of Nika, bred and owned by Manya Dujardin, Sanibel Maltese, Oxford, Connecticut.

Muriel Calhoun's Ch. Friar Tuck pictured winning on the way to his championship.

Oak Ridge Ciara, bred by Thomas and Carol Neth and handled by Sandy Tremont for owner Gail Hennessey of Wappingers Falls, New York.

Ch. Jaydora's Scarlet Touch, pictured winning at a 1978 show with breeder-owner Dorothy H. Hatley, Jaydora Maltese, Trinity, North Carolina.

Pagari's Struttin My Stuf, owned by Pamela Rightmyer of Xenia, Ohio. The sire was Ch. Maltara's Show Off ex Al Kay's Yasmin's Charm.

Ch. Kathan's Tangerine, ten months old, is sharing the spotlight with four year-old Stefanie DiGiacomo, daughter of Tangerine's breeder, handler, and co-owner Kathy DiGiacomo. Tangerine is also co-owned by Claudia Grunstra and Tom Pierro. This win was under breeder-judge Merrill Cohen.

Both later to become champions, these winners at the 1979 Lewis and Clark Kennel Club show were Tutees Chutzpah, handled by Angela Dahl, and Tutees Primrose Picca Dilly, handled by Cathie Phillips. Chutzpah is co-owned by Arvid Dahl and Trudie Dillon; Picca Dilly is co-owned by Rita Dahl and Marge Stuber.

On the right is Ch. Ginger Jake, U.D., photographed in the Bahamas at a dog show with his friend Ch. Joann's Merrylane Maximatch. Jake is one of the few dogs to be a winner in both the conformation and obedience rings. Owned and trained by Faith Ann Maciejewski of West Allis, Wisconsin.

Ch. Su-Le's Bananaquit, pictured finishing for championship at ten months of age, is owned by Kathy DiGiacomo, Kathan Maltese, Fair Lawn, New Jersey. "Banana" is a full sister to Su-Le's Bluebird and Bittern, and is the dam of Ch. Kathan's Tangerine.

Ch. Country Villa's Tinker Toy, photographed on the day he achieved his championship title, finishing with two 4-point and one 5-point major wins. The sire was Ch. Windsong Hey Mister Banjo ex Moppets Little Annie Fanny. Bred and owned by Delores Halley of Blue Grass, Iowa.

Ch. Kathan's Sunshine Superman, pictured here at ten months of age, finished for championship one month later. He was a Top Producer in 1982 with six champions to his credit. Bred, originally owned and handled by Kathy DiGiacomo, Superman is now owned by Barbara Bergquist.

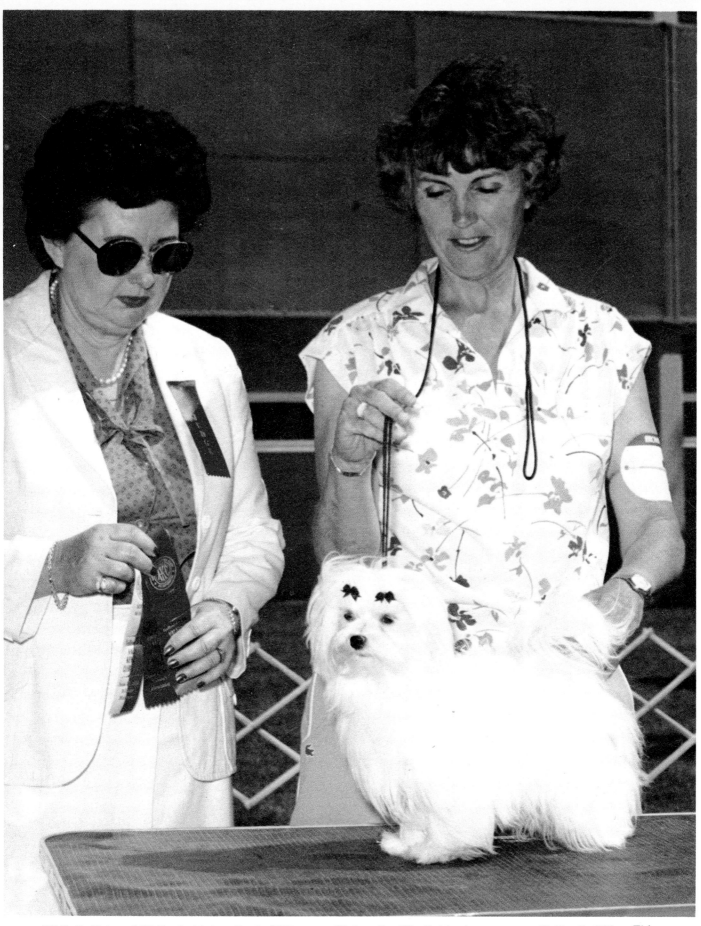

Dil-Dal's Tutees Lil't Rocket takes Best of Winners with handler Rita Dahl, who co-owns with Trudie Dillon. This win was at the Yellowstone Valley Kennel Club show under judge Jean Fancy.

Best in Show winner and American, Bermudian, and Bahamian Ch. Noble Faith's White Tornado is pictured winning the Breed at the 1983 Westminster Kennel Club show under judge Tom Stevenson. Barbara Dempsey Alderman handled for owner Faith Knobel of Ft. Lauderdale, Florida.

American, Bermudian, and Bahamian Ch. Noble Faith's White Tornado with his handler, Barbara Alderman. "Torre" is owned by Faith Knobel.

Ch. Su-Le's Jonina, Best of Breed winner at the 1978 American Maltese Association Specialty show, handled to this win under judge Jean Lepley by Annette Lurton for breeder-owner Barbara Bergquist of New Boston, Michigan.

MISSISSIPPI VALLEY KNL CLUB
ST LOUIS MISSOURI
JUNE 3 1979
TOY GROUP
UDGE
MR EDWARD W BRACY
HOTO BY
PETRULIS

A 1979 Toy Group win for Ch. Malone's Snowie Roxann, handled for owner Nancy Shapland by Peggy Hogg. Roxann's record was 52 Group Firsts, 11 all-breed Bests in Show and Best of Breed two years at Westminster. She is also a multi-Specialty show winner.

CHAPTER SEVENTEEN

Statistics and the Phillips System

Ch. March'en Bali Dancer is pictured winning under Irene Phillips Schlintz at a 1975 show. Bred, owned, and handled by Marcia Hostetler of Des Moines, Iowa.

As Maltese continued to grow in popularity, it was only natural that the entries at the dog shows continued to swell and competition was keen. The larger the entries, the more coveted the wins. In 1956, when Irene Phillips created her Phillips System for evaluating show dogs, Maltese fanciers fell right in line with her point system and began keeping records of their dogs' wins and compared them to others competing at the same time, as well as with other breeds of Toy dogs and even dogs of all the breeds.

Dog fanciers are still keeping score on the top winners in the breeds, and while many a "system" of making it to the top of a list has been recorded and publicized, there is no denying that they are all based on the original Phillips System—the most popular, fairest, and most recognized of all systems for naming the top-winning dogs in the country.

True, records are made to be broken, and we can all look forward to the day when another magnificent Maltese will come on the show scene and cut a path through the crowds of show dogs to triumph as the newest top-winning dog in our breed. There is always room for another great dog to bring additional glory to the Maltese.

As this book goes to press, we have a creditable list of Maltese who are doing themselves proud in the show rings. This book would be less than complete if it did not pay tribute in both word and picture to those dogs that have earned their titles by accumulation of Phillips System points.

In the mid-fifties, Mrs. John Phillips, a woman famous for her Haggiswood Irish Setter Kennels and a judge of many breeds, devised a point system, based on show records published in the *American Kennel Gazette*, to measure the accumulated wins of the nation's show dogs.

As in all sports, competition and enthusiasm in the dog fancy run high, and Irene Phillips—now Mrs. Harold Schlintz—came up with a simple, yet certainly true, method of measuring wins for this competition, which over the years has provided many thrills for dog lovers interested in the good sportsmanship so essential to a competitive sport.

The Phillips System, which Mrs. Phillips not only devised but also compiled during the early years, was sold as an annual feature to *Popular Dogs* magazine, whose editor at that time, Mrs. Alice Wagner, did much to make it the most important rule of success for a show dog. Later, when I took over as editor of *Popular Dogs* in 1967, I carried on the tradition and did the compiling of the figures as well. For the five years I was tallying the finals for the Phillips System, it was a constant source of enjoyment for me to watch the leading dogs in this country, in all breeds, climb to the top. Because I knew so many others felt the same way, and since the competition increased with each passing year, I felt that a healthy sampling of the Maltese which have achieved honors should be represented in this book so that they may become a matter of permanent record.

289

HOW THE SYSTEM WORKS

The Phillips System was designed to measure the difference between a dog-show win scored over many dogs and one scored over just a few dogs. For example, a Best in Show win over 1000 dogs should obviously have more significance than a Best in Show win over 200 dogs. The Phillips System acknowledged this difference by awarding points in accordance with the number of dogs over which the win was scored. Points were awarded for Best in Show and Group placements only. Best of Breed wins did not count.

The Best in Show dog earned a point for each dog in actual competition; absentees or obedience dogs were not counted. The first-place winner in each of the Six Groups earned a point for each dog defeated in his Group. The dog that placed second earned a point for each dog in the Group, less the total dogs in the breed that were first. Third in the Group earned a point for each dog in the Group, less the total of the breeds that were first and second. Fourth in the Group earned a point for each dog in the Group, less the total of the breeds that were first, second, and third.

Sources for the count were the official records for each dog show as published monthly in the *American Kennel Gazette* magazine, the official publication of the American Kennel Club. An individual card was kept on each dog that placed in the Group or won a Best in Show during the entire year. Figures were tallied for publication at the end of each twelve-month period, and a "special issue" of *Popular Dogs* magazine was devoted each year to presenting the Top Ten Winners in each breed.

In the beginning, only a few of the top dogs were published; but by 1966, the phrase "Top Ten" according to the "Phillips System" was firmly established in dog show jargon and the system had captured the imagination of dog fanciers all over the nation—many striving to head the list of the top-winning dogs in the country for that year.

The published figures included the total number of points (number of dogs defeated), the number of Bests in Show, and the number of Group Placements. It is extremely interesting to note that as each year passed there was a tremendous increase in the number of points accrued by the big winners—proof positive of the amazing success and increase in the number of entries at the dog shows from the mid-fifties (when the System was first created by Irene Phillips) to the mid-seventies, when it became a matter of record that the Number One dog in the nation had amassed over 50,000 points to claim the title of Top Show Dog in the United States that year.

THE FIRST MALTESE IN THE PHILLIPS SYSTEM

In 1956, the very first year the Phillips System burst forth on the scene, one of our little Maltese managed to make it to the list of Top Ten Toy Dogs.

1956

Number Eight on the list was Ch. Brittigan's Dark Eyes, owned by Anne and Stewart Pendleton from Louisville, Ohio. In 71 times shown, Dark Eyes won 71 Bests of Breed, 25 Group Firsts, 42 Group Placings, and 1 Best in Show. He was also Best American-bred Toy in 1956 at the Westminster show; Best of Breed at Westminster in 1955, 1956, and 1957; best American-bred Toy at Chicago in 1957; and Best of Breed Chicago in 1955 and 1957. (He didn't make the show in 1956!)

Weighing four pounds, two ounces, Dark Eyes had won his first Group at just six months and four days old.

During 1956, Maltese dogs accounted for two Bests in Show, 12 Group Firsts, 17 Group Seconds, 27 Group Thirds, and 12 Group Fourths.

1957

Once again this year Ch. Brittigan's Dark Eyes placed on the Top Ten Dogs list. This year he moved up to the Number Three position on the list, having won 7 Bests in Show, 19 Group Firsts, 8 Group Seconds, 3 Group Thirds, and a Group Fourth.

Dark Eyes accounted for all the 7 Bests in Show won by Maltese in 1957, but Maltese won a total of 25 Group Firsts, 32 Seconds, 34 Thirds, and 26 Fourths.

1958

There were two Maltese to top the list in 1958. Both were Villa Malta dogs, namely Ch. Bria of Villa Malta in the Number Six position and Ch. Musi of Villa Malta in the Number Seven spot. Bria won a Best in Show and 6 Group Firsts, 15 Seconds, 12 Thirds, and 8 Fourths; Musi won 11 Group Firsts, 14 Seconds, 10 Thirds, and 5 Fourths.

One of the early great Villa Malta Maltese, Ch. Bria of Villa Malta, owned by Margaret M. Rozik of Belle Vernon, Pennsylvania. Evelyn Shafer photo.

Both were bred and owned by Dr. and Mrs. Vincenzo Calvaresi of Bedford, Massachusetts. This was the year that Dr. Calvaresi was named the winner of the Gaines "Breeder of the Year" award.

Bria was owned by Mrs. John H. Luce of Orlando, Florida. First shown in 1958, Bria was undefeated in the breed after winning her championship.

1959

There were two more Maltese Dogs listed in the Top Ten Toys for 1959. Ch. Musi of Villa Malta moved from the Number Seven position the previous year to the Number Thirteen spot for 1959. In addition to a Best in Show win, Musi won 13 Groups, 22 Group Seconds, 10 Thirds, and 4 Fourths.

Another Villa Malta dog took over the Number Nine spot. Ch. Talia of Villa Malta made the list by winning 2 Bests in Show, 9 Group Firsts, 8 Seconds, 6 Thirds, and 2 Fourths.

This was the year that Ch. Musi of Villa Malta was listed among the Top Producers for the year, having produced ten champions.

1960

Two Maltese made it to the Top Ten Toys for the opening of the decade of the 1960s. A repeater from the previous year, Ch. Talia of Villa Malta was Number Eight this year, having won a Best in Show, 8 Group Firsts, 17 Seconds, 7 Thirds, and 2 Fourths. Another Brittigan Maltese appeared on the list in 1960, namely Ch. Brittigan's Sweet William. He won a Best in Show, 9 Group Firsts, 7 Seconds, 7 Thirds, and a Group Fourth.

Talia was to go on and win the Breed and a Group Third at the Westminster Kennel Club show in 1961.

1961

Ch. Brittigan's Sweet William had to carry the flag for the breed in 1961. He moved up to the Number Seven position as a result of his 3 Bests in Show, 7 Group Firsts, 18 Seconds, 5 Thirds and a Fourth.

It should be noted that during 1961, 25 Maltese dogs sired 36 champions during this year.

1962

In 1962 the Phillips System took on a new look in *Popular Dogs*. They published a list of the *Top Fifty* leaders in all-breed competition for this year. In the Number Thirty-four position was Ch. Aennchen's Smart Dancer. Dancer had won 3 Bests in Show, 20 Group Firsts, 8 Seconds, and 5 Thirds to make it to this spot on the charts. No other Maltese managed to place in the top fifty, but Smart Dancer was also Number Seven on the list of Top Ten Toy Dogs.

This was also the year that 44 Maltese sires produced a total of 55 champions.

Another Villa Malta great, Ch. Talia of Villa Malta, with handler Margaret Rozik winning the Toy Group under judge George Beckett at a 1960 show.

1963

While Smart Dancer had to be satisfied with the Number Ten position on the list of top dogs for 1963, there was cause for rejoicing in the Maltese breed because another Aennchen dog was to take over the Number Five spot in the Top Ten Toys. Ch. Co-Ca-He's Aennchen Toy Dancer waltzed into that position after winning 3 Bests in Show, 10 Group Firsts, 11 Seconds, 10 Thirds, and 6 Fourths. Smart Dancer also won 3 Bests in Show, 15 Group Firsts, 3 Seconds, and a Fourth.

Popular Dogs listed the top three dogs in each breed this year, not the top ten, and in the Number Three Maltese position was Ch. Lacy of Villa Malta—who won 5 Group Firsts, 7 Seconds, 4 Thirds, and 4 Fourths.

1964

The Top Ten Toy Dog category featured two Maltese. Ch. Co-Ca-He's Aennchen Toy Dancer was Number Six, and Ch. Lacy of Villa Malta was Number Ten.

Again this year, *Popular Dogs* featured only the top three in breed listings. Following the above two was Ch. Aennchen's Poona Dancer with 2 Toy Groups, 8 Seconds, 6 Thirds, and 7 Fourths.

Toy Dancer had won 4 Bests in Show, 14 Groups, 7 Seconds, and 2 Thirds. Lacy won a Best in Show, 5 Groups, 5 Seconds, 7 Thirds, and 4 Fourths.

1965

Two Maltese made the list of Top Ten Toys in 1965, and both bore the Aennchen's prefix.

American Best in Show winner Ch. Bobbelee April Love was exported to Akira Shinohara for his A-S Gloria Kennels in Japan.

Number Seven was Ch. Aennchen's Poona Dancer and Number Nine was Ch. Aennchen's Sari Dancer. Following those entries in the top three breed listings was another Aennchen dog, Ch. Co-Ca-He's Aennchen Toy Dancer.

Poona won 2 Bests in Show, 15 Group Firsts, 17 Seconds, 11 Thirds, and 5 Fourths. Sari Dancer won 2 Bests in Show, 8 Group Firsts, 7 Seconds, 5 Thirds, and a Fourth. Toy Dancer won a Best in Show, 5 Group Firsts, 9 Seconds, 4 Thirds, and 3 Fourths.

Three Maltese placed among the top sires for the year. Ch. Idnar's King Midas produced eight champion offspring. Ch. Aennchen's Shikar Dancer and Ch. Aennchen's Siva Dancer produced five champions each. Sun Canyon's Rena was a producer of three champions, making her a top dam.

This was also the year that Poona won the Toy Group at the Westminster Kennel Club show. She was co-owned by Frank Oberstar (who showed her) and L.G. Ward of Euclid, Ohio.

1966

Ch. Aennchen's Poona Dancer was riding high all through 1966 and managed to win 16 Bests in Show. She also won 50 Group Firsts, 17 Seconds, a Group Third, and 4 Fourths. She was Number Two Toy Dog for 1966. A new name appeared as the Number Eight Top Ten Toy Dog as Ch. Bobbelee April Love won a Best in Show, 13 Group Firsts, 10 Seconds, 2 Thirds, and 3 Fourths.

1967

This year *Popular Dogs* featured a list of the Top Fifty Dogs once again. It was my first year as compiler and I watched with great glee as Ch. Aennchen's Poona Dancer climbed all the way to the Number Three position in the all-breed competition! That automatically made her Number One Toy Dog, all-breeds. Poona won her spot with her 19 Bests in Show, 61 Toy Group Firsts, 11 Seconds, 3 Thirds, and 2 Fourths.

Two other Maltese also made the list of Top Ten Toys. In the Number Seven spot was Ch. Enricco, owned by F. Wiener and L. Rappond of California. Enricco won 9 Group Firsts, 12 Seconds, 5 Thirds, and 5 Fourths. Number Ten was Ch. Bobbelee April Love, owned by Mrs. M. J. Chaisson of Houma, Louisiana. The score here was 2 Bests in Show, 11 Group Firsts, 7 Seconds, 4 Thirds, and 4 Fourths.

1968

This year was quite a let-down. No Maltese placed in the Top Ten all-breed list or even in the Top Ten of the Toy Group. However, the Top Ten Maltese produced some very interesting and promising new names.

Number One on that list was Ch. Hi Ho's Hope Diamond, owned by H. Hines of New Orleans, Louisiana. Diamond finished her championship in 1965 at the tender age of thirteen months—then retired to motherhood. In 1968 she came back to the ring and soared to the top of the chart in the breed. Diamond did not win a Best in Show, but the points garnered in her 12 Groups Firsts, 9 Seconds, 7 Thirds, and 4 Fourths gave her the Number One rating. She was handled to this prestigious spot by handler Rene Roux.

The Number Two spot went to another newcomer, Ch. Pendleton's Jewel, owned by Dorothy White of Youngstown, Ohio. Jewel won 6 Group Firsts, 8 Seconds, 8 Thirds, and 3 Fourths. Dr. and Mrs. Kenneth Knopf of Forest Hills, New York, had the Number Three dog in Ch. Anna Maries White Panther. She had won 4 Groups, 9 Seconds, 6 Thirds, and a Fourth.

Poona, or Ch. Aennchen's Poona Dancer, came in at Number Four with 4 Groups and 2 Thirds. Number Five went to Ch. Aennchen's Sitar Dancer with a Best in Show, 5 Group Firsts, 3 Thirds, and 3 Fourths. This Aennchen dog was still owned by Mr. and Mrs. J. P. Antonelli of Waldwick, New Jersey. Number Six was Ch. Aennchen's Imp of Gwenbrook, who also won a Best in Show, 2 Groups, a Second, 3 Thirds, and a Fourth.

Number Seven was Ch. Bayhammonds Tina Dancer, owned by R. Gaudi of Fort Wayne, Indiana. Tina won a Toy Group, and had 6 Seconds, 6 Thirds, and 2 Fourths. Number Eight was Ch. Martin's Jingles Puff. It was 3 Group Firsts for Jingles, 2 Seconds, 2 Thirds, and 5 Fourths. Number Nine was Ch. Al Dor Jollo of Vegas, owned by R. and E. Hill of Las Vegas.

Number Ten was (last but not least) Ch. Joanne-Chen's Sweet Shi Dancer, owned by Mrs. Joanne Hesse of New Haven, Indiana. The association between Mrs. Hesse and Aennchen Antonelli was to make a bit of breed history in the future, but suffice it to say here that Sweet Shi Dancer was a Group winner and had 4 Seconds, 3 Thirds, and a Fourth to her credit by the end of 1968.

The late Aennchen Antonelli's Best in Show winning Maltese "Sitar" at the 1968 Staten Island Kennel Club show.

1969

In 1969 there was a star in the sky—or should we say a sparkling jewel? Ch. Pendleton's Jewel went all the way to the Number One spot in the Top Ten Toy Breeds that year for owners Dorothy and Norman White. She won 10 Bests in Show, 24 Groups, 13 Seconds, 6 Thirds, and 8 Fourths.

The Number Two Maltese was Ch. Martin's Jingles Puff, moving up from the Number Eight spot on the previous year's chart. Jingles won 2 Bests in Show this year and took 14 Groups as well as 38 Group Placements. Jingles was owner-bred and shown by Rena Martin of Highland Park, Illinois.

1970

At the beginning of the 1970s, Ch. Pendleton's Jewel had managed to climb to the Number Four spot on the Top Ten all-breed chart. This was due to the fact that he had won 16 Bests in Show, 41 Group Firsts, 13 Seconds, 1 Third, and 2 Fourths. Ch. Martin's Jingles Puff was once again in the Number Two position with 1 Best in Show, 8 Group Firsts, 7 Seconds, 7 Thirds, and 4 Fourths.

Number Three was Ch. Joanne-Chen's Maya Dancer, owned by C. Pierce of Oak Lawn, Illinois. Number Four was also a new name to the list, Ch. Su-Le's Wren of Eng, owned by Barbara Bergquist of Wyandotte, Michigan. Wren was also the winner of a Best in Show with 3 Group Firsts, 4 Seconds, 3 Thirds, and 2 Fourths.

Ch. Aennchen's Savar Dancer, the last of the Aennchen Maltese before Aennchen Antonelli's untimely death, is pictured winning the Toy Group at the Wallkill Kennel Club show—another in a long list of wins for this beautiful little Maltese.

Number Five was Mr. and Mrs. J. P. Antonelli's Ch. Aennchen's Savar Dancer with 5 Group Firsts, 4 Seconds, 4 Thirds, and 6 Fourths. Number Six was Ch. Sun Canyon Inca Idol, owned by M. Thompson of Sun Valley, California. Here the score was 3 Groups, 3 Seconds, 5 Thirds, and 1 Fourth. Number Seven was Ch. Mil-Ottie's Molly B, owned by D. Hochrein of Miami, Florida. Molly had 2 Groups, 9 Seconds, 1 Third, and 6 Fourths.

Number Eight was Ch. Joanne-Chen's Maja Dancer owned by Joanne Bell of Troy, Michigan. Maja won a Best in Show and a Group during 1970. Number Nine was Ch. Su-Le's Robin of Eng, owned by Barbara Bergquist. Robin took 2 Groups, 3 Seconds, 2 Thirds, and 2 Fourths. Number Ten on the list went to Ch. Spring Holly Passing Fancy, owned by D. Lewis and M. Middleton of St. Louis, Missouri. Holly's record was 2 Groups, 1 Second, 2 Thirds, and a Fourth.

Ch. Joanne-Chen's Maya Dancer, owned by Mamie R. Gregory and handled for her by Peggy A. Hogg, holds the all-time Maltese record of 43 Bests in Show, all-breeds. He was the top Toy for two years.

1971

Number One on the Top Ten Toy Chart was Ch. Joanne Chen's Maya Dancer, who garnered over 14,000 points for the year. Her 9 Bests in Show, 38 Groups, 11 Seconds, 3 Thirds, and a Fourth put her far ahead of the other Toys. Number Two spot went to the previous year's winner, Ch. Pendleton's Jewel, who won 2 Bests in Show, 10 Groups, and 4 Seconds. Number Three was Ch. Martin's Jingles Puff, with a Best in Show, 4 Groups, 9 Seconds, 2 Thirds, and 3 Fourths.

Number Four was Ch. Mil-Ottie's Molly B, also a Best in Show winner with 5 Groups, 7 Seconds, a Third, and a Fourth. Number Five was another Bobbelee dog, this time Ch. Bobbelee Hanky Panky, owned by R. L. Harrison and winner of 4 Toy Groups, with 6 Seconds, 2 Thirds, and 2 Fourths. T. Dillon and C. Phillips saw Ch. Coeur De Lion become Number Six. Also a Best in Show winner in 1971, Lion had 2 Groups, 4 Seconds, 2 Thirds, and 2 Fourths. Number Seven was Ch. Mike Mars Gwenbrook, with 1 Best in Show, 1 Group First, 1 Second, 3 Thirds, and 3 Fourths. M. T. Thompson's Ch. Sun Canyon White Cloud was Number Eight with 3 Group Seconds, a Third, and 2 Fourths.

Number Nine was Ch. Su-Le's Wren of Eng, winner of 4 Groups, a Second, 3 Thirds, and 2 Fourths. Number Ten position went to another new name . . . M. K. Calhoun's Ch. Duncans Nicholas, also winner of a Best in Show and a Group.

1972

Another top winner in our breed in 1972 and the second highest scoring show dog in the United States was Ch. Joanne Chen's Maya Dancer, defeated only by the ASCOB Cocker Spaniel, Ch. Sagamore Toccoa (who managed to accrue over 50,000 points). Maya's 45,000 plus was a tremendous victory when you consider that each point represents a dog defeated for the win. This placement on the charts automatically made Maya the top Toy dog, all-breeds, and Number One Maltese for the year. The score was 32 Bests in Show, 33 Groups, and 16 Placements.

Another Aennchen dog was Number Two. S. J. Knopf's Ch. Aennchen's Paris Dancer took 4 Groups, 9 Seconds, 9 Thirds, and 7 Fourths. Number Three was Ch. San Su Kee Ring Leader Too, owned by the Nelsons. Leader won a Best in Show plus 9 Groups, 2 Seconds, 1 Third, and 2 Fourths.

Number Four was D. K. Babcock's Ch. Su-Le's Bunting with 6 Seconds, 3 Thirds, and 6 Fourths. Number Five was Ch. Al Dor Pzazz, owned by A. and G. Hendrickson. Pzazz took 2 Groups, a Second, 2 Thirds, and a Fourth. Pzazz was the recipient of the California Maltese Club 1972 Ideal Dog Award. Bred by Dorothy Tinker and handled by Nancy Tinker, the owners were Art and Grace Hendrickson of Los Angeles.

Number Six was Ch. Martin's Posy Puff, owned by P. Rust. Posy had 4 Groups, 4 Seconds, 4 Thirds, and a Fourth. Number Seven was Ch. C and M's Torino of Camero with 3 Groups, 4 Seconds, and 2 Thirds. Ch. Coeur De Lion was Number Eight with 2 Groups, 2 Seconds, 2 Thirds, and 2 Fourths. Number Nine was another Su-Le dog, this time Ch. Su-Le's Roadrunner with 3 Groups and 2 Seconds. Number Ten was also a Bergquist entry, Ch. Su-Le's Martin, with 2 Groups and 2 Fourths.

At the first Independent National Specialty Show in 1971, held in New York City, Best Puppy from the regular classes was Ch. Su-Le's Bunting, bred and handled by Barbara Bergquist of New Boston, Michigan.

1973

By 1973 I had left *Popular Dogs*, and was no longer doing the finals for the Phillips System. The 1973 results in that magazine listed only the top ten dogs in each breed.

Ch. Cuddledoon Mayadolls Prince was Number One in Maltese with 3 Bests in Show, 9 Groups, 5 Seconds, 1 Third, and 3 Fourths. Dr. A. M. and N. D. King were the owners. Number Two was Ch. Bobbelee Hanky Panky, owned by R. L. Harrison, and a Best in Show winner. He also had 2 Groups, 12 Seconds, 8 Thirds, and 2 Fourths.

Number Three found Dr. Kenneth Knopf's Ch. Aennchen's Paris Dancer as a Best in Show winner with 6 Groups, 11 Seconds, and 7 Thirds. Number Four was Ch. Joanne-Chen's Maya Dancer, owned by Mamie Gregory, as a Best in Show winner with 3 Groups and a Second.

Number Five was Ch. Sun Canyon Jenelle, owned by M. F. Thompson, with 3 Groups, 4 Seconds, 7 Thirds, and a Fourth. The Number Six spot went to Ch. Pen Sans Moonshine, owned by L. C. Olive. Moonshine won a Best in Show and took 5 Groups, 2 Seconds, 3 Thirds, and a Fourth. Number Seven was Ch. San Su Kee Melody Too, owned by D. E. Palmersten, with 2 Group Seconds, 7 Thirds, and 3 Fourths. Number Eight was Ch. Maltacellos Issa of Buckeye, who won a Group and had 2 Seconds, 4 Thirds, and 4 Fourths.

Ch. Pen Sans Moonshine is pictured winning Best in Show under the late judge Louis Murr at the 1973 Wichita Kennel Club. Bred by Gloria Busselman of Richland, Washington.

Ch. Oak Ridge, Melissa, owned by Lin-Lee Maltese of Finleyville, Pennsylvania.

Two repeaters returned for the Number Nine and Number Ten positions. Ch. Martin's Posy Puff was winner of 4 Groups plus 2 Thirds and a Fourth for Number Nine. Ch. Al Dor Pzazz had 3 Groups, a Second, a Third, and a Fourth to be Number Ten on the list.

1975

By 1975 *Popular Dogs* was no longer being published and the rating system had gone over to *Showdogs* magazine with certain changes in point ratings. They featured the Top Twenty all-breed winners; however, none of our Maltese placed in this category. A new Sun Canyon entry, however, made it to Number Seven in the Top Ten Toy Group (and was the Number One Maltese). Ch. Sun Canyon Reach For The Stars was that entry, with a Best in Show, 9 Groups, 9 Seconds, 6 Thirds, and 5 Fourths.

Number Two in the Top Ten for the breed was Ch. Maltacellos Issa of Buckeye, and Number Three was Ch. San Su Kee Star Edition. Following were, in order, Ch. Oak Ridge Melissa, Ch. Feathers Merri Minx, Ch. San Su Kee Show Stopper, Ch. Salterr Glory Seeker, Ch. Lizaras Karousel, Ch. Su-Le's Martin, and Ch. Celias Mooney Forget Me Not.

1976-1977

1976 rati.. seem to be "missing." The next appearance of a rating "system" appeared in an August 1978 issue of *Shows and Dogs* magazine, giving the results of the 1977 finals. Once again no Maltese placed in the Top Ten all-breed lists. Number Eight on the Top Ten Toys list, however, was a Maltese given as Ch. Joanne-Chen's Mino Maya Dancer with over 9,000 points. We

Almost Ready for Open, a pen-and-ink drawing of a show Maltese by Kathy Blackard of Brooklyn, Connecticut.

can only surmise that this is the same Maya Dancer we have heard of before, but are at a loss as to the addition of "Mino." Was this an offspring or a typographical error? Since no further information was given, we cannot say.

With this lack of information, and no listing of any of the Top Ten in each breed, we can only regret the lack of credit that is due any of the winners. With the end of 1976, therefore we conclude a full two decades of rating system listings on our Maltese from the time Irene Phillips first conceived her idea in 1956. Many other systems and ratings have come and gone since that first one. While each tries to be different and better, we can only hope that it is still

providing the incentive to dog owners to breed better dogs for competing in the rings.

GREAT SHOW DOGS OF AMERICA—1955 through 1966

Irene Phillips Schlintz herself compiled an impressive feature on the Great Show Dogs of America from 1955 through 1966, and this was published in *Showdogs* magazine in the 1970s. But no system (and there have been many that have come and gone) has ever generated the excitement and respect that her original Phillips System did—and put competition at the dog shows on a new high level we will surely remember well into the future.

Three-year-old Stefanie DiGiacomo poses with three-month-old future Champion Kathan's Johnny Reb.

CHAPTER EIGHTEEN

The Maltese As a Breed

Marge Stuber's puppy, Primrose Angel Baby, with Marge Stuber's sculpture. Angel is just two months old in this photo.

Ask the owner of any breed of dog about temperament and they will invariably include "and wonderful with children" among the most desirable attributes. However, in the case of the Maltese it happens to be true!

Maltese love everyone, and make marvelous companions for people of all ages. They are long-lived little creatures and their stamina and spunk completely belie their size and the statement written by H. W. Huntington in 1897 wherein he described Maltese as "looking like spun glass." They may look like spun glass, but they certainly are more substantial and enduring!

Maltese are equally content to sit on your lap or on a chair beside you or hike at your heels in the woods or in the fields. They learn quickly because of their high intelligence, said to be the result of their long close association with their human counterparts over so many hundreds of years. They are easy to house train and, for their size, can withstand extremes in temperature if accustomed to it properly and gradually. They are not finicky eaters, and enjoy their food, especially if some treats come from your plate.

Even the stud dogs get along well with each other, and while they may be vocal about their opinions and likes and dislikes, they cannot be said to be argumentative in character. Their fondness and their speed when hunting or chasing small creatures is believed by some to lend authenticity to the idea that they do have a bit of the "terrier" in their background and personality.

The Maltese is truly a dog for all toy breed fanciers!

MALTESE STORIES

In discussing the exploits of our spunky little Maltese, it would perhaps be safer and more accurate to refer to these "reports" as Maltese *stories*. Certain "poetic license" seems to be taken when repeating the accomplishments or heroics of our little dogs.

For example, it is still the opinion of some that Grayfriers Bobby, the dog that stood watch at its master's grave for twenty years, dying there by the side of it, was a Maltese. Actually, it is said to be a Skye Terrier, not a Maltese. There are other stories about Maltese that have flung themselves into their master's grave, or have exhibited amazing feats of bravery in defense of their owners.

It is also interesting to note that during the height of their popularity, in their early days in Britain, these little dogs were readily for sale from the streethawkers and peddlers on the city streets. They were said to be good sellers because the brown eye-stain on the white faces made them look as if they had been weeping, which generated a great deal of sympathy among dog lovers.

Furthermore, it is written that if the dog hawkers were to make themselves out to be cruel people, the little dogs were quickly snapped up and taken home to be cared for more kindly. Edward Ash, in his *The Practical Dog Book* published in England in 1930 further states that one particular dog monger enjoyed special success when he repeatedly put red paint on a bandage and wrapped it around a dog's foot.

FAMOUS OWNERS OF MALTESE

There is nothing like movie stars being seen with their favorite dog to give the breed a tremendous boost in popularity. Over the years, the Maltese have had their share of this kind of publicity since a number of tinsel town's elite have chosen the breed as their companions.

We have mentioned elsewhere in this book the fact that Mary Carlisle and her mother were breeding Maltese dogs and brought fame to this breed. Actress Mona Freeman was another actress who toted her little Maltese around the set when making a picture. Mr. and Mrs. Gary Cooper were owners of at least one of Mrs. Blanche Mace's Maltese and also owned Tina of Yelwa. Singer Georgia Gibbs named her Maltese Henry, and Tallulah Bankhead named hers Dolores. Lee Remick owned a couple of them and was seen with two in a charming photograph in an issue of *Harper's Bazaar* magazine. Rosemary Clooney owned four Villa Malta Maltese back in the 1950s.

Rosemary Clooney with a Maltese she purchased from the Villa Malta Kennels. This photograph was taken in 1974.

TOTIE FIELDS AND HER MALTESE

Totie Fields, the comedienne, was a Maltese fancier and had several before her death. Her original Maltese was a gift from Mike Douglas, the TV star. During one of her appearances on the Mike Douglas show, Totie saw and fell in love with a little Maltese dog. Mike gave it to her, and she promptly named it "Mike" after him, even though it was a female.

Totie traveled everywhere with her little dogs and offered a substantial reward when one was stolen from her during a Las Vegas engagement. However, the little dog was never recovered.

She made a graduation gift of Ch. Al-Dor Cherry's Jubilee when her daughter Jody graduated from Smith College. Totie's own Al-Dor Ivy finished her championship in 1978.

The Las Vegas Maltese Association bestowed honorary memberships on Totie and her husband George.

MALTESE AND ROYALTY

Mary Queen of Scots (1542-1565) was well-known as a dog lover and managed to surround herself with dogs. She had Maltese sent over to her from France, and it is said to have been a little Maltese dog that was found under her skirts after she was beheaded. The exact breeding of the little dog she spent her last days with in her cell has always been open to speculation, but a Maltese is a possibility.

Giuseppe Verdi in the 1860s owned a Maltese named Loulou that went everywhere with him, including rehearsals and performances at the theatre. French novelist Louise de la Ramee, who wrote under the name Ouida had many, many Maltese as well as all breeds of dogs. A drinking fountain for dogs was erected in her honor at the time of her death at Bury St. Edmunds in England.

MALTESE PUBLICATIONS

Not too much has been written about the Maltese individually. There is mention made of them in books covering all breeds of dogs, but little on the breed specifically.

However, those who wish to keep up with the breed today can receive a Newsletter if they join the American Maltese Association. Membership information can be obtained by writing to the American Kennel Club, 51 Madison Avenue, New York, New York 10010, and requesting the name and address of the current corresponding secretary.

The late comedienne Totie Fields and husband George Johnston being awarded an honorary membership in the Las Vegas Maltese Association. Pictured with them is the organization's president Dorothy Tinker, from whom Totie bought three Maltese.

There are also two books by Marge Stuber entitled *I Love Maltese* and *Breeding Toy Dogs, Especially Maltese* that can be had by writing to her at her Ohio home. Her complete address too may be obtained from the American Kennel Club.

Dennis Carno wrote an update on Virginia T. Leitch's 1953 book *The Maltese Dog, A History of the Breed*. There are small paperback publications in the $1.50 to $5 price range available at pet stores that will give a basic outline of the breed and breed standard for those who wish to learn a little about Maltese.

Kathy DiGiacomo and Barbara Bergquist, both active breeder-owners and association officers, have collaborated in the writing of a moderately priced introductory book on the breed, entitled simply *Maltese*. Anna Katherine Nicholas, noted show judge, has contributed a much more definitive volume called *The Maltese*. Both of these books are heavily illustrated and available from T.F.H. Publications, Inc.

THE MALTESE IN ART

It was our original intention to include an entire chapter on the Maltese dog in art in this book. However, as research progressed, the number of paintings and art works became so enormous that it would be virtually impossible to include a list of them all. Therefore, while many art works will be featured in photographs throughout the book, no attempt will be made to chronicle the masterworks of artists down through the centuries. We will, instead, suggest that those who wish to obtain copies or information regarding this art can do so by consulting other publications.

One excellent source for photographic reproductions is the previously mentioned *The Maltese Dog, A History of the Breed*, by Virginia T. Leitch with a second edition revised and updated by Dennis Carno. This volume was published in 1970 by the International Institute of Veterinary Science in Bronxville, New York.

The second book contains a comprehensive list of paintings and artists, with titles, and is entitled *Maltese Dogs—The Jewels of Women.* This book by Miki Iveria was published by the Maltese Club of Great Britain and printed by J. Riches & Co. Ltd. It is truly a remarkable compilation worthy of mention and consideration in any discussion of the Maltese in art.

"The Prince of Hawaii," painted by Enoch Wood Perry in 1864, attests to the Maltese-type dog on this remote Pacific Island. This prince was heir to the Kamehameha dynasty (1790-1872) but died shortly after this painting was commissioned. It hangs in the Bernice P. Bishop Museum in Honolulu.

302

"Our Last Queen" is a portrait of George the Third's wife with her pet Maltese.

Ch. Sanibel Sweet Pea was captured in pastels by James Fischer.

Shaded from white to aqua to black, this Maltese batik on silk was rendered by artist Nancy Brown of Omaha, Nebraska.

An acrylic-on-wood painting of a Maltese in beautiful coat was done in 1983 by Kathy Blackard.

James Fischer's pastel rendition captures Ch. Kathan's Bristol Stomp in a typical pose.

This painting on slate is one of the art pieces in Norma Belford's collection.

This beautiful acrylic was done by Dr. Roger Brown of Omaha, Nebraska.

American and Canadian Ch. Su-Le's Sparrow was rendered in oils on canvas by Jacke Szuchs.

Maltese Batik, on silk, was created by Nancy Brown for Dr. and Mrs. T. Robert Bashara, owners of the model, Sunny Sunflower.

This hand-knotted Persian wool rug was designed by Susan M. Sandlin and executed by Mary M. Sandlin, The Original Petit Point kennels in Alexandria, Virginia.

Vicbrita Serena Primrose was sculpted larger than life by artist Lorraine West. Owned by Marge Stuber of Lima, Ohio.

Two ceramic figurines from the collection of Pamela Rightmyer, Sundaze Kennels, Xenia, Ohio.

Ch. Bar None Thunderbird pictured winning under judge Kathleen Kolbert with Michele Perlmutter handling. The Perlmutter children who help care for the dogs are, left to right, Rebecca, Jed, Billie-Rachal and Sunshine.

One of the ceramic Maltese from Norma Belford's collection.

A highly stylized ceramic sculpture owned by Delores Halley of Blue Grass, Iowa.

Weewyte's Pitter Patter, photographed in this charming portrait study by Olan Mills for breeder-owner Mrs. Kathy Blackard.

Tutees Primrose L'Espance (with Trudie Dillon) and American and Canadian Ch. Tutees Destiny of Artivanda (with Angela Dahl) at a recent Klamath Kennel Club show under judge Irene Phillips Schlintz.

Glossary of Dog Terms

Achilles heel. The major tendon attaching the muscles of the calf from the thigh to the hock.

AKC. The American Kennel Club. Address: 51 Madison Avenue, New York, NY 10010.

Albino. Pigment deficiency, usually a congenital fault.

Almond eye. The shape of the eye opening, rather than the eye itself, which slants upwards at the outer edge, hence giving it an almond shape.

American Kennel Club. Registering body for canine world in the United States. Headquarters for the stud book, dog registrations, and federation of kennel clubs. It also creates and enforces rules and regulations governing dog shows.

Angulation. The angles formed by the meeting of the bones.

Anus. Anterior opening found under the tail for purposes of alimentary canal elimination.

Apple-head. An irregular roundness of topskull. A domed skull.

Apron. On long-coated dogs, the longer hair that frills outward from the neck and chest.

Balanced. A symmetrical, correctly proportioned animal; one having correct balance of one part in regard to another.

Barrel. Rounded rib section; thorax, chest.

Bat ear. An erect ear, broad at base, rounded or semi-circular at top, with opening directly in front.

Beard. Profuse whisker growth.

Beauty spot. Usually roundish colored hair on a blaze of another color. Found mostly between the ears.

Beefy. Overdevelopment or overweight in a dog, particularly hindquarters.

Bitch. The female dog.

Blaze. A type of marking; white stripe running up the center of the face between the eyes.

Blocky. Square head.

Bloom. Dogs in top condition are said to be "in full bloom."

Blue merle. A color designation. Blue and gray mixed with black; marbled-like appearance.

Bossy. Overdevelopment of the shoulder muscles.

Brace. Two dogs (a matched pair) that move in unison.

Breeching. Tan-colored hair on inside of the thighs.

Brindle. Even mixture of black hairs with brown, tan, or gray.

Brisket. The forepart of the body below the chest.

Broken color. A color broken by white or another color.

Broken-haired. A wiry coat.

Broken-up face. Receding nose together with deep stop, wrinkle, and undershot jaw.

Brood bitch. A female used for breeding.

Brush. A bushy tail.

Burr. Inside part of the ear which is visible to the eye.

Butterfly nose. Parti-colored nose or entirely flesh color.

Button ear. The edge of the ear which folds to cover the opening of the ear.

C.A.C.I.B. Award made in European countries to international champion dogs.

Canine. Animals of the Canidae family which includes not only dogs, but foxes, wolves, and jackals.

Canines. The four large teeth in the front of the mouth often referred to as fangs.

Castrate. To surgically remove the testicles on the male dog.

Cat-foot. Round, tight, high-arched feet said to resemble those of a cat.

Character. The general appearance or expression said to be typical of the breed.

Cheeky. Fat cheeks or protruding cheeks.

Chest. Forepart of the body between the shoulder blades and above the brisket.

China eye. A clear blue wall-eye.

Chiseled. A clean-cut head, especially when chiseled out below the eye.

Chops. Jowls or pendulous lips.

Clip. Method of trimming coats according to an individual breed standard.

Cloddy. Thick set or plodding dog.

Close-coupled. A dog short in loins; comparatively short from withers to hipbones.

Cobby. Short-bodied; compact.

Collar. Usually a white marking, resembling a collar, around the neck.

Condition. General appearance of a dog showing good health, grooming, and good care.

Conformation. The form and structure of the bone or framework of the dog in comparison with requirements of the breed.

Corky. Active and alert dog.

Couple. Two dogs.

Coupling. Leash or collar-ring for a brace of dogs.

Couplings. Body between the withers and the hipbones.

Cowhocked. When the hocks turn toward each other and sometimes touch.

Crank tail. Tail carried down.

Crest. Arched portion of the back of the neck.

Cropping. Cutting or trimming of the ear leather to get ears to stand erect.

Crossbred. A dog whose sire and dam are of two different breeds.

Croup. The back part of the back above the hind legs. Area from hips to tail.

Crown. The highest part of the head; the topskull.

Cryptorchid. Male dog with neither testicle visible.

Culotte. The long hair on the back of the thighs.

Cushion. Fullness of upper lips.

Dappled. Mottled marking of different colors with none predominating.

Deadgrass. Dull tan color.

Dentition. Arrangement of the teeth.

Dewclaws. Extra claws, or functionless digits on the inside of the front and/or rear legs.

Dewlap. Loose, pendulous skin under the throat.

Dish-faced. When nasal bone is so formed that nose is higher at the end than in the middle or at the stop.

Disqualification. A dog that has a fault making it ineligible to compete in dog show competitions.

Distemper teeth. Discolored or pitted teeth as a result of having had distemper.

Dock. To shorten the tail by cutting.

Dog. A male dog, though used freely to indicate either sex.

Domed. Evenly rounded in topskull; not flat but curved upward.

Down-faced. When nasal bone inclines toward the tip of the nose.

Down in pastern. Weak or faulty pastern joints; a let-down foot.

Drop ear. The leather pendant which is longer than the leather of the button ear.

Dry neck. Taut skin.

Dudley nose. Flesh-colored or light brown pigmentation in the nose.

Elbow. The joint between the upper arm and the forearm.

Elbows out. Turning out or off the body and not held close to the sides.

Ewe neck. Curvature of the top of neck.

Expression. Color, size, and placement of the eyes which give the typical expression associated with a breed.

Faking. Changing the appearance of a dog by artificial means to make it more closely resemble the standard. Using chalk to whiten white fur, etc.

Fall. Hair which hangs over the face.

Feathering. Longer hair fringe on ears, legs, tail, or body.

Feet east and west. Toes turned out.

Femur. The large heavy bone of the thigh.

Fiddle front. Forelegs out at elbows, pasterns close, and feet turned out.

Flag. A long-haired tail.

Flank. The side of the body between the last rib and the hip.

Flare. A blaze that widens as it approaches the topskull.

Flashy. Term used to describe outstanding color-pattern of dog.

Flat bone. When girth of the leg bones is correctly elliptical rather than round.

Flat sided. Ribs insufficiently rounded as they meet the breastbone.

Flews. Upper lips, particularly at inner corners.

Forearm. Bone of the foreleg between the elbow and the pastern.

Foreface. Front part of the head; before the eyes; muzzle.

Fringes. Same as feathering.

Frogface. Usually overshot jaw where nose is extended by the receding jaw.

Front. Forepart of the body as viewed head-on.

Furrow. Slight indentation or median line down center of the skull to the top.

Gay tail. Tail carried above the topline.

Gestation. The period during which a bitch carries her young; normally 63 days.

Goose rump. Too steep or too sloping a croup.

Grizzle. Bluish-gray color.

Guard hairs. The longer, stiffer hairs that protrude through the undercoat.

Hare foot. A narrow foot.

Harlequin. A color pattern; patched or pied coloration, predominantly black and white.

Haw. A third eyelid or membrane at the inside corner of the eye.

Height. Vertical measurement from the withers to the ground or from shoulders to the ground.

Hock. The tarsus bones of the hind leg that form the joint between the second thigh and the metatarsals.

Hocks well let down. When the distance from hock to ground is close to the ground.

Hound. Dog commonly used for hunting by scent.

Hound-marked. Three-color dogs; white, tan, and black, predominating color mentioned first.

Hucklebones. The top of the hipbones.

Humerus. The bone of the upper arm.

Inbreeding. The mating of closely related dogs of the same breed, usually brother to sister.

Incisors. The cutting teeth found between the fangs in the front of the mouth.

Isabella. Fawn or light bay color.

Kink tail. A tail which is abruptly bent, appearing to be broken.

Knuckling over. An insecurely knit pastern joint often causing irregular motion while dog is standing still.

Layback. Well placed shoulders; also, receding nose accompanied by an undershot jaw.

Leather. The flap of the ear.

Level bite. The front or incisor teeth of the upper and lower jaws meeting exactly.

Line breeding. The mating of dogs of the same breed related to a common ancestor; controlled inbreeding, usually grandmother to grandson, or grandfather to granddaughter.

Lippy. Lips that do not meet perfectly.

Loaded shoulders. When shoulder blades are out of alignment due to overweight or over-development on this particular part of the body.

Loin. The region of the body on either side of the vertebral column between the last ribs and the hindquarters.

Lower thigh. Same as second thigh.

Lumber. Excess fat on a dog.

Lumbering. Awkward gait on a dog.

Mane. Profuse hair on the upper portion of the neck.

Mantle. Dark-shaded portion of the coat or shoulders, back, and sides.

Mask. Shading on the foreface.

Median line. Same as furrow.

Molera. Abnormal ossification of the skull.

Molars. Rear teeth used for actual chewing.

Mongrel. Puppy or dog whose parents are of different breeds.

Monorchid. A male dog with only one testicle apparent.

Muzzle. The head in front of the eyes; includes nose, nostril, and jaws, as well as foreface.

Muzzle band. White markings on the muzzle.

Nictitating eyelid. The thin membrane at the inside corner of the eye which is drawn across the eyeball. Sometimes referred to as the third eyelid.

Nose. Scenting ability.

Occipital protuberance. The raised occiput itself.

Occiput. The upper crest or point at the top of the skull.

Occlusion. The meeting or bringing together of the upper and lower teeth.

Olfactory. Pertaining to the sense of smell.

Otter tail. A tail that is thick at the base, with hair parted on under side.

Out at shoulder. Shoulder blades set in such a manner that the joints are too wide, hence jut out from the body.

Outcrossing. The mating of unrelated individuals of the same breed.

Overhang. A very pronounced eyebrow.

Overshot. The front incisor teeth on top overlap the front teeth of the lower jaw. Also called pig jaw.

Pack. Several hounds kept together in one kennel.

Paddling. Moving with the forefeet wide, to encourage a body roll motion.

Pads. The undersides, or soles, of the feet.

Parti-color. Variegated in patches of two or more colors.

Pastern. The collection of bones forming the joint between the radius and ulna, and the metacarpals.

Peak. Same as occiput.

Penciling. Black lines dividing the colored hair on the toes.

Pied. Comparatively large patches of two or more colors. Also called parti-colored or piebald.

Pig jaw. Jaw with overshot bite.

Pigeon breast. A protruding breastbone.

311

Pile. The soft hair in the undercoat.

Pincer bite. A bite where the incisor teeth meet exactly.

Plume. A feathered tail which is carried over the back.

Points. Color on face, ears, legs, and tail in contrast to the rest of the body color.

Pompon. Rounded tuft of hair left on the end of the tail after clipping.

Prick ear. Carried erect and pointed at tip.

Puppy. Dog under one year of age.

Quality. Refinement; fineness.

Quarters. Hind legs as a pair.

Racy. Tall; of comparatively slight build.

Rat tail. The root thick and covered with soft curls—tip devoid of hair or giving the appearance of having been clipped.

Ring tail. Carried up and around and almost in a circle.

Ringer. A substitute for close resemblance.

Roach back. Convex or upward curvature of back; poor topline.

Roan. A mixture of colored hairs with white hairs. Blue roan, orange roan, etc.

Roman nose. A nose whose bridge has a convex line from forehead to nose tip; ram's nose.

Rose ear. Drop ear which folds over and back, revealing the burr.

Rounding. Cutting or trimming the ends of the ear leather.

Ruff. The longer hair growth around the neck.

Sable. A lacing of black hair in or over a lighter ground color.

Saddle. A marking over the back, like a saddle.

Scapula. The shoulder blade.

Scissors bite. A bite in which the upper teeth just barely overlap the lower teeth.

Screw tail. Naturally short tail twisted in spiral fashion.

Self color. One color with lighter shadings.

Semiprick ears. Carried erect with just the tips folding forward.

Septum. The line extending vertically between the nostrils.

Shelly. A narrow body that lacks the necessary size required by the breed standard.

Sickle tail. Carried out and up in a semicircle.

Slab sides. Insufficient spring of ribs.

Sloping shoulder. The shoulder blade which is set obliquely or "laid back."

Snipey. A pointed nose.

Snowshoe foot. Slightly webbed between the toes.

Soundness. The general good health and appearance of a dog.

Spayed. A female whose ovaries have been removed surgically.

Specialty club. An organization that sponsors and promotes an individual breed.

Specialty show. A dog show devoted to the promotion of a single breed.

Spectacles. Shading or dark markings around the eyes or from eyes to ears.

Splashed. Irregularly patched; color on white, or vice versa.

Splay foot. A flat or open-toed foot.

Spread. The width between the front legs.

Spring of ribs. The degree of rib roundness.

Squirrel tail. Carried up and curving slightly forward.

Stance. Manner of standing.

Staring coat. Dry harsh hair; sometimes curling at the tips.

Station. Comparative height of a dog from the ground—either high or low.

Stern. Tail (or rudder) of a sporting dog or hound.

Sternum. Breastbone.

Stifle. Joint of hind leg between thigh and second thigh; sometimes called the ham.

Stilted. Choppy, up-and-down gait of straight-hocked dog.

Stop. The step-up from nose to skull between the eyes.

Straight-hocked. Without angulation; straight behind.

Substance. Good bone; on a dog in good weight; a well-muscled dog.

Superciliary arches. The prominence of the frontal bone of the skull over the eye.

Swayback. Concave or downward curvature of the back between the withers and the hipbones. Poor topline.

Team. Three or more (usually four) dogs working in unison.

Thigh. The hindquarter from hip joint to stifle.

Throatiness. Excessive loose skin under the throat.

Ticked. Small isolated areas of black or colored hairs on another color background.

Timber. Bone, especially of the legs.

Topknot. Tuft of hair on the top of head.

Triangular eye. The eye set in surrounding tissue of triangular shape. A three-cornered eye.

Tri-color. Three colors on a dog; typically white, black, and tan.

Trumpet. Depression or hollow on either side of the skull just behind the eye socket; comparable to the temple area in humans.

Tuck-up. Body depth at the loin.

Tulip ear. Ear carried erect with slight forward curvature along the sides.

Turn up. Uptilted jaw.

Type. The distinguishing characteristics of a dog to measure its worth against the standard for the breed.

Undershot. The front teeth of the lower jaw overlapping or projecting beyond the front teeth of the upper jaw when the mouth is closed.

Upper arm. The humerus bone of the foreleg between the shoulder blade and forearm.

Vent. Area under the tail.

Walleye. A blue eye; also referred to as a fish eye or pearl eye.

Weaving. When the dog is in motion, the forefeet or hind feet cross.

Weedy. A dog too light of bone.

Wheaten. Pale yellow or fawn color.

Wheel back. Back line arched over the loin; roach back.

Whelps. Unweaned puppies.

Whip tail. Carried out stiffly straight and pointed.

Wire-haired. A hard wiry coat.

Withers. The peak of the first dorsal vertebra; highest part of the body just behind the neck.

Wrinkle. Loose, folding skin on the forehead and/or foreface.

PERPETUAL WHELPING CHART

| Bred—Jan. | 1 2 3 4 5 6 7 8 9 10 11 12 13 14 15 16 17 18 19 20 21 22 23 24 25 26 27 | 28 29 30 31 |
| Due—March | 5 6 7 8 9 10 11 12 13 14 15 16 17 18 19 20 21 22 23 24 25 26 27 28 29 30 31 April 1 2 3 4 |

| Bred—Feb. | 1 2 3 4 5 6 7 8 9 10 11 12 13 14 15 16 17 18 19 20 21 22 23 24 25 26 | 27 28 |
| Due—April | 5 6 7 8 9 10 11 12 13 14 15 16 17 18 19 20 21 22 23 24 25 26 27 28 29 30 May 1 2 |

| Bred—Mar. | 1 2 3 4 5 6 7 8 9 10 11 12 13 14 15 16 17 18 19 20 21 22 23 24 25 26 27 28 29 | 30 31 |
| Due—May | 3 4 5 6 7 8 9 10 11 12 13 14 15 16 17 18 19 20 21 22 23 24 25 26 27 28 29 30 31 June 1 2 |

| Bred—Apr. | 1 2 3 4 5 6 7 8 9 10 11 12 13 14 15 16 17 18 19 20 21 22 23 24 25 26 27 28 | 29 30 |
| Due—June | 3 4 5 6 7 8 9 10 11 12 13 14 15 16 17 18 19 20 21 22 23 24 25 26 27 28 29 30 July 1 2 |

| Bred—May | 1 2 3 4 5 6 7 8 9 10 11 12 13 14 15 16 17 18 19 20 21 22 23 24 25 26 27 28 29 | 30 31 |
| Due—July | 3 4 5 6 7 8 9 10 11 12 13 14 15 16 17 18 19 20 21 22 23 24 25 26 27 28 29 30 31 August 1 2 |

| Bred—June | 1 2 3 4 5 6 7 8 9 10 11 12 13 14 15 16 17 18 19 20 21 22 23 24 25 26 27 28 29 | 30 |
| Due—August | 3 4 5 6 7 8 9 10 11 12 13 14 15 16 17 18 19 20 21 22 23 24 25 26 27 28 29 30 31 Sept. 1 |

| Bred—July | 1 2 3 4 5 6 7 8 9 10 11 12 13 14 15 16 17 18 19 20 21 22 23 24 25 26 27 28 29 | 30 31 |
| Due—September | 2 3 4 5 6 7 8 9 10 11 12 13 14 15 16 17 18 19 20 21 22 23 24 25 26 27 28 29 30 Oct. 1 2 |

| Bred—Aug. | 1 2 3 4 5 6 7 8 9 10 11 12 13 14 15 16 17 18 19 20 21 22 23 24 25 26 27 28 29 | 30 31 |
| Due—October | 3 4 5 6 7 8 9 10 11 12 13 14 15 16 17 18 19 20 21 22 23 24 25 26 27 28 29 30 31 Nov. 1 2 |

| Bred—Sept. | 1 2 3 4 5 6 7 8 9 10 11 12 13 14 15 16 17 18 19 20 21 22 23 24 25 26 27 28 | 29 30 |
| Due—November | 3 4 5 6 7 8 9 10 11 12 13 14 15 16 17 18 19 20 21 22 23 24 25 26 27 28 29 30 Dec. 1 2 |

| Bred—Oct. | 1 2 3 4 5 6 7 8 9 10 11 12 13 14 15 16 17 18 19 20 21 22 23 24 25 26 27 28 29 | 30 31 |
| Due—December | 3 4 5 6 7 8 9 10 11 12 13 14 15 16 17 18 19 20 21 22 23 24 25 26 27 28 29 30 31 Jan. 1 2 |

| Bred—Nov. | 1 2 3 4 5 6 7 8 9 10 11 12 13 14 15 16 17 18 19 20 21 22 23 24 25 26 27 28 29 | 30 |
| Due—January | 3 4 5 6 7 8 9 10 11 12 13 14 15 16 17 18 19 20 21 22 23 24 25 26 27 28 29 30 31 Feb. 1 |

| Bred—Dec. | 1 2 3 4 5 6 7 8 9 10 11 12 13 14 15 16 17 18 19 20 21 22 23 24 25 26 27 | 28 29 30 31 |
| Due—February | 2 3 4 5 6 7 8 9 10 11 12 13 14 15 16 17 18 19 20 21 22 23 24 25 26 27 28 March 1 2 3 4 |

Boys and girls together, photographed by owner Vera Rebbin.

Fantasyland Me Bunny, photographed at seven months of age. Bred by Carole M. Baldwin; owned by Mr. Ito of Japan.

Index

This Index is composed of three sections: a general index for informational matter, an index of persons named in the text, and an index of kennels mentioned.

Index of People

Abbey, L., 102
Alderman, Barbara Dempsey, 61, 92, 94, 153, 240, 286, 287
Amoni, Arivoldo, 110
Anderson, Grace Hendrickson, 99
Antonelli, Aennchen, 8, 9, 10, 11, 35, 36, 41, 43, 47, 89, 103, 133, 134, 221, 228, 293, 294
Antonelli, Joseph P. (Tony), 9, 35, 36, 41, 43, 47, 133, 134, 221, 228
Ash, Edward C., 23

Baker, Mr., 19
Baldwin, Carole M., 40, 55, 124, 164, 189, 197, 216, 252, 316
Baldwin, Thomas, 73, 211
Bashara, Dr. & Mrs. T. Robert, 305
Bashford, 81
Basiszta, M., 94
Bassett, Mrs., 26
Beam, Maxine, 66
Beattie, Mr., 19
Beckett, George, 291
Beeching, Madeline, 23
Belford, Norma, 123, 140, 307, 304
Bergquist, Barbara J., 8, 9, 56, 69, 79, 87, 157, 227, 248, 250, 253, 284, 287, 295, 301
Bergquist, Robert, 69
Bergquist, Susan & Lisa, 70
Bergum, William, 147
Bernfeld, Cyril, 95
Bevin, Edd, 114
Bissell, William, 116, 120, 167
Blackard, Kathy, 57, 63, 75, 179, 183, 217, 244, 297, 304, 307
Blackman, Mr., 19
Blackman, Mrs. Sarah, 19
Blanchard, Kathy, 13
Blumberg, Keke, 55, 78
Bodinius, Mme., 101
Both, Martin, 28
Bower, Mrs. Robert, 239
Brauer, Becky, 102
Brearley, Joan McDonald, 7, 9
Brickley, Rita, 89
Brierley, Mrs. I.C., 23, 26
Brown, Dennis, 43, 262
Brown, Nancy (Mrs. Roger), 36, 42, 90, 133, 134, 138, 176, 209, 224, 248, 250, 252, 303, 305
Brown, Pamela, 9, 43, 262, 267
Brown, Dr. Roger, 36, 42, 90, 133, 134, 138, 176, 181, 209, 224, 248, 250, 252, 304
Brown, Tracy, 43, 249
Brunotte, Andrena, 150, 154
Buffon, 15

Burke, Elsie, 84, 197, 203
Busselman, Gary, 40
Busselman, Gloria, 40, 52, 90, 99, 163, 296

Caius, Dr. Johannes, 16, 17
Calhoun, Muriel, 231
Callimachus, 15
Calvaresi, Dr. Vincenzo, 32, 33, 36, 158
Calvaresi, Mrs. Vincenzo, 32, 33
Card, Mrs. L.H., 23
Carey, Len, 251
Carno, Dennis, 301
Carson, Dorothy, 55
Cass, Glynnette, 80
Cecil, Gladys, 41
Charpie, Betty M., 50
Childs, Terry, 201
Clark, Ann Rogers, 210
Clark, Mrs. Boyd, 89
Clooney, Rosemary, 300
Cohen, Merrill, 86, 113, 280
Coleman, Linda & Lee, 61, 76, 77, 92, 144, 191, 206, 236
Coleman, Mr., 19
Constantino, J. Chip, 67
Corioll, Wendy & Jean, 99
Cotton, Winifred, 34, 35, 50
Cox, Elvera, 89
Craig, Robert & Eloise, 89
Crapo, J.M., 29
Crook, Marion, 23
Curry, Jonda & Allen, 49
Cutillo, Nicholas, 41-2, 50, 95, 255

Dahl, Angela, 76, 119, 147, 149, 225, 242, 281, 308
Dahl, Arvid, 60, 76, 281
Dahl, Rita, 60, 76, 94, 119, 149, 243, 281, 285
Darcey, Mrs., 26
Davis, Diane, 80, 139, 153, 203, 205, 211, 274
Dennam, Sandra, 99
Derhammer, Don, 209
Derhammer, Mrs. Don, 209, 250
Dewey, A., 19
Dick, Pauline, 157
DiGiacomo, Anthony, 165
DiGiacomo, Kathy, 9, 62, 78, 85, 87, 88, 91, 95, 129, 154, 165, 186, 202, 204, 211, 226, 238, 246, 278, 280, 283, 284, 301
DiGiacomo, Stefanie, 280, 298
Dillon, Trudie, 38, 94, 281, 285, 308
Dinsmore, Jo Ann, 28, 44, 45, 254
di Tavera, La Condesa Beatrice (Beatrice Brown), 14, 20
Dixon, Mrs., 22
Dollar, Danny M. & Edith N., 82

Downing, Melbourne, 231
Draper, Mrs. W.L., 31
Drobac, Betty, 258, 263, 270
Duncan, Fran, 89
Dujardin, Manya, 82, 85, 279
Duxbury, Melda Lee, 99

Eckes, Mrs., 89
Edwards, Vivian, 211
Egeberg, Knut, 119
Elder, Byron, 250
Engstrom, Anna, 69
Evans, Dr. J.S., 97
Evans, Virginia (Gini), 89, 97, 99

Faigel, Joseph, 250
Fancy, Jean, 285
Farmer, W.P., 31
Feldblum, Annette S., 72, 210
Feller, Adolph, 3
Ferguson, Ruthann, 79
Fernando, Don, 30
Field, Dr. William, 88, 153
Fields, Totie, 300
Fierheller, Glenna, 109, 112, 121, 188, 190, 255
Fischer, Elyse, 85, 86, 127
Fischer, James, 220, 273, 303, 304
Fish, Mrs., 19
Fishman, Mrs., 45
Floriabo, Bobbie, 99
Ford, Laura, 78, 247
Forest, Mrs. K.D., 22
Fraguada, Jose A., 109, 122
Fraser, Mrs. P.B. Gordon, 25, 101
Fraser-Newalls, Miss M., 22
Fuller, Lindy, 85

Garber, Madonna, 164
Garshi, Mrs. Kazumasa, 102
Geiger, Karol, 85
Gemmill, Randy, 190, 254
George, Earl, 19
Gibbs, Miss, 18
Gifford, Lady, 19, 21
Gilbert, Rita & Charlie, 223
Gilbert, Mrs., 22
Gold, Fay, 181
Good, Mary, 31
Grady, Arlene, 89
Graham, Earl, 231
Graham, Robert, 70
Graham, Vera, 124
Gregory, Joseph (Joe), 82, 171, 251
Gregory, Mamie R., 89, 96, 294
Grubb, Susan S., 85
Grunstra, Claudia, 62, 78, 247, 280
Halley, Delores, 80, 173, 233, 283, 307

Haney, Major Travis, 219
Hardy, Anna Mae, 39, 52, 91, 94, 99, 163, 208, 229
Harrington, Lillian, 134
Harrison, Roberta, 71, 99
Hartley, Mrs. Heywood, 80
Harvey, Miss A.J., 19
Hasegawa, Saichi, 102
Hatley, Dorothy H., 45, 279
Heald, Mildred, 40
Hechinger, Mary, 44
Hennessey, Gail, 9, 26, 88, 91, 146, 154, 172, 200, 201, 247, 279
Hensel, Richard, 84
Herrief, Vicki, 25, 26
Hesse, Joanne, 35, 36, 43, 44, 56, 89, 96, 99, 104, 249
Hodges, Mrs. G.A., 102
Hogg, Peggy A., 64, 65, 66-7, 89, 96, 144, 274, 288, 294
Hoh, Mary, 191
Holbrook, Gwen, 99
Hollis, Maxine, 133
Hood, Mrs. Acland, 22
Hood, Helen, 71
Hopple, Florence, 89, 99
Horlock, Mrs. R.H., 22
Hornemann, K.H., 101
Horney, Vivian, 89, 99
Horowitz, 22
Hostetler, Marcia, 3, 43, 44, 54, 72, 159, 171, 174, 175, 190, 235, 254, 289
Howell, Lani, 88
Howell, Patricia, 89, 99
Howens, W., 101
Hrabak, Shirley, 274
Hunt, Muriel, 88
Hunter, Mrs. C.M., 23
Huntington, H.W., 299

Ito, Mr., 316
Iveria, Miki, 302

Jackson, Russell, 89
Jacobs, J., 21
Jenner, Ed, 88
Johnson-Gil, Judith & Elaine, 71, 114
Jones, Corson, 271
Judd, Anna, 31

Kalstone, Larry, 34
Kalstone, Shirley, 99
Kannarr, Priscilla, 99
Kauffman, Sue, 144
Keasbury, Mrs. G., 30
Keenan, Sabrina, 146
Keller, Grace, 99
Kendrick, William, 69
Kenney, Linda & Nicky, 88
Kent, Duchess of, 18
Kerr, Lesley, 113, 147, 151

319

Index of Kennels

A Prayer for Animals

Hear our humble prayer, O God, for our friends the animals, especially for animals who are suffering; for any that are hunted or lost or deserted or frightened or hungry; for all that must be put to death. We entreat for them all Thy mercy and pity, and for those who deal with them we ask a heart of compassion and gentle hands and kindly words. Make us, ourselves to be true friends to animals and so to share the blessings of the merciful.

Albert Schweitzer